MOIDART

Among the Clanranalds

MOIDART
Among the Clanranalds

Charles MacDonald
Edited by John Watt

Birlinn

This edition published in 1997 by
Birlinn Limited
14 High Street
Edinburgh EH1 1TE

British Library Cataloguing-in-Publication Data
A Catalogue record of this book is available from the British Library

ISBN 1 874744 65 3

The Publisher acknowledges subsidy from

THE SCOTTISH ARTS COUNCIL

towards the publication of this volume.

Printed and bound in Finland by Werner Söderström OY

Contents

List of Plates

Memorial cross to Father Charles

Father Charles MacDonald

Thatched cottage at Kinlochmoidart, *c.* 1890

Father Charles and School Board outside Mingarry School, 1887

Roshven House, 1857–8

Eilean Shona House, 1893

Ardtoe, *c.* 1890

Castle Tioram from Dorlin House, *c.* 1890

Acknowledgements

FOR their kindness and generous help I should like to thank Hugh Cheape and Dorothy Kidd of the National Museum of Scotland; Fiona Marwick of the West Highland Museum, Fort William; Ian MacKenzie, Rona Talbot and Ian Fraser of the School of Scottish Studies and Ronald Black of the Celtic Department, University of Edinburgh; Monsignor Thomas Wynne, Arisaig; George Fox, Strontian; Charles MacFarlane, Glenfinnan; Norman H MacDonald, Edinburgh; and the following Seven Men, and Three Women, of Moidart: Iain, Mary, Allan and Margaret MacMaster, Mingarry; Allan MacDonald, Glenuig; Robert Fairley, Alisary; Alan Blackburn, Roshven; Mrs N D Stewart, Kinlochmoidart House; Fergie MacDonald, Mingarry; and Iain MacDonald, Glenuig.

ERRATUM

The Publisher regrets that the editor's name is misspelt and should read John Watts.

Dr John Watts is a graduate of Oxford and Glasgow Universities, a Fellow of the Society of Antiquaries of Scotland and a member of the Scottish Catholic Heritage Commission. He is the author of a historical novel *A Cairn of Small Stones*, and is presently writing the history of Scalan, the Highland seminary, due to be published shortly.

Introduction

CHARLES MacDonald was born in 1835 at Millburn, Inverness-shire, the sixth of seven children. At the age of twelve he was sent to Blairs College, the junior seminary of the Catholic Church in Scotland, where he spent two years before graduating to senior seminaries in France. His studies were completed at St Sulpice in Paris, whereupon he returned to Scotland and was ordained in August 1859. The following Spring he was sent to Moidart. It was his first, and as it turned out his only parish, for he remained there until 1892 when ill health, which had dogged him for some years, finally forced him to retire from active work. He died in Helensburgh just two years later.[1] He is buried on Eilean Fhìonain, the Green Isle in Loch Shiel, which has been a burial place for more than a millennium, and of which he wrote lovingly in his book.

Father Charles had already been a priest of Moidart for nearly thirty years when his book was published. The district he served, like the adjacent areas of Arisaig, Morar and Knoydart, was among the most rugged and remote in the Highlands, and this — as he remarks in the introductory chapter — was one of the reasons why its people had remained 'about the most conservative in the kingdom', whether in their loyalty to king and chief or to their faith. And yet, in his own time among them he had been witness to 'great changes' in the community and the way of life, symbolised for him by the recently built mansions of the new moneyed lairds, incomers all, which now stood in stark contrast to the roofless ruin of the ancient Castle Tioram of Clanranald.

It was in order to preserve something of a vanishing way of life that he put pen to paper, to record some of the traditions from the mouths of his parishioners, as well as the more recent events that he himself had witnessed. Most likely he had no thought of publication when he began, for we know that it was his friend Lord Howard of Glossop, owner of the Loch Shiel estate, who persuaded him to work up his notes into a book, and who met the costs of going to press.

The work he produced reflects its origins, for it really comprises a number of 'sketches', as he himself calls them, skilfully linked together. Each is a tale more or less complete in itself, so that the book can be dipped into, should the reader wish to follow a particular interest or remind himself of the details of a particular person, place or happening. On the other hand, the local setting for the main narrative, and its broadly chronological structure, held together by the continuous thread of the Clanranald line and those of its main associated families, give the whole a most effective and satisfying unity, a unity which holds even when the author allows himself an extended digression in place or time.

Father Charles enjoyed some but not all the advantages of the historian, for his home in Mingarry was close to the bearers of oral tradition, but far from the great libraries of the city. He was a well read man, nonetheless, and could quote where need be from the standard Histories of the day. And in any case, for his chosen subject the gain far outweighed the loss. He is said to have been a man of engaging conversation himself, and this quality comes through in his writing also. It is an engaging book. It has the warmth of the chapel house sitting-room about it, not least in its touches of gentle humour. Characteristically of a Highlander writing about the Highlands, it is essentially about people. It makes delightful reading.

Occasionally, the author offers us his own opinion, as for instance when he proposes a solution to the poverty of the small farmer. He acknowledges the efforts of the better landowners to improve their estates and support their tenants, but we know from surviving correspondence how much he regretted the arrival of these 'new Southern proprietors'. Some half century before his arrival in Moidart the Clanranald lands had been sold off 'piece by piece', and the old continuity had been replaced by the 'notorious mutability' of the new ownership. As a Clanranald, whose family had fought at Culloden, his heart was with the old: the social structures, the martial spirit, the leadership and the loyalties. The shepherd was as much the conservative as his flock.

In reading *Moidart, or Among the Clanranalds*, we feel we have made acquaintance not alone with the men and women described in it, but with the author also. But if so, it is not because he ever makes reference to himself. Indeed, of his own work among the people and his influence upon the Moidart of his day, he makes no mention at all. He writes of the whisky drinking which often led to disgraceful scenes at funerals, for instance, but he does not tell us that it was he himself who put a stop to the practice in Moidart. He refers to the different culture of the people across the River Shiel, but he says nothing of his own work for harmony between the two communities, when fights took place at the Old Bridge and he would stride in among his own flock and whip them home with a hazel stick.

By all accounts, in fact, he ran a tight ship in the parish. He had a quick temper to match his red hair and *An t-Sagart Ruadh* — the Red Headed Priest — was held in some respect by all. But there was affection in the name too, for he was very much a priest of his people. He had taken trouble to learn their Gaelic language, and they had taken him to their hearts. He could use the *caman* too, and it was *Maighstir Tearlach's* team that everyone wanted to play for in the annual Shinty match on the strand at Dorlin on New Year's Day. He was on close terms of friendship with the landowners, and partial to the entertainment of the Big House, spending 'weeks' every winter over at Dalilea, by his own account, playing whist and backgammon with the family. But he was equally at home among the ordinary people, and whenever they needed him he was there, whether at the far end of Glenforslan or up over by the Plate Rock into Glenuig. He is remembered as an excellent and intrepid horse-man, and he and his horse knew every bridle path — for those were the only roads — and overcame all obstacles meteorological, and at least once (so it is said) diabolical, to reach the sick and the dying.

These things are mentioned here, appropriately, because it is as much for the priest as for the author that Charles MacDonald is honoured in Moidart. But details such as these, preserved in local memory, can only make us wish that he had found space to include a great deal more in his book both of the events that he played a part in and of other happenings that he knew of. We would like to have heard about the cattle drovers, for example, who were still passing through Moidart in his day, though in much reduced numbers from the great age of droving, and used to camp on the brae above his church. And we wish he had given us more details of the mass emigrations following the potato famine, which halved the local population just a decade before his arrival there.

Themes such as these he would no doubt have developed in the sequel that we know he planned to publish, in the wake of the immediate and unexpected success of his book. Unfortunately ill health and an early death prevented his completing it, and it is thought that most of what he had collected was inadvertently destroyed in the clear-out of his effects.[2] One small manuscript which survived and was later published in the *Celtic Monthly*, appears to be part of the intended sequel: it comprises letters home from the Peninsular Wars, with comments by Father Charles, and in fact adds little of direct relevance to his theme.[3]

Those who seek further details of the Moidart of his day must look elsewhere. The local estate papers and other official documents provide a wealth of information, but not the lore and the stories that lie behind the records, the very things that a sequel might have given us.[4] Much is now lost irretrievably. But there are people living today – perhaps the last generation – who retain some of the old stories, so that it would yet be possible, and a task for someone, to fill out the details of his day, and bring the story forward into the present, by recording what does still remain in the memory of those few who have the knowledge to pass on.

Meantime, Father Charles' book stands as a unique and valuable source of the history of Moidart and Clanranald, and one which has itself now become a part of that history. It has taken on something of the status of a classic, partly no doubt because it is unique but also for its own inherent worth. It has certainly been treasured with a special pride of possession in Moidart, and by those who trace their roots to Moidart. But the author's fear that it would have little interest to others has proved unduly modest. The original edition very soon became unobtainable, and in answer to a wide demand it was later serialised by the *Oban Times* in the Old Country and by the *Casket* of Antigonish in the New. In 1989 a centenary facsimile edition was published and the eagerness with which it was received confirmed the book's continued widespread interest today.

The present edition has been prepared with that wider, modern readership in mind. For that reason it includes end-of-chapter notes and Appendices, to elucidate matters that the author could assume would be understood by his own local contemporaries, but which may present problems for some readers today.

The first of such problems is place names. Some will be familiar to everyone, and others to anyone with an interest in the Scottish Highlands, but a number are very local, and a few have now passed out of use altogether. West Highland place names are Gaelic (and/or Norse) in origin, but the better known ones, particularly, have usually been anglicised by map makers, and it is the anglicised form that the author uses where it exists. But many a place name, often too local to have figured on maps, has retained its Gaelic form.

Personal names are also Gaelic and follow the particular way of naming customary in Gaelic tradition. Surnames in the English sense are rarely used. Persons are known by their first name and further identified by a patronymic — the name of their father, father's father, etc — or by a nickname. Clan and family lines have always been accorded a great importance in the Highlands and, in a tradition until recently oral where memories were remarkable, people could trace their families back over many generations. The whole way of thought has been genealogical. Some readers may therefore find difficulty not only with the form of names but with what the author himself calls the 'bewildering genealogies' of the many branches of Clan Donald that occur in the book.

To complicate matters further, when Father Charles uses Gaelic, as in the case of some place names and most personal names, his spelling is very often at variance with that in use today — he even uses the letter 'v', for example, which does not now appear in the Gaelic alphabet.

To aid the reader, Appendix I contains every place and personal name mentioned in the text, arranged alphabetically and with page references, with their pronunciations where this is not obvious, and, in the case of Gaelic words, their standard modern spelling and English meaning. The place names also include gazetteer references corresponding to the maps of Moidart and the adjacent areas produced in Appendix II, so that they may be easily located. And to assist the reader through the bewildering genealogies, simplified genealogical tables of the lines of Clanranald and its prominent local cadet families are provided in Appendix III.

Upon occasion the author quotes from Gaelic poetry, and more rarely from Latin or French, and when doing so he hardly ever offers a translation. The omission has been rectified in the end-of-chapter notes. He also refers to the writings of contemporaries, mainly historical works that were the standard texts of the day but are now almost forgotten; again these are identified in the notes.

Finally, it has already been remarked that much of the book comprises brief sketches, because of the way the author gathered and presented his information. Often he only touches upon a matter, and leaves us a tantalising glimpse. This is especially so for wider happenings beyond Moidart which are not central to his theme, and for the more distant history that forms the subject of his earlier chapters. In several such cases some extra detail has been provided in the notes, and for those who wish to pursue these or other topics in greater depth the 'Suggestions for Further Reading' in Appendix IV offer a selection of the published sources available.

It is hoped that the notes and Appendices prove helpful. They have been kept separate from the text itself so as not to obstruct or deflect from Father Charles' narrative, but merely to support it. The book he wrote is the thing that matters.

Notes

1   For a more detailed account of his life the reader is referred to Iain Thornber's Biographical Note in the centenary edition (Edinburgh, 1989), based substantially on an earlier biography by Alastair Cameron ('North Argyll') with much additional material.

2   There are, however, those who believe that the MS was not in fact destroyed and has survived, and there are opinions as to its present whereabouts.

3   *Celtic Monthly,* six articles from February to August 1904. The letters are by John MacDonald, second son of Archibald MacDonald, Rhu, who figures at length in Chapter xii of the book. The first letter is dated May 1811. A copy is held on microfilm in the National Library of Scotland, Mf SP Serial 8, Reel 4.

4   Unfortunately, the most valuable source remains in manuscript and as far as I know unpublished. This is *The Clanranald MacDonalds of Moidart,* written by Colin S. MacDonald of Bracebridge, Ontario in 1955. The fruit of twenty years' research, and based on documentary material and personal interviews, it is particularly strong on those Moidart families who settled in Canada, providing valuable details of their lives both before and after emigration. A microfilm copy is held in the School of Scottish Studies, University of Edinburgh.

Chapter 1

Descriptive view of the "Rough Bounds" – Attachment of the natives to the cause of the Stuarts in former times – Raonuill Mor a' Chrolen and George III

THE Garbh-chriochan, or the "Rough Bounds," is a Celtic name which, from time immemorial, has been given to a large tract of country lying in the Western Highlands between Loch Suinart in the south and Loch Hourn in the north-east. The term is not inapt, for wild as many other parts of the Highlands undoubtedly are, the natural features prevailing throughout this region are exceedingly savage and rugged. To the traveller, for instance, sailing northwards round the Point of Ardnamurchan, they present a mass of dark hills coming down in broken ridges towards the coast, and crowding thickly behind each other until the higher peaks become mere points marking the outlines of the eastern horizon. At intervals between its two extremities the coast is opened up by certain arms of the sea, some of which shape themselves into broad deep bays, while others penetrate far into the land, disappearing among the mountains in narrow tortuous channels, their course obstructed by reefs and islets, and their shores fringed by woods representing every variety of native growth. The principal among them are Loch Suinart, Loch Moidart, Loch-nan-uamh, Loch Aylort, Loch Nevis, and Loch Hourn. The land is formed by them into so many peninsulas, thus adding to the difficulty of travel in a region where, from other causes, communication cannot be easy. On lines somewhat parallel are two magnificent stretches of fresh-water lakes, entering still farther into the interior. These are Loch Sheil and Loch Morar, the one eighteen the other sixteen miles long. The districts included in the "Rough Bounds" are Ardnamurchan,

Moidart, Arisaig, North and South Morar, and Knoydart. For bold and romantic scenery nothing can surpass them. They impress forcibly even those who make no claim to the imagination of the poet, and who know little or nothing of those special features which have such attractions for the eye of the artist. But on a closer inspection the land is found, as a rule, to be poor and barren. Some of the valleys are mere dead-flats of moss or moorland. This is particularly the case towards the western end of Lochshiel, where a very extensive tract of this character expands from both sides of the loch to the foot of the adjoining hills. The same features exhibit themselves on the southern side of the river Sheil, nearer the sea, and in a considerable portion of South Morar. The spurs which come down towards the coast are rough and rugged in their outlines. Sometimes they undulate in broad easy swells, exposing, at frequent intervals, all over their surface flat patches of rock from which every trace of vegetation and soil has been washed away. At other times the descent is more abrupt and rapid; portions of the hill sides are sliced off into precipices, from the foot of which, down to the end of the steep slopes, there are well-defined tracks, thickly covered with loose stones and large slabs detached from the heights above. All over these hill sides the incline is interrupted by smaller spurs, sharp and angular, which come straggling down towards the lower ground, the hollows between them giving shelter to thin lines of aspen and hazel, or serving as channels for the torrents which the frequent downpours peculiar to the West Coast perpetually feed and quicken. Against the face of the highest cliffs sometimes a solitary tree, rooted to a cleft in the rock, or perched on some tiny ledge, may be seen fighting for its precarious footing, and, although stunted and puny, holding its own against the breath of the storm-king. For a few hundred yards before the easier slopes touch the valley, belts of hazel, ash, mountain oak, and birch wood, with here and there a solitary holly, are not infrequent. But on the upper ranges the scene is desolate. Jagged peaks, lonesome corries, and stretches of coarse tableland, dotted with innumerable small lakes, whose solitude has charms only for the deer and the wild fowl, fill up the picture from one end of the Garbh-chriochan to the other. As one enters more deeply towards the east the scene softens a little. The long sapless heather and the precipitous character of the hills, give way to mountains more graduated in their descent, and covered almost to their summit with grass and ferns. Dividing glens wind in and out in every direction. Many of them are singularly picturesque and charming. But they are lonesome to a degree, and a heavy stillness, broken only at times by the barking of a shepherd's dog, seems for ever to hang over them. The biographer of St Columba, who seems to have had a personal acquaintance with the "Rough Bounds," characterises them as "aspera et saxosa,"—rough and stony. "Alio in tempore per asperam et saxosam regionem iter faciens, quae decitur Artdamuirchol" (Ardnamurchan). —*V: St Columbae,* lib. i., c. 12.[1]

Communications between one section and the other, as well as between the whole and the outer world, have at all times been difficult. No roads with any pretence to the name existed. Even now the deficiency is most marked; and whatever General Wade may be elsewhere, he is of no account here.[2] Morar and Knoydart suffer most, but in many other parts the natives have little reason to consider themselves better off. About the beginning of the present century a high road, leading from Fort-William and Strontian, was advanced a few miles into the Moidart district, but it stopped abruptly at the foot of a rock near the head of Loch Moidart, and from that time to this has only advanced half a mile farther. When forced to face these difficulties, some of the means adopted by the inhabitants of old are, without being original, sufficiently quaint to be remembered in these days of steamboats, railways, and motion at high pressure. It is said of one of the Glengarry chiefs that when he had occasion to travel into the Garbh-chriochan with his family, he used to pack his younger children into creels, and, tying these to the backs of ponies, make his way over hill and moor as best he could, very much as a native of Uist or Eigg does with his peats to-day. If the creel on one side of the pony outweighed the creel on the other, a few stones thrown into the latter made the scales even. It is no doubt partly owing to this difficulty of access that the inhabitants of these districts are about the most conservative in the kingdom,—conservative in religion, conservative in those old fashioned notions of loyalty to the crown, and of respect for their landlords, which, unfortunately, in many places are already things of the past. When the old faith went down under the Revolution which swept over Scotland in the sixteenth century, the changes which were brought about can scarcely be said to have acquired a footing north of the river Shiel. When the Stuarts claimed their own, and appealed to the loyalty of the Highland clans, none answered more readily than the Clanranalds, or their fiery cousins the chieftains of Glengarry. They and their followers were up with Montrose, Dundee, and with Mar; and among them was organised that last expedition which nearly set Prince Charlie on the throne.[3] Although the scenes in which the forefathers took such a part can scarcely fade from the memory of their descendants, still the traditional feeling of loyalty to the throne has not perished. It is as freely given to the reigning dynasty now, as it was given formerly to the unfortunate Stuarts. When George III expressed, on a certain occasion, a strong desire to see some of the surviving Highlanders who had been out in the '45, a certain number were brought forward, and among them a grim old warrior from Knoydart named Raonull Mor a' Chrolen. After putting some questions to the latter, the king remarked that no doubt he must have long since regretted having taken any part in that *Rebellion*. The answer was prompt and decisive. "Sire, I regret nothing of the kind." His Majesty, for an instant, was taken aback at such a bold answer, but was completely softened by the old man adding, "What I did then for the Prince, I would have done as heartily for your Majesty if you had been in the Prince's place." This is very much the feeling that animates all true Highlanders. It is the one at any rate that prevails in the "Rough Bounds," although, it must be confessed, the treachery shown in the massacre of Glenco, and the brutal severities exercised after Culloden, are apt to give a spasm even to the most honest loyalty. It is a sedative, however, to have the privilege of abusing and execrating the authors, without necessarily implicating or thinking ill of their connections and descendants.

The whole of the Garbh-Chriochan belonged at one time to the Macdonalds. Ardnamurchan was owned by an off-shoot of the clan called the MacIans. Moidart, Arisaig, Morar, and Knoydart were part of the family inheritance of the Clanranalds.

The MacIans were extirpated in 1625 by the Campbells; and of the vast estates owned by the Clanranalds only the ruined castle of Eilean Tirrim, and a small uninhabited island called Risca, remain to the family as sad memorials of their past greatness. After the destruction of the MacIans, Ardnamurchan was repeopled by a strange mixture of Hendersons, M'Phees, M'Lachlans, M'Naughtons, Camerons, and Macphersons. Their descendants are there to this day.

In the Clanranald districts the mass of the natives are still Macdonalds, although in certain parts Gillises and Kennedys are fairly numerous.[4] Almost all of them belong to the crofting class. Their small farms are generally situated on the margin of the moors, in the vicinity of the sea-coast, or about the lower end of the large fresh-water lakes. The more fertile straths and the glens are in the hands of the sheep farmers and the owners of the land. In the total absence of local industries, many of the crofts can only be regarded as negative blessings, for they are not adequate to the support of a family from one end of the year to the other. They can only prove satisfactory by being considerably enlarged; but the want of capital, sometimes on the part of proprietor as well as of tenant, has hitherto been the great difficulty. There are many landowners throughout these districts who, in the fullest sense, have striven to ameliorate the lot of the smaller tenantry, and whose sympathies go with the latter. But from one cause or another, and especially from faults committed during a generation for which the present owners are not responsible, their benevolent efforts have not been crowned with that full measure of success which one could desire.

The great changes which, within the last thirty years, have come over this wild part of the Highlands, are well contrasted by storm-beaten roofless Castle Tirrim on the one hand, and the group of handsome mansions which have sprung up in its neighbourhood on the other. Among these may be mentioned Dorlin House, belonging to Lord Howard of Glossop; the fine new mansion of Robert Stuart Esq., in Kinlochmoidart; the house of Professor Blackburn at Roshven; and a very stately pile, magnificently situated, built by the late Mr Astley of Arisaig. Other buildings, more in the villa style, such as are to be seen on Eilean Shona, Invermoidart, and on the Glenuig property, add to the contrast, and help to that train of ideas which the presence of the old and the new brought so prominently face to face with each other naturally suggests. The presence of danger, the apprehension of unwelcome visitors, the risks of a sudden attack, and a general distrust of men and the times, are as plainly indicated in the massive walls and in the impregnable situation of the old castle, as they are absent in its younger neighbours. No doubt there is a touch of romance at the thought of brave men encompassed with perils, and holding their own at the point of the sword, ready for all comers. But this thought finds little hold in the breasts of prosaic persons, who are grateful to a strong-handed Government for relieving them of the opportunity of proving themselves heroes, in exchange for the solid benefits of peace and the maintenance of social order.

In the following sketches the scene is principally limited to one only of the districts mentioned above, viz., to Moidart. They can scarcely be said to have any particular interest except perhaps for persons living in or acquainted with this district, and they make no pretence whatsoever to anything new or original. Unfortunately the extreme dearth of materials precludes their being anything else but sketches. What is accepted as more or less historically trustworthy has been published already by Gregory[5] and others, and is here repeated on their authority. The traditional part has been gathered from among the more intelligent of the natives, while the rest may be said to have come under the personal knowledge of the writer himself.

Notes

1   'On another occasion, while travelling through the rough and stony country that is called Artdamuirchol': Adamnan, *Vita Sancti Columbae*, translated and edited by William Reeves and published as *Life of St Columba* in *The Historians of Scotland* (Edinburgh 1874), vol vi, p. 14. The reference is book 1, chapter viii, and not as Charles MacDonald has it. Reeves' edition is more easily accessible today in the reprint of 1988 by Llanerch Enterprises, Lampeter, Dyfed, with the original chapter numbers but different page numbers.

2   General Wade is best known for overseeing the construction of a network of roads and bridges in the Highlands, to allow the rapid movement of Government troops against Jacobite clans, following the rising of 1715. Construction began in 1726 and took ten years. The Wade roads were the first other than bridle paths in the Highlands. The General was also responsible for enforcing the Disarming Act following the '15.

3   For the Clanranald involvement in Montrose's campaigns in 1644, see chapter v, pp 62ff; for their support of Claverhouse — Bonnie Dundee — in 1689, see chapter vi, pp 88ff; and for their involvement in the Jacobite rising of 1715 under the Earl of Mar, with the burning of Castle Tioram and the death of Allan Dearg Clanranald, see chapter vi, pp 91ff.

4   In the author's day there were Kennedys living in Eilean Shona and Glenuig — their families probably originated in Braes Lochaber, and came to Moidart after the '45. Gillis was a fairly common name in North and South Morar (the latter was their ancient home, where they had lived at least as long as the MacDonalds) and the few Gillises in Moidart in the nineteenth century would have been fairly recent arrivals from there.

5   Gregory, Donald, *History of the Western Highlands and Isles of Scotland from AD 1493 to AD 1625* (Edinburgh, 1836; 2nd edition, London 1881).

Chapter 2

THE etymology of the word Moidart, according to a writer in the "Statistical Account," is said to be a compound of "mùid"—sea spray, and "ard," —height, "Heights of the sea spray."[1] Very little is known of the early history of the district. In Adamnan's Life of St Columba, mention is twice made of the river Shiel, the present dividing boundary between Moidart and Ardnamurchan. The writer tells us that some of the saint's companions, who were keen fishermen,—"strenui piscatores,"—cast their nets into the river and captured five salmon. St Columba urged them to try again, assuring them of success. They obeyed, and duly landed a very large fish—or, as Adamnan describes it "mirae magnitudinis"—of extraordinary size. He calls the Shiel "fluvius piscosus"—a river abounding in fish; and the Latin term by which he describes it is "Sale."[2] Any one acquainted with the Shiel can well believe all that is said of it; but the example set by the saint's fishermen has been copied so closely, and pushed to such extravagant lengths, during the last forty or fifty years, that one wonders how the whole race of salmon frequenting its waters has escaped extermination. Even yet, under favourable circumstances, the angler's sport is sometimes splendid; and it will delight those who love the preservation of what ought to be a glorious river, to learn that a much more enlightened policy lately inaugurated in reference to the Shiel, is likely to make it once more what it was of old—"piscosus."

The second occasion in which Adamnan refers to the Shiel is

this:—Some of the buildings at Iona had gone out of repair, and a supply of wood for the necessary restorations was required. For this purpose twelve boats were sent out on a voyage, and, in due course, were laden with cargoes of oak, fetched from the mouth of the river Shiel—"ab ostio fluminis Sale." On the return voyage the weather at first was calm, so that the sailors were obliged to take to their oars; but a west wind suddenly springing up, they made for an island close at hand, called Airthrago or Airtrago, and sought shelter under it. Shortly afterwards the wind shifted to the south-east. This enabled them to hoist their sails and slip away to Iona, which they reached without any difficulty.[3] A few remarks on this expedition will not be out of place. Dr Reeves, the talented and accurate editor of Adamnan's work, finds some difficulty in admitting the Moidart Shiel to be the river in question, and is inclined to shift the scene elsewhere. He gives his reason in a note appended to chapter 45, book ii.—"The river Shiel, which connects the fresh-water lake of Lochshiel with the sea, ...is excluded from identification with the name in the text, because it was a S.E. wind which conveyed the party from it to Hy, whereas a N.E. wind would be required to do this from beyond Ardnamurchan. We must therefore leave this name unidentified." The Doctor's difficulty has been submitted to certain gentlemen living in the district, and who for years have been accustomed to sail along the Ardnamurchan and neighbouring coasts. Their verdict, founded upon practical experience, entirely does away with his objection. They declare that under a south-east wind, a vessel leaving Loch Moidart would fetch Ardnamurchan Point with slack sheets— well on, in fact, towards the north end of Mull; and that, by hauling closer, the rest of the journey could be accomplished without any alteration in the course, so that from Loch Moidart to Iona the whole journey could be made in one stretch. A west wind is a head-wind to any boat leaving Loch Moidart for the Point of Ardnamurchan, so that the boats to which Adamnan refers would be compelled either to turn back or to find shelter along the Ardnamurchan coast. Now there is an island which, supposing them to have left the mouth of the river Shiel, would have given them the shelter required. This island is only a few miles beyond the entrance of Loch Moidart, and is known under the evidently modern name of Eilean na-h-acarsaid, or "harbour island." Fishing vessels constantly fly to it under heavy westerly or southerly gales. Between Loch Moidart and this island there is a promontory called Rhu Ardtoe. The similarity between Ardtoe and Airtrago, the writer thinks, will strike any one who is accustomed to the abbreviations and other modifications which ancient names undergo in the course of centuries; and it is not improbable that the island bore in olden times the name of this promontory Airtrago— Ardtoe—which the Iona boatmen had just passed; or, that not knowing it by any specific name, they distinguished it by a name which they knew, viz., that of the Rhu not far from it. This transition does not seem more violent than that of Artdaibmuirchol and Artdamuircholl to Ardnamurchan. Yet when the biographer writes of Artdaibmuirchol, no reader of ordinary intelligence fails to understand what place is meant. Dr Reeves suggests that Airtrago may be identified with Arran; but, with all respect, this seems a very wild guess, for in this hypothesis how does he explain "ab ostio fluminis Sale"? Professor Mackinnon inclines to the idea that it must be sought for in Lorn. The objection to this is, that the identity of the river in which the salmon were caught is almost beyond dispute, the Moidart and Ardnamurchan Sheil being plainly indicated. This granted, it seems quite improbable that Adamnan, a few chapters afterwards, would use the same terms "Sale" and "flumen Sale" to signify a different river Sheil, without adding something to prevent the one being confounded with the other, if a difference really existed. It may occur to some that the Iona people must have somewhat laboured under a misapprehension, if they expected to get oak trees near the banks of the Sheil in sufficient quantities to reward them for undertaking such a long journey, for to-day, indeed, very little of the kind exists, and that little commands little or no value. But in those early times thick forests undoubtedly covered a large portion of Ardnamurchan and Moidart. In the moss flats near the river, the trunks and roots of noble trees, which are constantly met with by the natives when cutting their peats, bear witness to what once existed. It is also one of the great difficulties to be contended with in reclaiming land in that neighbourhood, to devise means by which these obstructions may be removed, for no proper drainage can be effected so long as they remain in the soil. This was especially the case when the present Cliff farm, situated on the banks of the river, was being brought under cultivation. Gunpowder had sometimes to be used. On one occasion a party of workmen employed in cutting a deep trench, a mile or so farther east, came upon a bed of acorns, blackened of course, but not decayed. The large trunks near them seemed to indicate a grove of oaks in the midst of the forest, some of them were imbedded to a depth of nine feet below the surface. Not far from this spot is a place still called Rhu Darach, or "oak point." When the MacIans of Ardnamurchan were chased from the sea and forced to give up their career of piracy, it is related of one of their bands that, being hotly pursued by a Government ship, and by some galleys belonging to the hostile clans, they ran their vessel ashore near Ardtoe, and taking to the woods between that place and Sheilfoot baffled the search of the enemy. They afterwards crossed the Sheil river, and became absorbed among the Clanranald Macdonalds. The large tracts of moss near the western end of Lochsheil are in reality overwhelmed forests. The natives have a tradition that these were set fire to by the Danes; but it is more probable that they were levelled under some tempest of greater intensity than usual. It was thus that a magnificent wood went down in Arisaig during a fierce hurricane which swept over the kingdom about twenty-seven years ago. On this occasion the few trees left standing could only be compared to the stalks of corn which escape the hooks of the reapers. The destruction of our native woods along this part of the coast was completed by the iron-smelting company established, about the middle of the last century, on the shores of Loch Etive. The fuel used for their purposes was charcoal, and to supply this charcoal almost all our woods were mercilessly cut down, and the country left denuded. In Glenuig, for instance, where scarcely a tree can be seen to-day, the woods were so thick that, many years after the '45, if the cattle strayed within them it was a task involving hours of worry and search to recover them. The same melancholy story is told of Roshven. The hill slopes, except in one corner, may be said to have been swept clean. Fifty years ago a bobbin manufactory was established at Salen-Suinart, and the surrounding copses were put under requisition; but the operations of the company were wisely kept under some kind of control, the result being that the wooded shores of Loch Suinart are now among the most pleasing features of that part of the country. But as these operations extended up the south side of Lochsheil, the fury of total destruction seems to have found vent once more. That side of the loch has never recovered, except near the entrance to Polloch. At the head of the loch, and within the site of the Glenfinnan Monument, there are some magnificent old Scotch firs, which, if they are remnants of an ancient forest, as is probably the case, give one some idea of what the country must have been in olden time when covered with such noble trees. Between the pass at the head of Loch Eilt and the inn at Kinloch-Aylort, both sides of the valley show signs of having been, ages ago, under forest. In some instances the pines are still upright, but they are lifeless trunks, worn to the core with age, hoary and weird-like in their decay. Many of the local proprietors have, within the last thirty years, given a good deal of attention to the rearing of young plantations. It is a most praiseworthy effort. As successful in this direction may be mentioned Mr Dalgleish of Ardnamurchan, Mr Macdonald of Glenaladale, Captain Swinburne of Eilean Shona, Mr Blackburn of Roshven, the late Mr Hope Scott, Lord Howard of Glossop, and Mr Astley of Arisaig.

From the light reflected by the ancient Irish annals, it seems pretty well settled that a considerable tract of debatable ground lay between the recognised territories possessed by the Dalriads and those still held by the Northern Picts, or "Cruithne Tuath." According to Mr Skene this intermediate belt included Morven. This would throw the natives of Ardnamurchan, Moidart, and of districts farther north, among those whose policy it would be to resist the encroachments of the Dalriads. The aggressiveness of the latter exciting the jealousies of the other party would naturally enough lead on to conflicts, the scene of which would often be within the debatable ground, or beyond its limits, according as victory weighed to either side. In this hypothesis, without however wishing to push it too far, we may perhaps be able to identify within our own neighbourhood one or two places mentioned in the ancient annals, and regarding which there is some uncertainty. Thus, twelve or thirteen years after St Columba's arrival in Iona, there is a brief record entered in Tighernach's annals, and worded Cath-locha-da Eiges—"battle of Loch da Eiges." If the event is not to be placed in Ireland, one would feel inclined, judging merely from sound, to place it in Morven, close to Loch Teagus. This narrow loch is a branch of Loch Suinart, and diverges into Morven opposite Glenborrodale of Ardnamurchan. According to the "Statistical Account" there is a vitrified fort close to the shore, and within a short distance of Rahoy.

In Adamnan's "Life of St Columba" we are told that, while in Ardnamurchan, the saint once overheard two of his companions discourse about two Irish chiefs supposed to be then living in Ireland, and, interrupting the conversation, said:—"My children, why do you talk so foolishly about two men whose heads, only recently, have been cut off by their enemies?" This announcement was confirmed that very same day by the arrival of some Irish sailors, who anchored their vessel at a place called Muirbolc or Muirbulg.[4] There is not much difficulty in identifying this spot. Dr Reeves says that Muirbolc signifies a sea inlet, and probably belongs to a sheltered bay in or near Ardnamurchan. At the entrance of Loch Suinart, and on the west side of Rhu Ardslignish, there is a pretty little bay called Camus-nan-Geall, and immediately above it a small farm, now added to the farm of Mingarry, called Bourbloige. But Adamman qualifies the name by a strange epithet, which has given rise to a good deal of discussion among commentators, viz., Muirbulg of Paradis*e-nèamh*. Perhaps the beauty of the spot may have struck the saint and his companions as in singular contrast to the rest of the country, for it is in the same chapter we read of Ardnamurchan being a "regio aspera et saxosa;" and, by way of marking this contrast, they may have compared the place to Eden. Or it may have merited the term from some remarkable event connected with the conversion of the natives dwelling in it, or from the presence among them of certain persons eminent for their piety. There is an ancient cemetery close to the bay, and, a little farther to the east, a well called after St Columba. It is very probable that the event recorded by Tighernach, under the year 731, has reference to Buorbloige: "Cath itir Cruithne agus Dalriada in Muirbulg ubi Cruithne devicti,"—Battle between the Picts and Dalriads in Muirbulg, where the Picts are defeated.[5] A similar entry is made in the annals of Ulster. From this it would appear that the Dalriads, after seizing the neutral ground, had crossed Loch Suinart, and continued driving the Pictish inhabitants still farther north.

When the Danes and other bands of northern searovers began their devastating visits to the western isles and mainland, they sometimes formed settlements on the lands from which the original owners were expelled. But these attempts were generally accompanied by conflicts, of which faint glimmerings reach us at times through local traditions. One or two such scenes are connected with Moidart. The first is placed behind the heights of Dorlin, near the border of a little lake called Loch-na-fala, or "the bloody loch." The natives are said to have been worsted in the engagement, but, in falling back, to have disputed the ground as far as Langal. When Somerled sometime afterwards attacked and defeated the invaders at Corran, he pursued them as far as the banks of the Shiel. The Danes crossed the river at the ford opposite the small village of Aharacle. On gaining the Lochshiel side they made a vigorous stand, but during the battle their leader Torquil was killed. This loss discouraged his followers, who, quitting the field, retreated to the hills, and made their escape to the sea-coast by the Scardoish pass and that of Briaig. It is a pretty strong corroboration of the truth of this tradition, that the name of the

Danish leader has clung to the place ever since. The etymology of the word Aharacle is Ath Thorguil, or "Torquil's ford." After Somerled's death, disputes arose between two of his sons—Reginald and Angus, and for some years a very unnatural war was carried on between them. The family historian of the Clanranalds states that they fought one of their battles in Moidart. But unless this has reference to the incident of Loch-na-fala, no trace of it can be found in the traditions of the district. Angus, with his three sons, perished in Skye in a conflict with the natives of that island; although in the annals of Ulster mention is made not of Angus's, but of Reginald's sons, as having been present on the occasion:—"Cath tucsat meic Raghnailt mic Somairligh for feraibh Sciadh du in ra marbhadh an ar," AD 1208. "A battle given by the sons of Reginald, son of Somerled, to the men of Skye, who were slain with great slaughter."—(Transl. by Mr Skene).[6]

The chief memorial connected with the ancient inhabitants of Moidart is a vitrified fort on Eilan-nan-gobhar. This island is situated opposite the modern mansion of Roshven, and forms part of Professor Blackburn's property. The fort, considering the many ages that have lapsed since its formation, is in a very fair state of preservation, and is an interesting relic of the past. It is perched on the top of a rocky eminence, and in its erection advantage has been taken of the natural means of defence offered by the locality. It is about one hundred and twenty yards in circumference. The walls vary in thickness, from five to six feet. The height however is inconsiderable, not exceeding on level ground three or four feet. Within the enclosure there are traces of four circular buildings, with a passage between them leading from N.E. to S.W. In one part there is a deep hollow, as if the earth had been scooped out, perhaps to mix with the materials that went to form the wall. A few yards farther away, on the N.E. side, there is another and smaller fort; the walls are partly vitrified, partly built up with massive stones. The approach to both forts is by a narrow steep gorge, the lower end of which shows signs of having been strongly defended. There is a small spring of water near the landing-place on the island. There are also signs of a spring higher up between the two forts, but this supply is said during periods of drought to dry up.

From Reginald—mentioned above—son of Somerled was descended John of Isla. This chief married his cousin Amie, a daughter of Roderick, one of Bruce's most faithful followers. When the Scottish king had secured the independence of the country, Roderick shared in the prosperity of his master, and seems to have been confirmed in his title to very large estates. These, including Moidart, Arisaig, Moidart and Knoydart, went at his death to his daughter Amie. By her marriage with John of Isla Amie had several sons, to one of whom, Reginald, the powerful family of the Clanranalds trace their origin.[7]

notes

1   *The New Statistical Account of Scotland* (Edinburgh and London 1845), volume vii, p. 120, Parish of Ardnamurchan: "'Mud' an old Gaelic word for sea spray, and 'Aird', heights, literally the heights of sea spray".

2   *Life of St Columba* Book II, chapter xviii, p. 49 in *Historians*, p. 82 in Llanerch edition. Father Charles mentions the heavy fishing of the river in his day, but does not mention his own exploits. Fishing was his favourite hobby, and it is said that the biggest salmon ever taken from the Shiel was caught by him, but was never officially recorded since he used a worm and not a fly to make the catch.

3   *Ibid*, Book II, chapter xlvi (not 45), p. 75 in *Historians*, p. 108 in Llanerch. 'Hy' is *Ì* ('island') by which name Iona was commonly known, its full name being *Ì Chaluim Chille* ('the Island of Columkille').

4   *Ibid*, Book I, chapter viii, p. 14 in *Historians,* p. 47 in Llanerch. Columba's prediction was in fact even more impressive than as described, since he also predicted the arrival that day of the Irish sailors bearing the news.

5   *The Annals of Tighernach* are printed in *Revue Celtique*, tome xvii, 1896. The entry for the year 731 is on p. 235. The actual wording is 'Cath ider cruithniu 7 Dal Riada im-Murbolg ubi Cruithne devicti'. The *Annals of Ulster* date the battle AD 730, the *Annals of the Four Masters* have it in 725.

6   *Annals of Ulster*, edition with translation and notes by W. M. Hennessy (volume l) and B. MacCarthy (volumes 2-4), 4 volumes (Dublin 1887-1901). The entry is for 1209, not 1208 as stated, and varies somewhat in spelling from the author's quotation.

7   It was customary to base the English equivalent of Gaelic names on the baptismal Latin, so the Gaelic *Raghnall* or *Raonull* (ie 'Ranald') was written in English as 'Reginald' from the Latin *Reginaldus*. The descendants of Reginald are therefore Clanranalds (*clann Raghnaill,* 'the children of Ranald').

Chapter 3

Origin of the Clanranald Family—John of Isla—Divorces his wife Amie—Withdrawal of the Latter to Moidart —Building of Castle Tirrim—Traditions connected with Castle Tirrim—Allan Mac Ruari—Noted for his Plundering Habits—Visits James IV. at Mingarry Castle—Subsequent Visit to Blair Athole, where he is seized and put to death—Execution of his Son— Ferocity of Allan-nan-Corc—Murder of Dugald at Inverailort—Origin of the Morar Family—Murder of Allan-nan-Corc by Allan Mac Dhughuill .

JOHN of Isla is known in Celtic history as the "Good John." When his life, however, comes to be scrutinised, it is questionable how far this distinctive epithet suits him. His treatment of Amie, after several years of wedded life, has a strong resemblance to that with which Henry VIII. favoured his legitimate consort Catharine of Arragon; the slight difference between the two cases being, that the English king acted from undoubtedly beastly motives, while John at any rate simply acted from ambition. With a view of furthering the family influence, John divorced Amie in order to contract a new alliance with a daughter of Robert II. The plea for this step was his sudden uneasiness of conscience in having married within the forbidden degrees of kindred, and so violated the decrees of the Church. It took many years apparently before the chief's delicate conscience wakened up to this sense of guilt; but, once wakened, it was of course a matter of urgent importance to prevent it from falling asleep again until the remedy had been applied. The angels themselves might be supposed to sympathise with "Good John" under such a load of mental distress, and to view with compassion the many sleepless nights which the thought of his union with Amie no doubt gave him. But, unfortunately for the worthy chief's good name, there are convincing proofs that, before marrying Amie, he had applied to the Papal Court, and received in 1337 the necessary dispensation, so that the marriage acquired the same binding force as that of any other marriage in which no canonical impediment existed. How he and the ecclesiastical lawyers came to an understanding on this point it is difficult to imagine. But they settled it somehow, to the disgrace and confusion of Amie, who immediately afterwards had to withdraw from the "Good John's" company. Celtic writers, in discussing this part of their task, are unanimous in affirming that the discarded wife's life was throughout thoroughly pure and reproachless. A curse seems to have attended John's unscrupulous conduct, for the eldest son born of the second marriage became entitled, through Mary Leslie, to the earldom of Ross, that bone of contention which, for nearly two centuries, kept the Western Highlands and Isles in a state of constant disorder, and did more to prevent the civilisation of the country than any other cause during that dark epoch. After the separation, Amie retired into Moidart, where without loss of time she seems to have set about building the present Castle Tirrim, ad 1353.[1] The site was chosen with considerable judgment. About three hundred yards from the cliffs of Dorlin, and immediately close to one of the inner channels formed in Loch Moidart by the island of Risca, there is a detached mass of rock rising abruptly from the edge of the salt water, and at ordinary tides almost surrounded by the sea. The only communication with the mainland is by a narrow sandbank, which at spring tides is covered to a depth of three or four feet. The castle is reared on the highest platform of these rocks. The position is almost unassailable. The outer walls of the building are pushed forward, so that in one part they overhang the sea; while in other parts any footing is almost impracticable, owing to the sudden slope of the rock towards the ground below. The approach itself to the main entrance is not very easy, and at one point where it trenches on the edge of the precipice facing the sea is decidedly dangerous. The walls of the castle are thick and massive. The inner court is lower by four or five feet than the block on which the main building rests. On this block there is a sort of terrace, upon which the doors of the dungeon, the kitchen, the tower, and of one or two other apartments, open. On this same terrace or landing, and directly in front of the entrance to the court, there is a flight of steps giving access to a room above the dungeon. Stone spiral staircases inside the building gave communication between the lower and the upper rooms, but they have mostly fallen down. The ceiling of the rooms is in most instances very low, not exceeding eight feet. In one of the ground-floor apartments— probably the kitchen—there is a well sunk in the solid rock, the depth of which is unknown. It is choked up, in a great measure, with stones and every kind of rubbish, yet the water rises to within a couple of feet of the top. From a slight inspection, it is clear that considerable additions have been made to the building as it originally stood,—the turrets, for instance, flanking the corners of the main tower. To strengthen one of these, a staircase originally giving access to some upper rooms and to the outer walls has been blocked up. It is probable too that the side between the tower and the kitchen was not built as at present until long after Amie's time. The name of the mason employed in constructing the turrets is still remembered, viz., David Paterson. He was a native of Bail-nan-cailleach, in Uist. He received a small plot of land from Clanranald at Scardoish, close to Dorlin. His grandson William was out in the '45; and another descendant, Christina Patterson, died at Langal about twelve years ago. One of the present Macdonald families at Langal trace their connection with him by the mother-side. It is said that Castle Tirrim, although attacked over and over again, was never taken except once. The story as given by the natives is interesting. For some political offence the Clanranald of the day was put under ban by Government. His estates were declared to be forfeited, and a commission was issued empowering the Earl of Argyle to reduce him *vi et armis*. Every one throughout the Highlands knows that such commissions never came amiss to the head of the Campbells; for if the business did not mean an accession of landed property, it meant at any rate plunder, which was the next best thing under the circumstances. The expedition in due course set forth, and, after reaching Loch Moidart, closely invested the castle. While the galleys anchored under that side of the walls fronting the sea, a strong detachment of fighting men was landed and posted on the narrow isthmus on the other side, thus cutting off all communication between the castle and the mainland. Some feeble attempts at an assault were made, but these, owing to the natural strength of the fortifications, were easily repelled. Seeing the impossibility of reducing it by storm, the besiegers determined to force it by starvation. After five weeks of impatient expectation they gave up even this attempt. One evening the landed force was recalled, the vessels got under weigh, and the whole expedition sailed away towards the open sea. After clearing the entrance of Loch Moidart they shaped their course towards the Point of Ardnamurchan, and soon disappeared from the sight of the besieged. The latter, delighted at such a happy riddance, lost no time in coming down from the rock, many of them seeking the inner parts of the country, where they expected to get tidings of their families. On the following day, great was the consternation of the district in learning that the castle was in the hands of the enemy. This was how it happened. After sailing a few miles homewards along the Ardnamurchan coast, the Campbells suddenly altered their course, and, availing themselves of the darkness, returned to Loch Moidart, which they entered —not however by the south channel, just quitted, but by the other—on the north side of Eilan-Shona. This channel, although much narrower, is deep throughout, except at the ford of Shona, and this part is practicable at high water for vessels of moderate draught. At the inner or eastern extremity of Shona the two arms of the loch unite. By this course the Campbells had simply to sail round two-thirds of the island, to find themselves once more in the exact position which they held a few hours previously. Not anticipating such an adaptation of Greek genius, the few men still forming the garrison were taken completely by surprise. After a short but futile resistance they were put to the sword. The triumph of the victors, however, was not of long duration. The whole of the Clanranalds, dispersed through the district, gathered in one body, and, making a furious attack, succeeded in forcing their way into the court. Here a desperate hand-to-hand fight took place, no quarter being given or taken on either side. Some of the Campbells, when the main entrance was assaulted, had not entered the court, but, slipping over the rocks, sought safety in the vessels, and thus escaped. The rest of their countrymen, however, cooped up within the walls, perished to a man.

In some of the later sieges which this redoubtable stronghold had to sustain, artillery had been brought to bear, doing considerable damage to its walls. The marks were particularly evident on the side facing Dorlin Cliffs, as well as on the side opposite the course of the river Sheil at low water. The breaches never having been properly repaired, were among the first parts of the building to give way, when neglect, and the action of frost and rain, began to convert it into a ruin. Last year measures were taken to arrest the progress of decay; and while the masons were engaged in filling up the parts injured by the guns, they found several cannon balls deeply imbedded in the wall. The iron was, as a rule, shattered into fragments, but in one or two instances the balls had split into halves. From these one was able to decide that the calibre of the shot used by the besiegers did not exceed nine pounds. Under the Regency of Mary of Guise there was a double expedition organised against the famous John of Moidart, one portion of which was to operate on land under the Marquis of Huntly, the other on sea under the Marquis of Argyle.[2] We are told that the vessels of the latter were equipped with pieces of artillery supplied by the Government; and although nothing of any grave importance resulted from these warlike preparations, there is little doubt that Argyle paid the castle a visit, and exercised the skill of his gunners against its walls. Amie lived for several years at Castle Tirrim, and, so far as is known, died within it. About the same time John built the Castle of Ardtornish, near the Sound of Mull, which for a long time afterwards was regarded as the family seat of the Lords of the

Isles. As most readers are aware, the chiefs holding these and similar strongholds exercised the most absolute sway over the inferior clansmen. They were the arbiters in all quarrels and disputes among their followers, and in cases where punishment was necessary the execution was often prompt and summary. At Ardtornish the criminal condemned to death was, if the tradition is to be credited, flung over a precipice close to the castle. In Moidart the last sentence was carried out on a low hill within sight of Castle Tirrim. It is still called Tom-a'chrodhaidh, or "the hill of hanging." One of the last scenes of feudal justice, or perhaps barbarity, witnessed on its summit, was the hanging of thirteen Mackenzies. These unfortunate men had been made prisoners during a raid carried by the Clanranalds into Kintail. But the affair turned out disastrously for the invaders. In revenge, the prisoners had to be sacrificed. Perhaps death, in most instances, was preferable to any lengthened confinement in the dungeon of Castle Tirrim, for the place is a dark, dismal, and revolting hole. The walls sweat with damp; while the earthen floor, being on an inclined plane, is moistened into mud by the water oozing from the rock. There is a narrow slit in the wall, giving admission to a faint gleam of light, but this in no sense relieves the obscurity of the interior; the roof is vaulted. It is said that among others who made acquaintance with the miseries of confinement in this dungeon, was a certain chief of the Clan Macintosh. This person, who had suffered cruelly from the forays of the Macdonalds, wished to place himself beyond their reach, and accordingly built himself a castle on an island of Loch Moy. Having established himself in these safe quarters, he, in rather a jubilant frame of mind, expressed a decided conviction that the Macdonalds were no longer a source of uneasiness to his mind. A wandering ministrel who overheard these remarks reported them to Clanranald. The latter, Allan MacRuari, a bold and reckless plunderer of the first class, chose to look upon the matter as a kind of affront offered to himself personally, as well as to the clan at large, and determined to vindicate his title of still being a terror to the Macintosh chief by taking summary proceedings against him.

Putting aside all consideration of the distance between them, and of the extreme difficulty of effecting a surprise, he set out with a chosen band of followers. After a few days of stealthy but rapid marching, they reached Loch Moy during the night, found means of crossing to the island, surprised the castle, and captured its owner. With the same rapidity Allan made his way back to Moidart, and deposited his captive in the gloomy dungeon of Castle Tirrim. The Macintosh chief was detained there for a year, when Clanranald dismissed him with a suitable little homily, to the effect that over-confidence was a mistake at all times, even when cherished behind the strong new walls of Castle Moy. The Moidart people have a tradition that a murder of more than ordinary atrocity was once committed in the dungeon, and that in consequence the blood of the victim cannot be wiped out of the soil. No doubt there have been wicked scenes enough enacted there, but the rest is pure legend. However, there is something constantly oozing from the ground near the door, which has a very strong resemblance to blood, and which no doubt has given rise to the story. When the earth saturated with the substance is cleared away, the undersoil, although at first entirely clean, and presenting no abnormal hue, becomes gradually tinged with a dark rusty colour.[3] The resemblance is so striking, that one of the Glasgow analysts, some years ago, was persuaded to carry some of the stained soil away, with a view to subjecting it to a more minute examination. But on applying the usual tests it was found, as anticipated, to be some other substance having no affinity to blood. A part of the court was, in later times, occupied by a wooden building which gave access to the top of the walls, and in which one or two rooms were fitted up, probably for the use of the men keeping guard. When the castle was set on fire in 1715, the ruins at this corner were piled up many feet in height, the remains of heavy calcined beams being very conspicuous. The late Mr Hope Scott, who then owned Dorlin, had all these cleared away, and while the men were at work some very interesting discoveries were made. A lump of metal, with faint fragments of canvas or leather adhering to it, was found to consist of a number of Spanish dollars, which on being detached and burnished resembled the five-shilling pieces lately in circulation in this kingdom. They were beautiful coins, of solid pure silver, and were issued under different reigns in the 17th century. They were probably brought to Castle Tirrim by Allan Clanranald, who had served under the Duke of Berwick, and who had hurried home to take part in the insurrection of 1715, and in whose lifetime the castle was burnt.

Several other coins were picked up on the same occasion, such as a small silver piece having a St Andrew's cross on one side, and the letters M.R. on the other; a large copper coin, coated with silver, belonging to the reign of Charles II; and several smaller ones, belonging to that of William and Mary. Perhaps it was more in unison with the character of this building to alight upon pieces of chain-shot, for instance two four-pounders linked together, the rusty head of an ancient battle-axe, stag's horns and the like, —all which were disinterred from the rubbish with which the court was encumbered. The Spanish dollars, nearly two dozen in number, were handed over to Admiral Sir Reginald Macdonald, the lineal representative of the chief who left them in Castle Tirrim one hundred and seventy-four years ago.

The roof of the Castle was covered with slates of a pale-green colour.

John survived his first wife several years. After his death his body was taken from Ardtornish and deposited in Iona, with no ordinary state and ceremony. The chroniclers seemingly forgot his faults under the strong light of his real virtues, and have left to posterity a character painted in very bright colours. He was the first who received the title of "Lord of the Isles."

Donald, the oldest son by the king's daughter, married the Countess of Ross, and through her founded his title to the earldom of that name. The claim was admitted, but the great accession of property which in this way came into the family of the Lords of the Isles, was more than enough to excite the jealousy of the Scottish kings, who could ill afford to see a subject, already semi-independent, become so powerful. Hence the origin of that protracted struggle between themselves and the Lords of the Isles, which, as stated before, involved every part of the Western Highlands and Isles for nearly one hundred and fifty years in scenes of rapine and bloodshed. This miserable contest goes a long way to explain the utter state of barbarism to which this part of the kingdom was then reduced. The Highlanders, in spite of their personal or tribal feuds, naturally rallied round him whom they regarded as their lawful prince, and opposed to the utmost both the forfeiture and the invasion of his claims. On the other hand, kings like James I, James II, and James IV, were not persons to relax in their efforts to make the authority of the crown absolute and respected everywhere throughout the kingdom. The struggle ended disastrously for the Lords of the Isles, and in the abolition of their title. This period may be divided into a series of seven or eight great insurrections, organised by–

Donald, 2nd Lord of the Isles	AD 1411
Alexander, 3rd Lord of the Isles	AD 1429
Donald Balloch, Lord of the Isles	AD 1431
John, 4th Lord of the Isles	AD 1451
Sir Alexander of Lochalsh	AD 1497
Donald Dubh, or the Black	AD 1503
Sir Donald of Lochalsh	AD 1513
Donald Gorm of Sleat	AD 1539

These are followed by the troubles which ended in the ruin of the Islay family, and in the transference of their estates to the Campbells. The civil wars commenced under Charles I perpetuate the confusion, until, after the rising in '45, the whole clan system becomes completely annihilated.

In these various insurrections the Clanranalds took a very active and prominent part, with the result that several of the Castle Tirrim chiefs came to a violent end. Such for instance was the fate of Alexander, son of Godfrey, who is mentioned as a leader of two thousand men. He with several other chiefs had been enticed by James I to Inverness; but once within the clutches of the treacherous king, they were hanged without mercy. The next, Allan MacRuari, fared no better. But his was a stirring and adventurous life, consecrated almost throughout to fighting and rapine. He carried his forays into Ross, Cromarty, Moray, and Argyle, while few places nearer home, not owned by his own clan, escaped his attentions. The island of Mull especially suffered from his depredations. The galleys of this chief were ranged on the side of Angus, son of John, fourth Lord of the Isles, at the battle of Bloody Bay, near Tobermory, and helped to win the battle on that disgraceful occasion. He was, moreover, accused of having laid sacrilegious hands on Iona itself, of having burnt a church dedicated to St Finnan at the head of Loch Lochy, and of having in his excesses spared neither priests nor laymen. There is a poem preserved to us in the collection of the Dean of Lismore, and translated by the late Rev. T. M'Lauchlan, in which this chief's iniquities are rather fiercely dealt with:–

> The one Demon of the Gael is dead,
> A tale it is well to remember;
> Fierce ravager of Church and Cross,
> The bald head, heavy, worthless boar.
>
> Mac Ruari, from the ocean far,
> Wealth thou'st got without an effort,
> 'Tis a report...
>   Bald head Allan, thou so faithless,
> That thou hast, not thine only crime,
> Ravaged Hy and Relig Oran.
> Fiercely didst thou then destroy
> Priests' vestments and vessels for the mass.
> Thou art Irish Gall's great curse;
> Thou art the man whose heart is worst
> Of all who followed have thy Chief.
> There was the Abbot's horrid corpse,
> Beside that other lawless raid

Against Finan in Glengarry,
Have cursed thy bald head, Allan.

Thine own country and thy friends
Thou hast cruelly oppressed.
The last of thy goodness was lost
Between the Shiel and the Hourn,
Worthless, cruel son of Ruari.

It is of Allan the story is told, that being at sea on one occasion, and having met unexpectedly a large number of Maclean galleys which it was hopeless on his side either to fight with successfully or to fly from in safety, he hit upon the following stratagem which helped him out of the difficulty. Feigning death, he caused his followers to have him duly covered over like a real corpse, while the piper commenced playing the lament suitable to so melancholy an occasion. Upon the Macleans approaching near enough to inquire whence the vessel came and whither it was bound, they were told that the Moidart chief had died, and that his remains were now being taking away to be buried in Iona. The hostile galleys passed on, no one on board being sorry to hear that Allan had at length gone to the shades. The story adds that Allan, taking advantage of the absence of so many of the islanders, landed in Mull, and kindled a few bonfires to celebrate his resurrection.

When James IV visited Mingarry Castle, in Ardnamurchan, in 1495, Allan was induced to come forward like a dutiful subject to do homage to his majesty. No doubt the persuasions of his father-in-law, M'Ian of Ardnanmurchan, who was a strong supporter of the royal policy, had a good deal to do in deciding him to take this step; and it was probably out of consideration for his host that James gave Allan the friendly reception which the latter is stated to have received. Perhaps, too, there was a sincere desire on the part of the king to reclaim this wild chief from his lawless ways. But it is much to be feared that Allan was too deeply imbrued to be made a saint of so suddenly; for some years afterwards, having accepted an invitation to visit the king at Blair-Athole, he was at once thrown into prison. He was tried, for form's sake, and condemned to have his head cut off, a sentence which was at once executed, AD 1509. Allan was twice married, first to a daughter of MacIan of Ardnamurchan, next to a daughter of Lovat.

His son Reginald, called Raonuil Bàn, although at first treated with some show of favour, fared no better than his father. For some crime, real or imaginary, he was hanged at Perth, AD 1513.

The next, Dugald, was slain by some of his own clan. The family chronicler ascribes the cause to Dugald's own folly, inasmuch as he had goaded the clansmen to desperation by his supposed cruelty and tyranny. Local traditions, however, put a very different complexion on this matter according to this version, Dugald fell a victim to a conspiracy organised among some of his nearest relatives, who wished to establish his uncle Alexander as chief at Castle Tirrim. There is no allusion to cruelty of any kind on the chief's part, so that one is tempted to impute the evil name under which he suffers to the industry of the chroniclers, who wished to cloak a wicked crime, and prevent it being reflected on the family which it was their business to glorify and flatter. The person selected to work the plot was a notorious scoundrel named Allan-nan-Corc, or "Allan-of-the-knife."[4] He was a near relation of the Castle Tirrim family, and it was probably due to this connection that his crimes escaped so long the punishment which they deserved. This ruffian still lives in the memory of the Moidart and Arisaig natives as a distinct model of ferocity and low cunning. In dealing with those opposed to him, his habit was to "knife" or dirk them off-hand when he could do so without much risk to himself, but to employ stratagem and the most treacherous artifices when having to do with persons capable of offering serious resistance. He is said to have murdered his own brother. His character was so well known, that few either in Moidart or Arisaig were rash enough to incur his hatred or trust his friendship. There is a story that this amiable character, on having once quarrelled with a certain neighbour, sought every opportunity of giving him the happy despatch; but the other being a person of singular prudence and great courage, and being moreover backed by a strong party of friends, was able to meet Allan successfully at every point. Rather disgusted at this failure, Allan had recourse to the serpentine qualities of his nature, and by a sudden show of friendship endeavoured to throw the other off his guard. Approaching him one day, he, with an air of sincere candour, protested that he would far sooner have the other as a friend than a foe, and was quite prepared to live on terms of amity for the future. He went the length of partaking of the other's hospitality, and with the consumption of his host's victuals all the venom of his nature seemed to change into honey. Before departing from the house, he extorted a promise that as he had taken the preliminary steps towards cementing their peaceful union, the other should show an equal amount of confidence in his late foe, and partake of his hospitality by coming to Allan's house on a fixed day. There was no demur to this, and at the appointed time the neighbour boldly presented himself at Allan's door. He was received most graciously, conducted to the best room, and invited to seat himself on a most tempting-looking couch covered with Allan's plaid. But the preparations were too elaborate, or there was a taint of treachery in the air perceptible to the acute senses of the visitor, for before sitting down he removed the plaid, and made the discovery that the couch was a snare. It had no bottom, or support of any kind inside. It was clear that Allan's delicate intention was not only to despatch his newly-acquired friend, but to despatch him in a very undignified position. Drawing his sword, the intended victim made his exit, assuring the unabashed host that no doubt the dinner would have proved excellent, but that the furniture was not by any means to his taste.

When the plot against Dugald's life was fully matured, advantage was taken of the chief's visit to Arisaig, where he used to reside for some weeks during the year, to put it in execution. It was known that Dugald was to return by Kinlochaylort, and the confederates determined to surprise and attack him in the difficult ground between Roshven and Inveraylort. For some days they took up a position among the woods at Alisary; but the chief not appearing, they moved on towards the head of the loch. Concealing themselves on the north side of the Bealach Breac, they waited until Dugald, with a few attendants, was seen to cross the bay, and when near the foot of the Bealach they rushed upon him. The attack was so sudden that the attendants gave way almost at once, the chief himself being compelled to seek safety in flight. He was pursued as far as Polnish, where he was hit between the shoulders by an archer in Allan's train. After falling, he was finished off by Allan's own dirk. The place is still called Corrie-Dhughaill. The body was then dragged down to the sea-shore, and left to be devoured by the ravens, Allan vowing that whosoever ventured to give it Christian burial should be made to feel the fullest measure of his vengeance. The chief's bailiff, however, M'Isaac, the tenant of Lochans, on hearing of the murder, crossed over to Kinlochaylort, and had the body brought down to Roshven. Here he was met by some Smerissary people, whom he persuaded to assist him in transferring the remains to Eilan-Fhionnan, in Lochshiel. For this act M'Isaac was freely threatened by Allan and his gang, but the mass of the natives were evidently favourable to M'Isaac, so that the murderers had to content themselves with threats which the other could afford to despise. Dugald had been married to a daughter of Lochiel, but his wife died shortly after the birth of their only son Allan. So long as this boy stood in the way, the conspiracy which destroyed the father could only be looked upon as half successful; and there is no doubt that, with men like Allan-nan-Corc engaged in it, the rest of the business would prove of the utmost ease. But a Cameron girl, who had accompanied her mistress to Castle Tirrim, suspecting their designs fled with the child to Lochaber, and confided it to the care of the grandfather or to one of the uncles. He was brought up among his mother's friends until he reached the age of manhood. His claims were then made known, and pressed at Castle Tirrim. Probably there was considerable demur on the part of those who had profited by the father's murder, and the negotiations became tedious. This not suiting the Camerons, a party, formed principally of Camerons and Macmillans, from Loch Arkaig side, were placed

at young Allan's service, with instructIons to take vengeance on his
father's murderers. They began with Arisaig, where, it was
rumoured, Allan-nan-Corc and some of his old band were then
living. The Camerons reached on a Sunday morning, when most of
the people were assembled at mass. This, in their opinion, was an
excellent opportunity of paying off old scores, so they suggested
that the church should be set on fire, and the worshippers
slaughtered while rushing out. But young Allan resolutely opposed
this, alleging, and with reason, that many of the Macdonalds had no
sympathy with Allan-nan-Corc's doings, and that to strike at them
in the way proposed would be to destroy the innocent with the
guilty. Seeing him in this humane frame of mind, the Camerons
were unable to control their disgust, so bidding him henceforth
follow his own devices, they returned at once to Lochaber. A
compromise was ultimately come to between the leaders of the
Camerons and the people of Castle Tirrim, by which Morar was
detached from the Clanranald estates and handed over to young
Allan, Dugald's son. Before this however takes place, the young
chief is made by the popular tradition to go through certain
romantic adventures; while a Nemesis is brought on the scene, in
which Allan-nan-Corc has to expiate his misdeeds before dropping
out of sight. The Highlanders have acted up to Horace's rule in this
narrative, "Nec Deus intersit, nisi dignus vindice nodus inciderit."[5]
After the departure of the Camerons, young Allan was for some
time a wanderer between Arisaig and Knoydart, until he made the
acquaintance of a very charming damsel who used to tend her
father's goats on the hills above Strath Arisaig. The pleasure of her
company was evidently a distraction to his cherished thoughts of
killing old Allan-nan-Corc, and, of course, ought to have been
avoided. But the worthy chief was not altogether master of
himself,—in fact, he was desperately in love, and for the moment
could think of nothing else but of Chloe and her charms. At this
serious crisis he rather complicated matters, by suggesting that the
lady should marry him, and that he should be introduced to her
friends. To this she readily assented; and then the great discovery

came like a thunderbolt on Allan, that she was the daughter of his father's murderer, Allan-nan-Corc. The power of Cupid must be very great, for, rather than lose his pearl, young Allan swore to forego his vengeance, and patch up a truce with old Allan-nan-Corc *ad vitam*. They were duly married, and lived for some months happily together under Allan-nan-Corc's roof. But one morning the young couple had a tiff, in the course of which the gentleman so far forgot himself as to give the lady a push which nearly sent her into the fire. Boiling over with indignation at such ungallant conduct, she cried out that if her father, who was then at the. other end of the house, saw how his daughter was treated, he would certainly do to Dugald's son what he did to Dugald himself. This stirred up the whole memory of the husband's past grievances. Rushing towards the place where the father was, he, without a moment's hesitation, plunged his dagger into the old man's breast and despatched him. By way of softening the tragedy, and giving the victim a decent departure out of life which his previous crimes scarcely warranted, old Allan-nan-Corc is represented at the moment of the assault made by his son-in-law to have been on his knees piously engaged at his morning prayers. Perhaps such a finale is not inappropriate, for it forms no part of the exigencies of the situation that the great enemy of mankind should have it all his own way.

Notes

1 Archaeological evidence in fact dates part of the castle from the mid thirteenth century, a hundred years before the building work undertaken by Amie. The first written record of it dates from 1373.

2 The expedition, which took place in 1554, is described more fully in chapter iv, pp 44ff.

3 This has been seen by people living today.

4 Allan-nan-Corc — this appears to be a misprint for 'Allan-na-Corc' (*Ailean na Cuirce*) — 'Allan of the Knife', since this is how the author translates the name, and how it always appears in tradition. *Ailean nan Corc* would translate 'Allan of the Knives'.

5 "And let no God be brought in (to the action) unless a tangle develops worthy of his intervention to unravel it" — Horace, *The Art of Poetry*, 190.

Chapter 4

*Selection of John of Moidart to be leader of the Clan—
His Imprisonment—Claim of Ranald Galda—His Expulsion from Castle
Tirrim—Battle of Blar-nan-leine—Annihilation of the Frasers and Death
of Ranald—The Strontian Worthy—Tradition regarding him—
Protracted Contest between John and the Government—Final Triumph of
the Former—His Death at Castle Tirrim—Buried in Eilean-Fhionnan—
Desecration of his Remains—Succeeded by his son Allan—
Destruction of the Clanranald Macdonalds in the Island of Eigg—
Sir Donald Macdonald—Compelled to submit to the Policy of James VI.*

AFTER the murder of Dugald, a good deal of obscurity hangs over the family-history of the Clanranalds. On the one hand, the legitimate heirs—viz., Allan, who, as we have seen above, had to content himself with Morar, and Ranald Galda, a son of Allan MacRuari, executed at Blair Athole—seem to have been obstinately excluded from the succession; while on the other, Alexander the usurper, or whatever he was, was unable to transmit the title to any of his own legitimate children. The probability is, that the tribe was in a more than ordinary state of confusion, if not of actual chaos, and that a majority of the more influential families among them by way of restoring some degree of order and of putting themselves in a position to hold their own against hostile clans, determined to select as chief the one best fitted for the office, irrespective of any hereditary rights or of lineage. If such was their aim, they certainly succeeded; for John of Moidart, the object of their choice, stands out unquestionably as the ablest as well as the most intrepid of all those who at any period ruled the clan. He was a natural son of Alexander, by a native girl Diorbhail, or Dorothy, daughter of a small tenant living at Brunery in Kinlochmoidart.[1] The distinguishing points in John's character were boldness, energy, fertility of resource under difficulties, prudence, and a tenacity of purpose, which the wholeweight of the Government of the day failed to shake. John was established at Castle Tirrim in 1530, shortly after Alexander's death. His name occurs during the same year in a paper presented to King James V., and signed by several other chiefs, among them MacIan of Ardnamurchan, in which the parties offer to do homage personally to his majesty, provided they receive a guarantee that in going and coming they shall not be molested by their redoubted foe the Earl of Argyle. The king assented at once to this, and made their journey safe by exacting hostages from the earl. During the next ten years we hear of no disturbances in which John or any of his people took part. In 1540, the king, while making a tour round the north of Scotland, received the homage of most of the insular and mainland chiefs. A considerable number met him in the island of Skye, and on this occasion the Moidart chief failed not to appear also. The treatment, however, which they received from the king was worse than a political blunder, it was a downright breach of trust. Glad to find so many within his grasp, the foolish king, without any sense of honour, carried them away south and committed them to prison. This opportunity was not lost upon Ranald Galda, who immediately came forward and urged his claim to the estates. His mother being a daughter of Lovat, Ranald was, while yet a child, removed to the north and brought up among the Frasers; but during the long period of his minority, as well as for years afterwards, his name seems to have almost lapsed from the memory of the Macdonalds. Either through personal indifference, or through the neglect of his mother's friends, no serious steps had hitherto been taken towards securing him in his rights. The oblivion into which he had fallen is pretty well expressed by the epithet which his re-appearance among the Clanranalds procured him, viz., the Galda, i.e. stranger. However, he was undoubtedly the heir, and as such, in the event of John's never coming back to his country, he had a fair prospect of being acknowledged chief.[2] But the Galda's character was misunderstood from the very beginning. While preparations were being made at Castle Tirrim to give him as hospitable an entertainment as the circumstances justified, he was heard to give utterance to certain ideas which bordered so closely upon what may be termed domestic meanness, that the guests rose up as one man and drove him with contempt from their sight.[3] The inference in their minds was, that a chief of such contracted views in matters pertaining to the kitchen, must be utterly wanting in the serious qualities necessary to uphold the reputation of a warlike race. But in this they were mistaken, as the event afterwards proved, and as some of them to their cost had to acknowledge. The indignity, however, offered to their relative was too much for the equanimity of the Frasers. They determined to force the Galda upon his unwilling clansmen, and to have him reinstalled in triumph at Castle Tirrim. But at this juncture the king died, and John of Moidart was liberated, or made his escape from prison. On reaching Moidart he resumed at once the leadership of the clan.

In preparing for the Frasers, John had the support of the Keppoch Macdonalds and of the Camerons then, according to Gregory, he and his friends, instead of waiting to be attacked, carried the war into the enemy's country, seizing and wasting Abertarf, Stratherrick, Glenmorrison, and Glen Urquhart. In their extremity the Frasers invoked the aid of Huntly, who, levying several hundred men, united his forces to theirs, and compelled the invaders to fall back towards the western end of the great glen. Some writers assert that they penetrated into Moidart itself, and actually reinstated the Galda, who, when all was over, accompanied the Frasers on their return home as far as the Lochy, doing this as a matter of courtesy to his northern friends. But this is very improbable, for there is no mention of a Fraser garrison ever having been left at Castle Tirrim, and for the Galda to come back without friends to support him must have meant certain destruction to himself. It is also most unlikely that the Macdonalds and the Camerons would have allowed an enemy to penetrate through the defiles of their wild and rugged country, without flinging themselves upon them and doing their best to cut them in pieces. The approach to Castle Tirrim by land would be almost impossible to any enemy, however well equipped and numerous, with an energetic leader and a strong clan in front to bar the way.[4] In fact no assailants would be rash enough to run the certain risk of being surprised in such dangerous ground. Whenever Castle Tirrim was attacked, it has always been, so far as known, by sea, the only side by which access was practicable. It is pretty certain that Huntly and Lovat, after reaching the western end of the glen, hesitated about proceeding any farther. Their campaign ended in a sort of demonstration, and, so far at any rate as the Gordons were concerned, had a strong resemblance to the warlike energy of the famous king who marched his troops up a hill and then marched them down again. Unable to fight on their own terms, the invaders made up their minds to withdraw. Huntly returned home by Glenspean; but Lovat, in spite of the earl's remonstrances, separated himself from the Gordons, and chose the line of the present Caledonian canal as being the nearest route to his own country. All are agreed that this was a most fatal mistake on Lovat's part. It gave the Macdonalds and the Camerons the opportunity which they keenly wished for. Pressing forwards on the north side of Loch Lochy, they intercepted Lovat at the head of the loch, thus compelling him either to fight or to surrender. It is certain that the Frasers, in point of numbers, had little or no chance of coming out of the business victoriously; but they had nothing of the stuff about them that shrinks from peril, and, like brave men, determined to cut their way through the opposing ranks, or die in the attempt. A most furious and sanguinary hand-to-hand fight ensued. Owing to the heat of the weather, the combatants threw off their upper garments, and fought, like butchers, in their shirt sleeves. Hence the name by which the battle has been handed down in history, Blàr-nan-leine, or "battlefield of the shirts." Lovat and Ronald Galda are said to have given proof of the most indomitable courage. Indeed, whether from personal animosity, or from that reckless disregard of life which the fighting habits of the age instilled, both sides, once engaged, grappled with each other in a desperate murderous struggle, neither seeking nor giving quarter. The whole field became a shocking scene of slaughter. Before the sun went down the Frasers were annihilated almost to a man. Tytler pithily remarks, that the parties fought rather for extermination than for victory.[5] Lovat, Ranald Galda, with nearly three hundred Frasers, were left dead on the field, and it is not improbable that an equal if not a greater number of the Macdonalds and Camerons perished along with them. It is generally believed in Moidart that Ranald Galda fell by the hand of a Strontian man called Mac Dhonuill Ruaidh Bhig—"son of little Red Donald." This individual received a deep cut in the head from Ranald's sword, and, after the engagement, was carried down to his native place at the head of Loch Suinart. His wound was at first carefully attended to by a local surgeon, but some of the Strontian people being deeply incensed at Mac Dhonuill Ruaidh, bribed the surgeon to put him out of the way. The cause of this animosity is attributed to the patient's insufferable vanity, inasmuch as he harped, in season and out of season, on his own personal valour in having overthrown and slain such a formidable opponent as Ranald, whereas his friends were perfectly aware that it was more by a trick, not to call it treachery, than by fair fighting that he succeeded as he did. For, during the fight, Ranald having cut down several of his adversaries, was about to perform the same office on the person of Mac Dhonuill Ruaidh, but the latter, dreading the encounter, shouted to Ranald to beware an enemy who was about to strike at him behind his back. Ranald instantly wheeled round to meet this supposed foe, but while doing so the Strontian man leaped forward and plunged his weapon into his side. The unfair deed was not unpunished. Ranald, by a supreme effort, dealt his assailant a desperate back stroke with his sword, which caught the assailant on the skull and deeply gashed it. He then fell down, and expired within a few minutes. Others say that some of the Strontian natives were in favour of Ranald, owing to his being the legitimate heir, and would have preferred him to John of Moidart; hence their anger at their neighbour for the part which he played in bringing about his death. The surgeon having been bribed, continued for some time his apparently friendly attentions to Mac Dhonuill Ruaidh Bhig; but one day while dressing the wound, he contrived by a somewhat rough and careless manipulation to open it afresh. The agony roused the victim to such a pitch of fury, that, snatching a dirk suspended near the bedside, he made a furious lunge at the surgeon's breast, and, as the story goes, drove the weapon home to the mark. It was his last effort; after two or three gasps, the son of little Red Donald went away to rejoin Ranald. His body was buried in Eilean Fhionnan. Many years afterwards the remains were disturbed in the process of making room for other and newer occupants, and, through some neglect, the skull of Mac Donuill Ruaidh was not recommitted to the earth. It lay for many a day among a heap of other bones under the altar slab of the ruined church of Eilean Fhionnan. It was often handled by the natives of Moidart, Ardnamurchan, and Suinart, whose curiosity was of the keenest in examining the cut left on it by Ranald Galda's sword. It has disappeared since, but whether carried away, or buried once more, it is impossible to say. There is one old man still living, a native of Dalnambreack, who saw it in his younger days, and which, in its presence, listened to old men repeating the tradition concerning it. It is also a tradition that Ranald's sword was taken down to Strontian, and preserved in some family of that neighbourhood for a long time.

There is another story connected with the battle of Blàr-nan-leine, at which one might be tempted to smile if only the real atrocity of the whole business could be kept out of sight. Two champions, a Macdonald and a Fraser, having singled each other out for mutual destruction, apostrophise each other in this fashion. The Macdonald, while delivering a vigorous lunge with his broadsword,—"Take that from Clanranald's blacksmith!" The Fraser, parrying the thrust, and then swinging his battle-axe over the Moidart man's head,—"And thou, receive this from MacShimie's (Lovat's) blacksmith.'" When the day was over, these two worthies were found lying beside each other, both dead, their bodies shockingly mangled.

This fight took place at the head of Loch Lochy, in the summer of 1544.

After the victory John withdrew into Moidart. His title to the Clanranald estates, so far at any rate as the tenure depended on the sword—and not upon "sheepskin," as the Highlanders termed it— was now secure. But he and the other two chiefs, his friends, had to face the fiercest resentment of the Government. The authorities were filled with horror at the details conveyed to them of the engagement, and vowed the amplest vengeance against the guilty parties. But if it is a far cry to Loch Awe, it is a cry farther still to Loch Arkaig and Loch Shiel. They made the attempt and failed, except in so far that they wasted Keppoch's lands, and hanged some of his people who fell into their hands. During the following year, many of the principal Highland chiefs passed over to Ireland, where they were to be initiated by certain emissaries of Henry VIII into some nefarious plot against the Scots Government. John, Maclean of Ardgour, Maclean of Kingairloch, MacIan of Ardnamurchan, and Glengarry were also present; but the meeting broke up in confusion, without any definite plan of action being agreed upon. So far as the Moidart chief was concerned, it had the effect of making him a still more conspicuous mark for future vengeance. He was outlawed, his property was declared confiscated, and his head would have been a welcome present to the Government. Shortly afterwards, Huntly, aided by the Macintoshes, appeared for the third time in the neighbourhood. Owing to a want of caution on their own part, or to putting too much trust in promises, Lochiel and Keppoch were seized, taken away to Elgin, and hanged. The expedition, however, left the Clanranald district unmolested. The co-operation of Macintosh on this occasion was about the worst turn which he could possibly have given to the interests of his own clan, for it gave rise to a feud between the latter and the Keppochs which, stimulated by minor disputes regarding land, lasted more or less actively for more than a hundred years. It was brought to a crisis in 1688, at the battle of Mulroy, on which occasion the

Macintoshes were defeated and compelled to fly. This battle is memorable as being the last of the kind fought among the Highland clans. In 1548 a free pardon is given to John. The Government in fact was unable to reach him in the wilds of Moidart. In 1552 he received a summons to meet the Regent Arran at Aberdeen. But this he flatly refused to comply with, knowing to a certainty that if he ventured within reach of the law his neck would be placed in jeopardy. His own early experience, and the example of his ancestors, were there to warn him. "Why don't you come into my grotto?" said the lion, in Lokman's fable, to the fox who kept at a respectful distance. "Because," replied the father of stratagems, "I see signs of many visitors having entered your house, but none of any having ever come out." For this act of contumacy John was outlawed again. A new expedition was organised against him, but, like the others, it collapsed. In 1554 Mary of Guise determined in earnest to have the Moidart chief thoroughly crushed and brought to justice. For this purpose orders were issued to have two separate forces prepared, the one to act by sea, the other by land. The former was entrusted to the Earl of Argyle, who, in addition to his own galleys, had a ship and artillery furnished by the regent. He was to enter Loch Moidart and attack Castle Tirrim. The second force was entrusted to Huntly. It was to consist of his Lowland retainers and of such friendly clans as could be pressed into the Government service. These were to penetrate into Moidart as best they could, and to chase John among the fastnesses of his own country. But John was not intimidated by all these preparations, nor moved one hairsbreadth out of his dogged obstinacy. Full of self-reliance, and trusting to the fidelity of his supporters, he determined to resist the invaders and keep them out of the country to the full extent of his resources. Having placed a strong garrison in Castle Tirrim, he took up a position with the rest of his fighting men towards the eastern end of Moidart, so as to watch Huntly's movements in the quarter where the earl was most likely to appear. But in a short time his apprehensions on this score were completely laid at rest. None of the Highland clans could be induced to give the earl any assistance, owing to his extreme unpopularity after the death of the Macintosh chief through whose means he had been able to trap Lochiel and Keppoch. This chief had been executed at Huntly's instigation, on a charge of conspiring against the earl, although the Government, by reversing the decision of the jury, expressed pretty plainly its opinion of the amount of truth contained in the charge. The Lowland followers being mostly mounted on horseback refused to proceed farther than Abertarf and Huntly knowing, even if they could be induced to continue the expedition, that Moidart was not altogether the place to capture John by a cavalry raid, had nothing for it but to abandon the enterprise and retrace his steps. The regent was deeply incensed at this conduct. She caused Huntly to be seized, imprisoned, and heavily fined. After coming out of prison, a sentence of banishment to France for five years was pronounced against him, and this was only remitted by his paying the Government five thousand pounds. The earl urged in his defence that if he had proceeded against John at the head of a body of mountaineers, and unsupported by Lowlanders, his own life would have most certainly been sacrificed; but the Government chose to consider this plea unsatisfactory. On the western side Argyle's efforts proved also a complete failure. There are no historical details left of his proceedings; but, as shown in a previous chapter, Castle Tirrim had been at one time severely bombarded, a battery raised between its eastern face and Dorlin Cliffs playing upon it on the land side, and a vessel anchored in the bed of the river firing at it on its southern exposure, and it is probable that the epoch must be referred to this expedition of Argyle. In any case, the besieged refused to surrender. John, relieved from his anxiety created by Huntly's rumoured approach, would naturally turn his attention to Argyle's proceedings, and, by hastening down in this direction, compel him at any rate to withdraw the land battery. It was part of the earl's instructions to chastise, if he could, some of the insular chiefs, especially Macdonald of Sleat and Macleod of Harris and, seeing the futility of trying to take Castle Tirrim, he no doubt continued his journey to deal with them. But although baffled in her projects,

Mary of Guise was more determined than ever to secure the person of John of Moidart. By putting a good deal of pressure on the Earl of Athole she persuaded this nobleman to enter into her schemes. Athole, however, was quite conscious of the difficulty of reducing John by force, and mistrusted any attempt of the kind, so he tried the arts of diplomacy. He opened up a correspondence with John, and, by promises of friendly intermediation, and assurances of being dealt leniently with by the Government, succeeded in persuading the chief to appear before Mary of Guise, together with two of his sons and some of his kinsmen.

It is stated that they were received by the regent with affability, even with kindness. But he and his relations had to go to prison all the same. Not relishing this sort of treatment, and being little prepared for it after the assurances given by Athole, John and his companions determined to make their escape at the very earliest opportunity. Either by knocking down their jailers, or by the secret co-operation of the latter, they found means of breaking through their prison hars, and soon were back to their friends in the west. John was once more outlawed. Pains and penalties, including forfeiture of possessions, were hurled against him; but, safe in his own country, he seems to have treated the southern not only with defiance but with contempt. The last we hear of him in the public records is from an entry made during a Session held at Edinburgh in 1567. The minute states that "my Lords" are requested to report by what means John of Moidart and Mackay may be "dantonit."[6] Considering that twelve years had elapsed between John's having taken leave of his jailers and the call for this report how to "dantonit" him, we may be sure that John had not been idle; but what the precise nature of his doings was, or in what direction they tended, we have no means of judging. Holding his own by the sword, he no doubt kept his weapon freely employed at the cost of his enemies. Tytler, in the following remarks, hits upon a truth which seems too often to escape the notice of those writers, for instance Hill Burton, who are so savage upon what they are pleased to call Highland lawlessness:—"In the meantime the kingdom became disturbed in the north, where the fierce and powerful Clan Ranald, under their leader John of Moydart, resumed their career of misrule and spoliation. The general policy pursued in these districts was that introduced by James IV. It was the practice of this monarch to keep the various clans in subordination by encouraging their mutual rivalry, and employing them as checks upon each other. In the event of any sept rising into dangerous pre-eminence, or, as was not unusual, into open rebellion, one of the most powerful northern nobles, Athol, Huntly, or Argyle, was intrusted with a commission of lieutenancy, and, on repairing to the disturbed districts with an armed force, they engaged some of the rival clans to assist in putting down the insurrection. There can be no doubt that such commissions, of which the powers were indefinite, had been often abused to the purposes of individual ambition. The great lords looked for forfeiture of the lands of the Highland chiefs to reward themselves and their followers, and, on many occasions, rather encouraged treason than promoted submission. It was a consequence of this miserable system that these continued in rebellion, not so much from any unwillingness to acknowledge the authority of Government, as from a dread of the influence and misrepresentations of their enemies" (Vol. iii., p. 75).[7] John was not "dantonit" by "my Lords" in spite of their cumulative wisdom. On the other hand, he was too much respected or feared to suffer much annoyance from his neighbours. He died at Castle Tirrim in 1584, having ruled the clan for fifty-four years. His body was conveyed to Eilean-Fhionnan, and buried in the church of that island dedicated to St Finnan. He was the last chief of the Clanranalds buried in the same spot, most of his successors preferring Toghmore in Uist as their final resting-place. It is with much regret that one has to add, that the remains of the illustrious chief were in course of time disturbed and thrown out by some insignificant families of the district, who had the audacity to claim this part of the church as a proper place to intrude their own nothingness and that of their miserable relatives. How the rest of the Moidart people came to tolerate such a violation of their greatest chief's grave is simply inexplicable. John's own descendants too seem to have shown considerable callousness in the matter, for although it may be pleaded on their behalf that, living in Uist, they could scarcely have been cognisant of such doings, still they had factors or bailiffs in Moidart, whose duty should have been, among other essential matters, to see that the dust of the family ancestors was not desecrated. Old Moidart men aver that the chief's skull and part of his bones were to be seen in that ghastly heap under the altar; and this was for many years the common belief of the whole district, until they were collected and committed once more to the earth in the little chapel used by the Kinlochnoidart family as their burial-ground. The body originally rested under one of those beautiful Iona stones with a sword carved upon it immediately in front of the altar. The idea traditionally preserved to us of John's figure is that of a man of great stature, in a frame well knitted together, powerful, and equal to any amount of exertion.[8] He was the first called captain or chief of Clanranald, a title which has ever since been retained in the family.

John was succeeded at Castle Tirrim by his oldest son Allan, a person of whom little good can be written. It was under this chief that the tragedy took place in Eigg by which the whole population of that island was by one fell act completely destroyed. The island had been visited by a party of Macleods, who offering, as alleged, some rudeness to the women, were seized by the islanders, bound hands and feet, and conveyed to their boat, which was then sent adrift and left to the mercy of the winds. Fortunately for the victims the boat was driven ashore in Skye, where they were rescued. Their chief however determined to retaliate, the more readily so as a bitter feeling for some time had been cherished in his breast owing to the shameful treatment which his sister, who was married to Clanranald, had been undergoing from her husband. The island was in consequence invaded by a large force of Macleods; but the natives, old and young, had taken refuge in a large cave close to the sea-shore, the existence of which was unknown to the enemy. They would probably have escaped, but, after a day or two, one of their number left his hiding-place to see if the invaders had departed. He was perceived, and tracked to the cave. Unable to get inside, the Macleods piled up a mass of combustible matter at the entrance, and setting it on fire smothered the helpless victims within.[9] The floor of the cavern was strewn over with their bones, which no one dreamt of disturbing until tourists commenced to visit the spot. These began to carry them away as curiosities. To put a stop to this scandal, the present proprietor of the island caused what remained of them to be gathered and buried under a heap of stones, where they are so far beyond the reach of the remorseless spoiler. The invaders burnt everything on the island, the church among the rest. It was probably owing to this that Allan, after having established a new colony, built another church, dedicated to St Donnan,[10] the ruins of which are still to be seen. This chief died in 1593.

His successor Donald—or Sir Donald, as the family genealogist is careful to qualify him—had a very difficult part to play. This was due to the strong measures which James VI. brought to bear on the Highlands, and on the leading families among the clans during the last twenty years of his life. Determined to make the authority of the crown dominant where it had been so long resisted, he had at first serious thoughts of extirpating most of the native population and of supplanting them by colonists drawn from the Lowlands. If the idea could be carried out without entailing too much trouble, there is no doubt that this odious personification of sense and folly would only have been too happy to realise it. As it was, he made an attempt, fortunately unsuccessful, by sending a large body of adventurers to seize the island of Lewis. The expedition, however, ended in the destruction of almost all those who took part in it. Tytler states that these colonists, who after the conquest of the island were to hold the land as tenants of the crown and pay the rents which the king should fix, forwarded their first instalment in the shape of a sackful of "humanheads."The tenancy went no farther; but the idea was transferred by James to Ulster, to be, in the days of Cromwell, completed among scenes of such atrocious barbarity as seem never to fade from the memory of Ireland. Even Hill Burton, who certainly loathes the Celt, and whose history teems with a certain cynicism that is most objectionable to many of his readers, can afford to discuss James's idea of "planting" in the proper tone. "This word has a peaceful and gentle sound, like the soothing shape in which the discreet surgeon announces that he has to perform some painful and critical amputation. In its full meaning, it was the removal of the race in possession of the soil, and the planting of another. Whether driven forth as wanderers elsewhere, or put to death in their old homes, the first step in the process was one of sheer cruelty to the natives" (Vol. vi.). Although compelled to abandon this iniquitous scheme, James applied himself to others with unremitting energy, all of which aimed directly or indirectly at the breaking down of the chiefs' feudal power, and at the establishment of the common law over their subjects. He derived most of his information regarding the state of the Highlands from one Andrew Knox, Protestant bishop of the Isles,[11] and upon the information thus supplied made many statutes for the supposed welfare of the natives, which were communicated to them through his ecclesiastical emissary. This personage is one of the prominent figures of the time, but his character, whatever it may have been in other respects, is not one to commend itself either for candour or honest dealing. To curry favour with his royal master, he stoops at times to tricks which, in a person of his character, are doubly disgraceful. Gregory tells us that a large number of the chiefs had assembled on a certain occasion at Aros Castle, in the Sound of Mull, to meet Lord Ochiltree and the bishop, who had certain instructions from James which it was judged wise or necessary to impress upon the native mind. When these instructions were given, and the assembly began to break up, the bishop suggests a little plot to his brother commissioner, the execution of which he fondly imagines will both please and tickle the king. The chiefs are courteously invited to step on board Ochiltree's vessel, first to have their untutored minds enlightened by a pious discourse from the bishop, and next to have their carnal appetites refreshed by the good things of Ochiltree's table. All the chiefs, and among them

Clanranald, complied, but Macleod of Harris suspecting some plot declined. While their attention was divided between the overflowing piety of the preacher, and the grosser things of earth, the guests were startled at being told that they must consider themselves prisoners until his majesty decided how to deal with them. The vessel set sail, and the trapped natives, after reaching the south, were thrown into jail. Despicable tricks of this nature never commend themselves to persons of ordinary morality and judgment, for, exclusive of the meanness, they offend common sense, inasmuch as they are likely to do far more harm than good to the cause in whose favour they are practised. Yet Scots kings and their agents have, over and over again, distinguished themselves in this unpleasant manner when dealing with the Highlander; and when the latter, taught by experience, became suspicious and refractory, and held aloof, the upholders of royalty go into hysterics over his conduct, or shout themselves hoarse in decrying him. The narrower-minded and the more contemptible among them sometimes apply terms to the mountaineer and the islesman which, one is tempted to think, would be strong enough if hurled at the worst species of wild beasts. Such language, when the cause which provokes it can be traced nearer home, is simply revolting. While the chiefs were kept in confinement, James continued issuing decrees for the better management of their properties, to which they were obliged to subscribe. Some of these regulations were no doubt wise, but others seem rather ludicrous, inasmuch as they belong properly to the small economies of a private household. Among the more important may be noted the following:—

The chiefs are ordered to appear once a year before the Privy Council at Edinburgh.

On such occasions they must bring a certain number of their relatives along with them. This number is specified for each chief by the council. Clanranald had to bring two.

Their children above nine years of age must be sent to school in the Lowlands, to be thoroughly instructed in reading, writing, and speaking the English language.

No child can be served heir to its father if it has failed to receive this education.

No chief can retain for his service more than one galley.

No fire-arms are to be used—not even in hunting.

As James was one of those absolute monarchs who, according to a certain writer, consider themselves born booted and spurred to ride mankind by the grace of God, one learns without any feeling of surprise that the Highland chiefs are requested to consider him as the head of the Church, and that their scruples, if such existed, of abandoning the old faith are amply satisfied by his royal mandate to conform to the new. In this sense they are enjoined to build kirks and manses.

Among minor details, they are to reduce the number of their retainers, to build "comelie" houses, to eschew idleness, to turn their swords into spades and ploughshares, and to develop themselves into diligent farmers, and skilful gardeners. Clanranald is ordered to remain at Castle Tirrim, with a view to developing the agricultural resources of its neighbourhood; but as rocks are likely to be ever more plentiful than cornfields at Dorlin, he receives permission to expend his energies over Howbeg in Uist. In this enchanted isle he has further opportunities of applying himself to a reasoned study of bucolics.[12]

In 1551 the Scots Parliament was so scandalised at the prodigious appetites of its Lowland subjects, that it deemed it necessary to put them under some restraint.

With much zeal therefore it launched into the question of plates and cookery, expanding or contracting the exact lines within which the stomach of an earl, baron, burgess, archbishop, bishop, or abbot might be reasonably mortified. In a very enlightened spirit it allowed the higher dignitaries from six to eight dishes at table, the lower ones from three to four. The working classes were left to their own discretion, probably because the *res angusta domi* was more than a sufficient barrier to their straying from the healthy path. James, drawing his inspiration from these acts, thought that the Highland chiefs might be profitably fettered by something of the kind. Although pretty abstemious in one sense, they were not looked upon as models of sobriety. They are cautioned therefore against excessive drinking, which, among other evils, "draws nomberis of thame to miserable necessitie and povartie, sua that they are constraynit, quhen they want from their awne, to tak from their nichtbours." Macleod and Maclean are liberally treated; each of them may drink four tun of claret in the year. Clanranald is more restricted, he must not consume more than three. Inferior personages are condemned to one.

There is not much mention made of uisge-beatha. The British Solomon, not being able to dive into the future, was evidently unconscious of the great ravages to be made on his Celtic subjects from this enemy some day, otherwise they would have heard of it before he took his departure to Paradise.

Donald was not deficient in the warlike courage of his race. He gave sufficient proof of this by chastising the laird of Barra, who had the temerity to invade Uist, and to seize some of the Clanranald property, while the chief was absent on the mainland. Donald, after routing the Barra men, hunted their leader through the outer isles until he vanished.

The pressure of the king's policy, however, was too much for him. He had to surrender to the force of circumstances, and acknowledge himself vanquished. It is quite edifying to read of the punctuality with which he reports himself each year to the Privy Council at Edinburgh. No pious Turk bound to the holy shrine of Mecca could have done better. If ever any qualms assailed him at the thought of John of Moidart's grandson being so thoroughly subjugated, or if his spirit revolted at the possibility of a Clanranald being rated by the southerner one degree of less importance than a Macleod or a Maclean, he found balm perhaps in the dignity with which James now invested him. He was knighted,—although one of the last Glengarries, with less than the coolness of Midshipman Easy, would like to have argued that point. Before removing from this troubled scene, Sir Donald professed himself a reformed chief—externally at any rate. He died in 1619, and was buried in Uist.

Notes

1   According to a local tradition John was a year in his mother's womb, due to the malign influence of a local woman, and when born at last he already had one tooth.

2   Ranald Gallda was younger than Alexander, being the son of Allan by his second wife.

3   When the suggestion was made that an ox be slaughtered for the feast, Ranald's reply was that a few hens would be enough. This earned him a new nickname — *Raghnall nan Cearc* ('Ranald of the Hens').

4   The only land approach to Castle Tioram for a large body of men was through the steep sided defile known as *Glac Mhór,* which could be defended quite easily.

5   Tytler, Patrick Fraser, *The History of Scotland from the Accession of Alexander III to the Union.* This book ran to several editions and, as we know from the exact page reference in Note 7 below, it was the four volume Edinburgh edition of 1864 that the author used. The present reference is to volume iii, p. 25.

6   Dantoned, i.e., subdued.

7   Tytler, PF *op. cit.* The Hill Burton referred to by the author is Burton, J. Hill, *History of Scotland from Agricola's Invasion to the Revolution of 1688,* 7 volumes (Edinburgh 1867-70), volume vii.

8   A doctor who visited Eilean Fhìonain and examined bones said to be John's calculated, from the length of the shin bone, that John would have been about 6'4" tall.

9   According to a near contemporary document the number killed was "395 persones, men, wyfe, and bairnis". The date was 1577.

10   St Donnan — an Irish monk who followed Columba to Iona and later established a monastery on Eigg with fifty-two companions. The house was raided by Danes on Easter Sunday 617 or 618. Donnan was permitted to

finish the Mass and bring the brothers to the refectory, which was then set ablaze by the raiders, those who tried to escape being put to the sword. Kildonan on South Uist, as well as Kildonnan with its ruined chapel on Eigg, is named after the saint, whose feast day is 17 April.

11 Andrew Knox was born about 1558, and educated at Glasgow University. He was made Bishop of the Isles in 1605, and Abbot of Icolmkill. He was afterwards translated to the See of Raphoe in Ireland, being succeeded in the Diocese of the Isles by his son Thomas. He died in 1632.

12 These arrangements are the Statutes of Icolmkill (Iona) of 1609, with additions in 1616. The text of the Statutes can be found in the *Register of the Privy Council of Scotland*, ed. D. Masson (Edinburgh, 1889), pp 26-30.

Chapter 5

The M'Ians of Ardnamurchan—Their Contests with the Campbells—
Assisted by John Clanranald—Their Extirpation—A Remnant
incorporated among the Macdonalds of Moidart—Taking of Mingarry
Castle by MacColl—Devastation of Ardnamurchan and Flight of the
Campbells—John Clanranald unites with MacColl in assisting Montrose—
Siege of Mingarry Castle by the Campbells—Raised by the sudden Return
of Clanranald—Visit of MacColl to Castle Tirrim—Frightful Foray into
Argyllshire, conducted by Montrose—MacColl, and Donald, son of John
Clanranald—Inverlochy and other Battles—Plundering of the Minister of
Kilmuir's Lands in Skye by John Clanranald—Extraordinary Traditions
regarding Donald Clanranald—Recent Discovery of large Sum of Money
stolen from this Chief—His Unpopularity among the Clansmen—His
Death in the Island of Canna—Raonuill—Mac-Ailein-oig

JOHN, his son, was compelled to follow his father's example in recognising the power of the Government; but before succeeding to the estates he had made an effort towards driving out the Campbells, who at this time were weighing heavily upon his kinsmen the MacIans of Ardnamurchan. The effort was scarcely successful. The Campbells came back in force, this time with all the authority of the Government to support them. After their return, the condition of the MacIans rapidly changed from bad to worse, until at length the whole tribe was banished from the district. The scene which closes over this branch of the Macdonalds is a very melancholy one. Their chiefs had at one time been the staunch supporters of the crown, and had often done such service to the latter as to provoke the resentment of other clans to whose detriment these services had been rendered. Some of the kings looked upon them with considerable favour; James IV, for instance, twice visited their celebrated stronghold at Mingarry, receiving during his stay the submission of the principal surrounding chiefs, and converting MacIan's castle into a sort of regal court. The loyalty of the MacIans sometimes went so far as to put them in the light of being regarded as policemen to the Government,— their zeal not stopping at the apprehension of even their own kinsmen, whose heads were thus brought to the block. After the disaster at Flodden, when the Government was too helpless to protect its friends anywhere, some of the persecuted clans determined to wreak their vengeance on MacIan. They landed in Ardnamurchan, and, in a pitched battle fought at Craig-an-airgiod, slaughtered the chief, several members of his family, and a large number of his people. For some time the clan recovered a certain amount of influence, but owing to a series of weak chiefs, and to the breaking out of dissensions among the leading families, it gradually waned, until latterly it became of little or no account. The dissensions referred to culminated in a tragedy, which is well remembered as Faothal Dhonuill Chonullaich, from the place where it occurred, viz., at the head of the bay between Kintra and Gorteneorn. The young MacIan chief of the day had been at variance with his uncle, but their differences having been brought to an amicable settlement, he went for a short time to Lochaber, where he married Lochiel's daughter. The uncle, however, was determined to have himself acknowledged as chief, and, watching his opportunity, surprised and remorselessly slew his unsuspecting nephew as the latter was conducting his bride to her new home. The punishment was not long of coming. Lochiel came down with several followers, and in the hot pursuit after the uncle overtook him in Morven. Driven to bay the murderer made a good fight of it, but his partisans were overthrown, and himself left mortally wounded on the field. There is rather a wild fiction regarding his last moments, which however is always quoted by the story-tellers of the country. It is mentioned in the Statistical Account:—"As he (the murderer) lay dying, he requested Lochiel to receive his sword, being unwilling to yield it to one of inferior station. As Lochiel approached, he made a blow at him, with such force as to cut several ant-hills in its sweep, though it missed Lochiel."

The way in which the Campbells came to interfere in Ardnamurchan is this:—A daughter and heiress of MacIan, for some reason or other, resigned her own rights in favour of one of the earls of Argyll, who thereby acquired the superiority over Ardnamurchan and Suinart. This superiority was not acted up to until many years afterwards, when the MacIans were becoming weak. In 1612, during the minority of the son of the victim in the above-mentioned tragedy, Archibald, fourth Earl of Argyll, sent Donald Campbell of Barbreck to seize Ardnamurchan and to levy the rents as his commissioner. Campbell, naturally of a cruel and harsh disposition, performed his task with such severity as to bring himself into odium with the whole population. In 1618 John Clanranald went over to their assistance, and drove Campbell out. The latter, however, was immediately reinstated by the Government. From commissioner he became tenant of Ardnamurchan. Goaded to desperation the people, in 1624, revolted again. According to Gregory, five or six score of them "seized, manned, and armed an English vessel, and betook themselves to a piratical life." Their depredations were so extensive, that these rovers became the terror of the West Coast, from the Mull of Cantyre to Cape Wrath. Their rapacity made no distinction between native, southern, or foreign craft. The Government was compelled to take vigorous measures against them. It fitted out some armed vessels, which were ordered to seek the pirates in their haunts, and either destroy or chase them from the seas. At the same time, it empowered some of the more influential Campbell families, under Lord Lorn, to proceed by fire and sword against that portion of the insurgent tribe which still remained in Ardnamurchan. Some of the insular chiefs, who had suffered from the pirates, gladly co-operated in these efforts. The pirates found this combination too strong for a continuance in their lawless course. They were chased from the Western Isles, and, in their extremity, were forced to seek refuge in Ardtoe Bay, where, running their vessels aground, they fled over to Moidart, to be hidden away among Clanranald's people. Their pursuers then joined the Campbells under Lord Lorn, so that between them the rest of the MacIans were completely exterminated. For his services on this occasion Lorn is said to have received the thanks of the Privy Council. Shortly afterwards Campbell became proprietor of Ardnamurchan, on condition of his paying a certain feu-duty to the Argyll family. One of his first acts following upon this change in his fortunes, was to introduce into the depopulated district a new colony, composed of persons more in sympathy with his own views regarding politics and religion, or at any rate much more pliant than the MacIans. They were a strange mixture—a sort of *omnium gatherum*—taken from the smaller clans, except the Camerons, dispersed through Argyleshire and Perthshire. It was no doubt by way of confirming them in these views that a minister was installed at Kilchoan, AD 1629, the first of the kind ever introduced, so far as known, into Ardnamurchan. The experience of the reverend gentleman was at first not quite encouraging. It is stated that he had to preach to empty benches, while the ancestors of our friends the Maclachlans and Hendersons remained outside the church amusing themselves by "putting" the stone. But the minister was equal to the occasion. He could "put" the stone too, and to some effect, for he "put" it farther than any of them. A pastor who could do this was clearly deserving of a congregation; so we are not astonished to learn that on subsequent occasions the young men went inside to prayers first, and "put" the stone afterwards, a proceeding quite orthodox, at least for those times, although only *secundum quid* now.

There is no mincing the fact that Campbell was a person of extraordinary energy, and of very great abilities, a type in his way of some of the remarkable men whom the troubles of the times brought to the front. But the direction given to those abilities is not such as to make him particularly admired by the kinsmen of the unfortunate MacIans. He was the natural son of that Campbell of Cawdor who was murdered, it is believed, at the instigation of young Campbell of Ardkinglass, AD 1591. Before finishing his career he was knighted by Charles I, AD 1628. He is commonly known as Sir Donald Campbell, Bart. of Ardnamurchan and Suinart.

John, in spite of the deep irritation felt at the proceedings taken against his friends in Ardnamurchan, was obliged to smother his wrath, for the forces brought into his neighbourhood were too formidable to warrant any interference on his part without being well supported by some of the other branches of the clan. But this support was not available at the time. When however the opportunity of retaliating did present itself, the Macdonalds seized it with alacrity, and did their best to make the Campbells go through the worst ordeal that had ever to be faced by that race.

During the bitter contests between the Campbells and the Macdonalds of Isla, the latter, on being defeated, involved the Macdonalds of Colonsay in their ruin. The island was seized and appropriated by the Campbells, while the laird, old Coll mac Gillesbuic, surnamed the Left-handed–Coll Ciotach, being stripped of everything, was driven into exile. A son of the latter, Alexander, took refuge in Ireland, where he was well received by the Macdonalds of Antrim. The wrongs endured by the family had made a deep and lasting impression on Alexander's mind. By constantly brooding over them, every other feeling seems to have been absorbed in the one intense desire of being revenged on the enemies of his race. Although bold, skilful, energetic, and possessing many of the qualities fitting him to lead an irregular host, he seems to have been unable to turn these to any higher aim than to indulge his cherished passion for retaliation. This weakness proved his own ruin afterwards, as well as the ruin of a far more capable and chivalrous leader, the celebrated Marquis of Montrose, with whom he was sent to co-operate by the Earl of Antrim in the attempt to restore the Royalist cause in Scotland during the time of Charles I. Alasdair was, on this occasion, placed at the head of a large body of Irish mercenaries, and proceeding to the western coast of the Highlands, first landed in Morven, where he seized the Castle of Kinlochaline. Coming on to Ardnamurchan, he lost no time in attacking Mingarry Castle, which was then held by the Campbells and some men picked from the colony imported by Sir Donald. Under a threat, which was not an idle one, of having the place set on fire and of smothering the defenders in the flames, Alasdair compelled the besieged to surrender at discretion. The castle was then garrisoned by some of Macdonald's own levies, and put in a condition to resist a siege in the event of the enemy attempting to retake it. The whole of Ardnamurchan was at the same time severely scourged by Alasdair and his men, the district, so it is stated, being given over to fire and sword. No doubt the cruelties endured by the previous inhabitants, the MacIans, were an incentive. While thus busy vindicating the old *lex talionis*,[1] Macdonald approached Clanranald regarding the main object of the expedition, and soon came to an understanding by which the Moidart chief and his followers were to give active support to the Royalist cause. He then set sail for the districts farther north, where he could communicate with the Macdonalds of Sleat and with the Macdonalds of Glengarry. It required very little inducement to bring the latter into the movement, and this being settled Macdonald landed the bulk of his forces, making his way to Athole, where Montrose was waiting for him, through Lochaber and Badenoch. John Clanranald reached the general's headquarters much about the same time. They were soon plunged in the busy campaign which the genius of their leader was preparing for them. By a sudden march Montrose came up to the Covenanters at Tippermuir, broke their ranks with the greatest ease, and in the headlong flight which followed destroyed two thousand of their number. After seizing Perth, and levying a heavy fine from the citizens, he marched into Aberdeenshire, met the Covenanters again, defeated them, and sacked the city. Clanranald, having lost a good many men during these engagements, returned to Moidart for reinforcements. It almost looks, however, as if the accusations of the Whig writers were more or less well founded, viz., that he and part of his men came back with the object of depositing with their families some of the plunder taken from the Lowlander. In any case the return was fortunate, for after reaching the district Clanranald learned, to his great surprise, that Mingarry Castle was closely invested by the Campbells, and that the siege had now been going on for seven weeks. Without losing a moment he burst into Ardnamurchan, surprised the besiegers, and compelled them to take to their galleys. The fort was re-victualled, while the defences were renewed in case of the siege being resumed. These operations were scarcely concluded when Macdonald himself appeared on the scene. He had heard of the straits to which the garrison had been reduced, and, fearing for the safety of his men, hurriedly left Montrose's camp, journeying day and night, so as to be in time to avert the threatened calamity. He met Clanranald while the latter was returning from Mingarry and about to cross the Sheil on his way to Castle Tirrim. Having his apprehensions thus relieved, the Irish leader accompanied Clanranald to Castle Tirrim, where he remained for several days, the Highland chief showing every attention which friendship and hospitality could suggest for the entertainment of his visitor.

The siege, until opportunely raised, threatened to be a very serious business for the defenders, for not only were the provisions running short, but the supply of water had become most scanty, so that the necessity of a capitulation was latterly becoming imminent. If this had come to pass, the probability is that every one belonging to the garrison would have been immediately hanged by the Campbells. The consciousness of this fate in store for them made the Irish more determined to hold out to the last extremity, bearing their privations manfully, until actual famine should compel them to surrender. But whatever their own sufferings were, those endured by certain prisoners shut up along with them were much worse. These unfortunate persons had been passengers on board a vessel captured by Alasdair on his way to Scotland. Three of them were Presbyterian ministers, who some time previously had been preaching the doctrines of the covenant in Ireland, and who at the time of the seizure of their vessel were coming back to Scotland. In a certain sense they were valuable prizes, for they might be used for the safety of Alexander's own friends if the latter were unfortunate enough to fall into the hands of the enemy. They were accordingly committed to Mingarry Castle. During the siege they were forced to subsist merely on a little barley-meal, and on some muddy water collected within the precincts of the fort. Some time afterwards the wife of one of the ministers was set at liberty, together with most of her companions, but the ministers themselves were confined as closely as ever. One of them succumbed to his sufferings towards the beginning of winter. Six months afterwards another gave way. The third would probably have fared no better, were it not that he was so far fortunate as to find himself exchanged for some prisoners held by the other side, and consequently set at liberty. He had been kept within the walls of the castle for ten months. While these men fared so badly, the minister of the parish, Mr M'Calman, seems to have steered through the difficulties of the situation with considerable success. It is not known how, but the fact seems to be well established that he found favour with Alasdair, and was not molested by his wild subordinates. Possibly he may have been a genuine sympathiser with the king's cause, or the exigencies of the situation may have dictated an exhibition of sympathy which, under other circumstances, would have been withheld. His conduct, however, at this trying juncture found little favour among his own friends, for in 1650—that is to say, six years afterwards— they excommunicated him for having "complied" with Alasdair. It is satisfactory to learn that the sentence was ultimately reversed, when the Presbytery, taking a more lenient or sensible view of the case, granted M'Calman a "testificate," which seems to have been a sort of refrigerator to the scorpion's sting.

During his stay at Castle Tirrim, Alasdair—or, to give him his rank, the Lieutenant-general—was very favourably impressed by the character of the chief's oldest son Donald. The latter was scarcely twenty years of age at the time, and had hitherto not been allowed to take any part in the campaign. But he had abilities which the keen eye of the experienced soldier was quick to discern, and won him favour. These, and the youth's ardent desire to see active service, induced Macdonald to plead with the father that Donald might be allowed to accompany him to Montrose's headquarters. After some hesitation the chief consented, and soon afterwards the lieutenant-general and Donald, together with a large number of Clanranald's men, set out for the camp. On their arrival, Montrose organised that terrible irruption into the heart of Argyllshire which the Campbells, owing to the advanced state of the season, it being winter, deemed almost an impossibility. Almost the whole of Argyllshire was swept from one end to the other. Hundreds of the inhabitants were put to the sword, their dwellings given to the flames, and their cattle in vast herds driven away by the invaders. Inverary was burnt to the ground, and Argyll himself only escaped capture by making a precipitate flight in one of his boats across Loch Fyne. This dreadful raid was planned in the most deliberate manner, Montrose dividing his forces into three bodies, one of which was commanded by himself in person, another by the lieutenant general, and the third by Clanranald. One may easily imagine how bitterly it was felt by the hapless natives, who, taken unaware, found themselves so suddenly reduced to face cold, famine, ruin. The following extracts taken from different authors, and quoted by Mackenzie in his history of the Macdonalds, give a vivid idea of what the desolation must have been:—"The clans laid the whole face of the country in ashes, killing whom they met marching to Inverary (amounting, it is said, to 895 men-at-arms), sweeping off its flocks and herds from every valley, glen, and mountain that owned the sway of MacCailin mòr." "They spared none that were fit to carry arms;...they put to the sword all the men whom they met going in arms to the rendezvous appointed by Argyll, nor did they desist till they had driven all the men fit for service out of the country, or forced them to retire to lurking holes known to none but themselves. They drove all their cattle, and burnt their cottages and their villages to the ground; thus retaliating upon Argyll the treatment he had given to others, he himself being the first who had practised this cruel method of waging war against the innocent country people, by fire and devastation." Another writer states:—"They left no house or hold, except impregnable strengths, unburnt, —their corn, goods, and gear, and left not a fourfooted beast in his haill lands; and such as would not drive, they houghed and slew, that they should never make stead."

It was one of the worst episodes of the kind that had ever occurred in the western Highlands. But three years previously this same Earl of Argyll, at the head of four thousand men, had burst into the Braes of Angus, devastating the lands of the Ogilvies by fire and sword without any mercy. It was in this raid that he burnt the "Bonnie House of Airlie," under such circumstances of inhumanity as to make his name infamous among posterity. His cruelties were so great that the Committee of Estates, who first prompted him to make the raid, were obliged to pass a special act of indemnity to protect him from the consequences of his behaviour on this occasion. For instance, the act wished to shield him "for demolishing (houses, towers, &c.) to the ground, or burning of the same, or putting of fire thereintil, or otherwise sacking and destroying of the same howsoever, or for putting of whatsoever person or persons to torture or question, or putting of any person or persons to death," &c. A recent writer adds:—"The Ogilvies had their revenge when the territory of the marquis was overrun by the fierce and ruthless clans that followed Montrose, and carried fire and sword throughout the whole estate of the clan Campbell."

After having thoroughly scourged the Argyll districts in this merciless manner, Montrose and his followers withdrew to Lochaber, taking their enormous booty along with them. Argyll, as may naturally be supposed, lost no time in gathering all his available men, and making otherwise ready for punishing his enemy. He reached Fort-William about the end of January 1645, while Montrose was preparing to march against Inverness. The Royalist leader, however, on hearing of Argyll's pursuit, wheeled round, and making one of those rapid marches for which he became celebrated, fell upon Argyll at Inverlochy on the 2nd of February, and, with little loss on his own side, cut to pieces fifteen hundred of the Campbells. The rout was complete, the earl, rather shamefully flying from the field and taking refuge on board his galley. Three months afterwards, viz., on the 4th May, Montrose defeated General Urry at Auldearn. On the 2nd May he broke General Baillie's army at Alford. On the 15th August he came up to Baillie again, and almost annihilated him at Kilsyth. It is estimated that on this occasion six thousand of the Covenanters were slain. In all these engagements the Macdonalds, under their young leader Donald, took a conspicuous part. After Kilsyth most of the clans, and among them the Macdonalds, withdrew to their native districts. The Irish leader behaved no better, his intense desire to give still further worry to his enemy in Argyllshire being the real motive, as alleged, of his leaving the victorious general. The result of such dastardly conduct was ruinous to Montrose. Deprived of the greater number of his followers, he was left helpless in face of General Leslie, who completely crushed him at Philiphaugh. With this defeat the Royalist cause in Scotland became hopeless. The lieutenant-general was not long afterwards pursued by Leslie in Argyllshire, and compelled to fly to Ireland. His aged father, Coll MacGillesbuic, fell into the hands of Leslie, who handed him over to the Campbells, and these gentlemen, as might have easily been foreseen, made quick work of him. They hoisted him up to the mast-head of his own galley, and hanged him without pity. Cromwell's Ironsides having got possession of Scotland, General Monk was detached to keep the Highlands in awe; and it is said by some that in the performance of this duty he was helped by certain Government ships cruising off the west coast, one of which entered Loch Moidart and cannonaded Castle Tirrim. Although there is no direct evidence of such a visit, certain circumstances have lately come to light which give it a considerable amount of probability. It seems that John Clanranald, for reasons best known to himself, thought it necessary, or at any rate useful, to make a raid in Skye, selecting for this purpose the lands owned by Mr Martin Macpherson, Protestant minister of Kilmuir. The details are so far given in a paper in the possession of the family of Sleat, and read by a Skye gentleman about a year ago before the Gaelic Society of

Inverness. The Moidart chief carried away on this occasion:—

    20 cows with stirks, valued at 20 merks.

    20 yeld cows,   "   15 merks.

    14 three year old cows, ,,   12 merks.

    60 sheep,   "   2 merks.

    20 lambs,   "   10 pennies.

    13 horses,   "   12 pennies.

    3 bolls of corn, &c.

    Barley crop, &c.[2]

In addition to these, his reverence claims compensation for a kiln, &c., not forgetting expenses incurred in the attempt to obtain justice. This raid took place in 1658; and, if brought to Monk's notice, would likely enough procure Clanranald the honour of a salute from one of Cromwell's ministering angels.

John died in the island of Eriska, 1670.

His son Donald commenced his career, as we have seen, under circumstances which brought out in an eminent degree some of the traditional virtues of the family; and although these, with the return of quieter times, were naturally more or less restricted in their scope, one would have expected the development of others suitable to his altered position and likely to do him honour. Even if this tribute cannot with any truth be paid to him, the memory at any rate of his gallant deeds performed while leading the clan under Montrose ought to find him a high place in the esteem of the Macdonalds; for undaunted courage, and a leaning to warlike enterprises, have at all times acted like a talisman on the ordinary followers of a Highland chief, so much so that their presence often condoned, or at any rate helped, to keep out of sight blots of a serious and most objectionable character. Yet it is a fact, so far as Moidart is concerned, that no chief of all the Clanranalds is painted in such black colours, or has left such a detestable memory behind him, as John's son, the friend of Alasdair MacColl. "Savage" and "cruel" are the two distinguishing characteristics which the traditions of the people stamp upon his name. That the stories are often gross exaggerations goes without saying. Indeed, an advocate on behalf of the chief might make out a fair case for his client, by pointing out that if he was stern and cruel at times, he had at least a certain amount of provocation to be so. No doubt, too, the cruel scenes with which the campaigns of Montrose early familiarised him hardened his disposition, and made certain views of retributive justice seem reasonable enough to himself while to others they would appear extreme. His despotism over the clan was much on a par with the despotism of other feudal chiefs, when their acts, uncontrolled by any higher principle, wanted also the salutary fear of assassination.

Here are some of the traditional stories current in Moidart connected with this chief's name:—On one occasion a serious theft of money belonging to Donald had been committed within Castle Tirrim, suspicions as to the guilty party pointing to the chief's valet, to another man, and to a girl known as James's daughter. After a searching examination, Donald was unable to bring the theft clearly home to any of them, and, in spite of every effort, failed to recover the money itself. Smarting under the double disappointment, and determined not to be baulked in his vengeance, he gave orders to have the whole three put to death. The two men were hanged on Tom-a-chrodhaidh, the usual place of execution; but a severer sentence was awarded to James's daughter. Having been bound hands and feet, she was ferried over to a rock about two hundred yards from the castle, and left there to perish under the flowing tide. To make her doom surer of fulfilment, she was tied by the hair of her head to the seaware growing on the rock. She was drowned, of course. The rock is still called Sgeir nighinn-t-Sheumais,—"the rock of James's daughter." It is right in front of Invermoidart House, but is only visible at low water. A very singular discovery corroborates part of this tradition. Some years ago the late Lord Howard of Glossop was anxious to open up a pathway along the cliffs north of Dorlin House overhanging Loch Moidart, and while the work was being carried out the labourers came upon a heap of loose stones piled up in the line of the proposed path. On dispersing these, their astonishment was great to find a large quantity of silver coins lying underneath. The number was over one hundred and fifty. They all belonged to the reign of Queen Elizabeth. They are about the size of shilling pieces, very thin, largely alloyed—in fact, of base metal. On the obverse side, the image of the queen is well executed, and very distinct. She has a double frill round the neck, and on her head the crown surmounted by a cross. On the reverse side, there is a shield quartered by a cross, the arms of which cut each other in the centre of the coin, and traverse the full diameter of the surface. The quarters are filled up with leopards, or lions and lilies. The inscription on the obverse side is, "Elizabeth Angliae Fr. et Hiberniae Regina;" on the reverse, "Posui Deum adjutorem meum." One of these coins in the hands of the writer is dated 1583. Considering that the coins lay buried for more than two hundred years, one is surprised to find them in such an excellent state of preservation. The spot where the discovery was made is almost midway between the castle and the rock on which the girl perished. Donald had also to deal with his female cook in a fashion which, if applied to her innumerable cousins engaged in the same estimable profession, would no doubt excite their strongest reprobation. This valuable domestic of Castle Tirrim was apparently given to snuff, and invariably kept a "mull" of her own. In times of scarcity, however, she made no scruple of helping herself to some of her master's, who loved a pinch also. One day, in a fit of mental abstraction, the old lady appropriated the box itself. The act was clearly proven, and so forthwith the delinquent was ordered by the inexorable judge to be led away to Tom-a-chrodhaidh. The victim evidently resented the sentence, for, on being conducted outside the castle, she refreshed her nose with a last pinch, and then, rather wastefully, chucked the box into the sea, where it yet remains to be found. The audacity of pocketing such a valuable article deserved condign punishment, and the reader should withhold his sympathy, for the last spiteful action of this cook points to a person of a very low moral tone. Like most of his ancestors, Donald was a great hunter, and his favourite gun was called "A' chubhag," i.e., the

Cuckoo. This weapon he cherished with as much affection as he cherished his wife. It was his inseparable companion, for it hung near his pillow at night, and leaned on his arm by day. Indeed its memory is far more revered than its master's, while its exploits are a source of wonder and entertainment to the audience for whose benefit the local seannachies have no doubt preserved them. Of course our ancestors were not inexpert at drawing the long bow; but the admirers of "A'chubhag" can stretch a mile or two with incomparable ease. To appreciate the nature of these performances, or rather to get at a conception of them, the intelligent reader should first prepare his mind by a careful study of the history of that interesting gentleman Baron Munchausen, and then conjure up, by the help of a lively imagination, all the feats which a weapon like the "Cuckoo," in the hands of a chief like Donald, would be most likely to do. The process will give results which, if not quite true,—for truth is stranger than fiction,—will go some length in lowering his opinion of the present age, which wisely shakes its head at the idea of there being Purdies and Lancasters in Moidart two or three hundred years ago. Persons trained in the superior school of thought characteristic of Munchausen's countrymen, will readily admit the verisimilitude of a history evolved on such principles, for it is philosophical in the highest degree, being deeply founded on the inner consciousness of somebody or other. If ever they make a feint of stumbling at the crowning point of belief, it will probably be due to the paucity of deer horns found among the ruins of Castle Tirrim, especially in the ashpit in front of the old kitchen,—this paucity, as they may object, being scarcely adequate to the full concept of the "Cuckoo's" capabilities. But the argument, besides being of a purely negative character, is illusory; for, in chief Donald's time, the manufacture of hartshorn created a demand for deer horns among the Highland chemists,[3] and the supply was one of the perquisites of the Castle Tirrim cook, whose salary was not high. Besides, it is well known that bones of this class were highly prized by the natives, who, submitting them to some primitive sort of Papin's digester, were able to help themselves to a jelly which, when properly sweetened and flavoured, was eaten by their sick friends as a specific for consumption. When Donald began to show signs of corpulency, and consequently found it rather inconvenient to chase the "fleet dun deer" among the hills of Moidart, he used to spend hours together sitting on the battlements of Castle Tirrim, with the "Cuckoo" on his knees, taking observation of every living creature on the sea beneath him, or on the land on each side of it. Seals, gulls, herons, and especially thieves of his own species, were careful, on such occasions, to keep out of sight, knowing full well what the penalty would be if the "Cuckoo" came to be levelled against them. One day it happened that the chief's keen eye alighted on a suspicious-looking object crouching on a rock not far from the smithy between Dorlin and Scardoish. It had every appearance of being a thief watching an opportunity to pounce on some small four-horned sheep which were browsing a few yards off, and which formed part of the property of the chief himself. The necessity of suppressing such a crime was pressing; so "Cuckoo" was immediately brought to the level, and, in the language of Nimrod, the object was bowled over with unerring accuracy. In its fall it went headforemost into the well or small pool of water lying at the foot of the rock. On some of the castle people hurrying to the spot, they were rather taken aback at discovering the "Cuckoo's" prey to be one of the chief's best followers, a young man, who, not having much to do, and finding the day rather wearisome, had sought a little enjoyment by sunning himself in the vicinity of Donald's sheep. This discovery would no doubt have shot pangs of remorse through the breast of any other leader, but Donald's philosophy strengthened him against any such internal attacks. To his mind the "Cuckoo's" intervention was quite justifiable, —for if the young man was innocent, his sudden removal made him continue so by taking him away from the danger of temptation; if he was guilty, he only got what he deserved. From the circumstance of the head having stuck in the well, while the feet seemed to stick in the air, the pool was called Tober-nan-ceann, Donald's frightened subjects not venturing to express themselves more minutely regarding the occurrence.[4] The spot is cherished by the Dorlin gardener, who not only drinks bravely himself from its refreshing water, but gives an unlimited supply to his kale and carrots and other vegetables out of it. Sometimes, when the object was within convenient reach, and where delicacy of operation was a question of minor importance, the chief gave tbe happy despatch by means of his trusty dirk. Thus, while travelling among his dependents in Uist, he one day stumbled upon a party of islanders reposing from the fatigue of cutting peats, and indulging themselves in the luxury of a meat dinner. One of the party, an old man, after finishing a shoulder of mutton, being curious to know the future, held the bare bone up before his eyes and gazed intently upon it. "What do you see there?" growled Donald. "I see," replied the seer, "what Clanranald would be sorry to know." "Declare it at once!" said his master. "Bithidh gibein air gach gadan do dh'fhearran Chlann Raonuill fhathast"— "Clanranald's property will break up into little fragments yet." According to some, the prophet added: "Alas! alas! the day when Raonull-nan-Roanuillich shall come to be at the head of the race."[5] Six inches of cold steel driven into his breast sent a true but imprudent soothsayer to Hades. Some authorities, however, refer this slight ebullition of choler to an earlier chief of the Macdonald race, so it is but simple justice that the son of John should have the benefit of the doubt; he has enough sins of his own to answer for, without saddling him with those of his ancestors. It is a more serious charge laid against Donald's memory, that, through a singular want of discrimination, he once went so far as to make an attempt on the life of a priest. Of course it is intelligible enough that an irascible creature like this hero should sometimes take to carving laymen's flesh, even with barely sufficient reasons to justify such an amusement; but to indulge himself in the same form on the sacerdotal body, looks almost as if he meant to push liberty to extravagance, or at any rate to the verge of license. In presence of the many distinct enactments bearing on this point, and sternly forbidding it, one is forced to conclude that Donald, on this occasion, simply acted *suadente Diabolo*. The reverend gentleman who was unlucky enough to incur his wrath was the priest of the little island of Canna, and the origin of his offence was this:— Donald had immured a native lady in the castle of Coroghon, for what crime no one now knows, and seemed disposed to keep her there for the rest of her life. Perhaps this was better than pitching her into the sea,—a finishing which, as we have seen, would have cost him little. But the pastor, rather imprudently, as some people will think, took to denouncing the deed, and one Sunday, in a very energetic sermon, gave a full portrait of the chief, painted in unmistakable black colours. Donald hearing of this incipient treason, armed himself with the "Cuckoo," and set sail for the island with the object of bringing his reverence to reason. But, at the very first sight of the Chief's galley, the priest fled to the western side of the island, where there are facilities for hiding. Donald pursued, and for some time it was a very interesting game, such as is sometimes seen between a keen hunter on the one side and a lively but prudent rabbit on the other. There is no doubt as to how the business would have ended, for Donald was in earnest, and the "Cuckoo" was ready. But the islanders, after the first day's hunt was over, sought the priest in his hiding-place, and quietly wafted him away to Rum or Skye, where Donald had no jurisdiction. From this point the chief's life becomes decidedly darker, not to say ominous. We hear less of the "Cuckoo," but a great deal of another companion, whose presence would not be obtruded on the reader were it not that the omission might be interpreted as a mark of disrespect to the traditions of the country, while Donald's history might justly incur the censure of being wilfully mutilated if the details held back came afterwards to be known by some inquisitive critic. This companion comes on the scene in a very unpleasant guise, viz., in that of a huge black toad; and here the chronicler may venture upon the remark, without thinking of the pun, that it was truly the *bête noir* of the latter portion of the chief's life, for it haunted him wherever he went, and made itself as much at home at Castle Tirrim as the owner himself or any of the few living creatures supposed to be favoured with his friendship or familiarity. Its true character may be inferred, by contrasting its performances with the habits of the species more commonly met with on earth. For instance, when the chief clandestinely sets sail for the island of Uist, leaving the familiar sound asleep in a corner of the courtyard of Castle Tirrim, he and his crew may be disgusted, but they are not surprised, to find it sitting on the shore of Loch Boisdale quietly waiting their arrival, and hopping towards them the moment they set foot on the island. When, on another occasion, Donald contrives, by a little artifice, to imprison and doubly lock it within the dungeon of the castle, and then with a chuckle launches his birlinn on a short excursion to Arisaig, he scarcely gets beyond the coast of Eilean-Shona when the creature is seen swimming in pursuit, gallantly breasting the waves, and, on reaching the vessel, showing every sign of enjoying the expedition more than any on board. How the unfortunate Clanranald came to be burthened with such an uninviting guest is a mystery that can never be solved. Months and years were spent in trying to dismiss it to the region whence it came, but although Donald hit upon many devices, he so far failed to hit upon the true one likely to have any real mesmeric influence over it. His enemies secretly rejoiced, while the few friends still clinging to him mourned each day as they noted the deep gloom which now settled over their chief's brow. To complicate matters, the familiar began to show signs of resentment, both at the attempts which Donald made to shun its company, and at the disgust which every one at Castle Tirrim openly expressed at its presence. The voyages to the outer isles came to be attended with unusual dangers, or adverse winds protracted them to an undue length, or some calamity was sure to happen which made Donald and those along with him heartily wish they had never quitted dry land. Its malevolence, for instance, is firmly believed to have been at the bottom of a furious storm which once overtook the birlinn between Arisaig and Rum, and which raged with such violence as to threaten to engulf every one on board. During the worst of those miserable hours, the monster was seen to swim incessantly round the ship, sometimes plunging deep under the billows, sometimes riding on their crests with the strength and ease of a porpoise; but the malignant glances shot from its wide staring eyes so alarmed the crew, that they implored the chief to take it on board, as a measure likely to propitiate it, and to avert from themselves what seemed to be certain destruction. Whenever their vessel plunged its bow under a deeper sea, or whenever it heeled over as if never to right itself again, the seamen renewed their entreaties, and each time with greater vehemence. But Donald was obdurate; he was evidently in one of his worst reckless moods. At length the squalls came down so fast and furious that the helmsman abandoned his post, and, with the rest of the crew, openly mutinied. In this extremity Donald tried his own hand at the helm, but the effort brought conviction even to his mind, that with such powerful agencies fighting against him it was hopeless to think of success. Turning in the direction of the monster, he, with some kind of naval blessing which the howling of the winds prevented the bystanders from catching, sullenly and reluctantly signalled to his tormentor. The latter, eyeing the chief, accurately interpreted the sign, and, without waiting for a second invitation, nimbly climbed on board, with this result that the storm instantly subsided, and the voyage ended in safety. After years of misery the chief succeeded in getting rid of this uncanny beast, but its disappearance, like its coming, is enveloped in mystery. According to popular belief it was devoured by a lion, the said lion being presented to Donald as a gift from the contemporary Earl of Argyll. If this is true, the Campbells have more good in them than the Macdonalds have ever given them credit for; but the Moidart natives, when coming to this part of the story, always pretend to have a difficulty in understanding,—first, how any Campbell, especially the head of the clan, could have been gifted with so much Christian magnanimity as to be able to heap up coals of fire in such an othodox fashion on the head of Alasdair MacColl's friend and partner; second, how the Campbells, although unquestionably persons of superior knowledge and ability, contrived to be so deeply versed in a certain art as not only to circumvent, but to chase ignominiously into their proper quarters, the emissaries of darkness itself. Unable to solve these serious problems, many suspect that the lion never came from Argyllshire at all, but was a *donatio inter vivos* made by some African prince, who hearing of the Moidart chief's great trouble, and touched with compassion, thought it an opportune moment for exhibiting Africa's skill in dealing with evil spirits. As an argument on behalf of this theory, they allege that so early as 1105 a *camel,* which certainly had no connection with Argyllshire, but which probably came from Egypt or Bactria, was presented, according to the Innisfallen annals, to Murdoch O'Brian, an Irish chief, by the King of Alban. Now if a camel could travel so far in the twelfth century, why could not a lion come from the African jungles in the seventeenth? A smaller section, who think themselves critics, suggest that the monster perhaps was swallowed up by that angry lion which figures on the Clanranald coat-of-arms. This idea, being strictly clannish, is steadily gaining ground.

There are proofs that Donald appreciated in the proper spirit his delivery, for, some time afterwards, we hear of his voluntarily submitting to considerable personal sacrifices in his anxiety to promote Christian observances among his neglected followers at Castle Tirrim. It had always been one of his Draconian laws, in dealing with those attached to his service, that when there was no work there should be no pay. In itself no maxim could be truer, and the patronage extended to it all the world over is a clear proof that Donald's appreciation of natural laws was, in this instance, both solid and discreet. But there is a little difficulty; if the daily wage is so small that even the thrifty workman has to consume it all on his daily wants, it stands to reason that the day of rest, on which none must work, is likely to prove for the straitened workman a day of hunger and discontent. This truth apparently got the length of Neil MacCormick's understanding, after first troubling him considerably in the region of his stomach. Neil was an Irish carpenter, whom Donald had brought over from County Donegal to repair his birlinns or to build new ones, according as the state of the Castle Tirrim exchequer permitted. But Neil's pay was almost phantasmagoric when gauged by the many wants of real life, or at any rate he brought himself to believe so; but being an Irishman he launched on an erratic course of his own, by way of protest against Donald's tightness, and with a view to ameliorating his own condition. If he had lived in present times, Neil no doubt would have adopted the vulgar fashion of going on strike, and done his best to fight against starvation by starving himself worse than ever. But in those days the merits of this kind of homoeopathic treatment were not so obvious, people not seeing their way so readily to the belief that live chicks can be got out of addled eggs, or that the human body can be made considerably taller by cutting the legs off and reducing it so many inches. Neil's plan was to work another day, and so he took to working on Sunday. The shock to the chief's recently awakened religious feelings was very great, and on ascertaining through his major-domo that Neil was the delinquent, he summoned the latter into his presence and lectured him soundly on his profanity. Among other things, he put the question pointedly whether or not he realised his miserable condition, and the severe punishment due, both in this world and in the next, for taking such liberties with one of the commandments. Neil no doubt knew he was a sinner, but when he heard the chief talk of punishments in this world, he began to have visions of Tom a-chrodhaidh and of the "Cuckoo," and a cold shiver passed through his whole frame. It was with considerable trepidation, therefore, that he managed to explain that the wretched pittance awarded to his services during the six days compelled him to hunger and fast on the seventh, and that if he sinned the blame was to be laid at the door of the chief's own conscience. How this explanation would have served Neil at any other time it is useless to speculate, but Donald was then struggling from darkness to light, and it is to his credit that, after some cogitation, he apprehended the difficulty. He would probably have increased his servant's pay, but the times were hard; while his savings, in the shape of those precious coins issued by good Queen Bess, had all vanished under the dexterous fingers of the thieves in his own household. He did however the best thing under the circumstances, he ordered MacCormick to be supplied with two good meals every Sunday from the kitchen of Castle Tirrim, and only reminded him occasionally of the necessity of repentance.

The circumstances attending Donald's final departure are somewhat perplexing; but, after mature consideration, the reader will probably acknowledge that the transition, although surrounded with extraordinary peril, was a safe one. The tradition is very distinct on the point. Donald was seized with his last illness in the island of Canna. About midnight, that is to say three hours before the end came, his attendants were startled by a loud shrill whistle which suddenly broke on the stillness of the night, wakening the sleeping natives from Sandy Island to the Point of Garisdale. It roused Donald himself from the stupor which for some time had been creeping over him. He sat up in bed, at first wildly staring around him, then scanning more carefully his attendants, as if half expecting to see some one else among their number. While thus occupied, the whistle was repeated,—this time louder, sharper, and with sufficient strength to make the house slightly tremble. The chief leaped to the floor at once, and made a frantic effort to rush outside. One of his cousins, however, a powerful member of the house of Morar, threw his arms around him, and after a sharp tussle dragged him back to the bed, where he kept him down until the paroxysm had subsided. While this was going on in the chief's apartment, some of the natives, more courageous than the rest, ventured a few yards beyond their doors to ascertain the cause of the noise. This was what, by the moonlight, they saw: a tall dark personage standing out against the sky on the highest peak of the promontory overhanging Canna Harbour—his face turned towards the chief's house—his head bare—his ears, preternaturally long and pointed, erect, as if ready to catch some response to a preconcerted signal. After a long pause, this being was seen to stamp impatiently on the ground where he stood, then to stride furiously towards the house. After a few steps, however, he stopped abruptly; twice or thrice he looked nervously, first in the direction of the beautiful cross standing near the old churchyard, then towards Rudhasgor nam ban naomha, where the ruins of an ancient convent lie, a little more to the south-west. Apparently reassured, he allowed his attention to be wholly concentrated on the chief's house, towards which for several minutes his gaze seemed as it were fascinated. At length turning round, and giving a toss to his head, he commenced pacing up and down the promontory, the occasional quick jerky movements of his hands and arms giving sufficient proof of a mind ill at ease and much perplexed. Disobedience to his summons had clearly not entered into his calculations. Now the exercise which he was giving himself might, under other circumstances, have done him good, but taken in a raw cold atmosphere like that of Canna, in the small hours of the morning, the effect on his temperament was simply disastrous. We all know how severely the livers of our countrymen become damaged after a few years in India. But a longer residence in much hotter climates, is sure to result in a derangement of the system intensely replete with gall and bitterness. The effect on the dark personage waiting for Donald was at any rate most unpleasant. Losing all sense of self-control, he flew to within a short distance of the dwelling; then, applying both hands to his mouth, he gave utterance to a series of such unearthly roars as to shake the very island to its foundations. They were like the roars of a famished lion pacing the desert in quest of a meal. The poor natives almost abandoned themselves to despair; while the sick man's attendants, all save the brave Morar man, seemed paralyzed with terror. Donald himself, whose every feature was convulsed with horror, bounded once more to the door. The spell under which he laboured seemed to endow him with an energy which no ordinary mortal could withstand. Grappling with his cousin, who tried to bar his exit, and who offered the most desperate resistance, the chief would no doubt have made his escape, and so gone to a terrible doom; but at the very moment when he seemed to prevail, an old barn-cock belonging to the vicinity crowed lustily three times. At the first crow, the chief gave a start, and paused in thc struggle; at the second, he heaved a deep sigh of relief; at the third, he suffered himself to be quietly reconducted to his bed. Once comfortably placed below the blankets, he appeared for some time to mutter as if in prayer,—then, beckoning to his cousin, he shook him gratefully by the hand. He also nodded kindly to the rest of the company. Then, with a childlike smile on his countenance, he slept for ever.

When the uproar created by the third summons had subsided, the dark personage was seen to retreat hurriedly to his original position at the top of the promontory. He then took a flying jump over the precipice into the sea; but before doing so he turned once more towards the chief's house, and shook his fist energetically at it. He skipped over the waves in a straight line towards the island of Rum, where he was lost sight of. But there is no doubt that he haunts that neighbourhood to this hour, for when sailors, and especially the Canna people, attempt to take the south-west end of the sound separating the two islands, they are pretty sure to be harassed and tormented by the furious boisterous squalls sweeping down from the elevated corries of A'bhrideanach. If, on the other hand, they take the eastern end of the same channel as the safer of the two, they are seldom allowed to pass without receiving striking proofs that their enemy is on the watch, especially close to Rhu Shamh-nan-Insir, and that they had better sail with discretion. This lesson, so often repeated, has not been thrown away upon them.

Donald died in the year 1686. His remains were carried away with much solemnity and interred at Toghmore in the Island of Uist, where the adversary has not dared to disturb them. The name of his undaunted relative of the house of Morar should not be allowed to perish. He was Raonull Mac Ailein Oig, concerning whom a few additional details have been preserved,—for instance, that, without having studied at Padua, he developed an extraordinary knowledge in dealing with the powers of darkness; again, that although no friend to witches, he still kept on good terms with ancient beldames possessing the faculty of second-sight, and that to this prudent friendship he owed his personal safety when nine of his companions perished in fording the river Lochy.

Clanranald gave him a farm in the island of Eigg, where he spent most of his life. In his old age he became blind and bedridden, and, like many another estimable benefactor, had to suffer somewhat from the neglect and ingratitude of his own family. These persons, however, he always tried to reform in his own way, first by mildly enticing them within reach, and then by soundly punching their heads when they could not escape from his hands.

Notes

1   *Lex Talionis* — the law of retribution, with punishment appropriate to the injury.

2   Value of Scots money:

> 12 pennies = 1 shilling
> 20 shillings = £1 Scots
> £12 Scots = £1 Sterling
> 3 Merks = £2 Scots
> 18 Merks = £1 Sterling

3   Hartshorn — grated horn was used at the time in the production of ammonia.

4   *Tobar nan Ceann.* In 1663 Alexander MacDonald of Inverlair and his six sons murdered Alexander of Keppoch and his brother Ranald. The murder was avenged two years later when fifty men, led by Archibald, brother of Sir James MacDonald of Sleat, killed all seven at their home at Inverlair, cutting off their heads. Returning to Glen Garry with the trophies, Archibald washed the heads in a well beside Loch Oich, which since that time has been known as *Tobar nan Ceann*, the 'Well of the Heads'. This event, known throughout the Highlands, must have taken place about ten years before the less famous killing by 'the Cuckoo' described here. Probably it suggested the name for the well to Donald's tenants, who apparently were not only unwilling to name the owner of the head, but even to narrow the matter down to a single head!

5   *Raonull-nan-Roanuillich*, (misprint, for *Raonuillich*) — ie, Ranald Clanranald. The prediction refers to Reginald George, in whose time the estate was sold off piecemeal (cf, chapter xii, pp. 202f).

Chapter 6

Allan Clanranald—His Chivalrous Character—Joins Dundee, and fights at Killiecrankie—Enters the French Service—Distinguishes himself under the Duke of Berwick—Is wounded—Castle Tirrim seized, and garrisoned by part of an English Regiment—Clanranald joins the Standard of the Earl of Mar— Orders Castle Tirrim to be set on fire— His Death on the Field of Sheriffmuir—Grief among his Adherents.

IT is not advisable that any chronicler should, either at the beginning of a chapter or elsewhere, stretch his wings and soar away into the regions of general speculation called Philosophy. The disgusted reader might reasonably enough object to follow, or the aeronaut himself might burst his own balloon and come down much quicker than he mounted. This last catastrophe would of course be extremely humiliating, but nature often puts an obstacle to its occurrence by giving the writer no wings to speak of, or at any rate by tying him rigidly down to the condition of a respectable pullet. It is thought necessary to make this remark, lest the reader take alarm, or think himself aggrieved, by having his attention drawn away for a few minutes from the subject-matter of the Clanranalds to such dry sticks as notions and realities, cause and effect, and the singular inconsistencies attached to them. The flight will be a short and a low one, while the digression itself will prove in reality a kind of steppingstone between the two chapters. When a lady once hauled up from the deep a large fish, the chief characteristics of which were a long tail, an enormous head, and a phantom body, her triumphant remark: "Regardez donc, quel ange!" was scarcely applicable, and the shock to any well-balanced mind would have been severe, had it not been mitigated by her French companion's rejoinder: "Oui, madame, c'est vrai; mais avouez que c'est un ange déchu."[1] It is a startling fact, and no doubt rather inexplicable, that Irish patriots are seldom brought within the touch of real misfortune until they are thoroughly made acquainted with the inside of *Mountjoy;* and the saturnine Yankees, who ought to see the fitness of things in a better light, vivify their criminals by sending them to the *Tombs.* One is hopelessly astray in the regions of nomenclature when "Hero," "Fury," and "Lion" turn tail, and vanish before the attacks of a warlike sheep with a lamb trotting by its side. A maritime metaphor like the "Ocean's Bride" ought, in all conscience, to prove exhilarating to the dullest mortal, for his imagination, so far as he can lay claim to any, gets a whiff of poetry and ozone at one and the same time; but the mind undoubtedly becomes embarrassed when a dusty collier from North Shields or Ardrossan parades the title,— notions and realities are plainly at war. Cause and effect are sometimes equally puzzling. It is a proverb of very respectable standing that "Like begets like," and its truth is wonderfully borne out by the earnestness with which we are invited to accept, almost as a first principle, its illustration in this other: "Montes parturiunt et nascitur ridiculus mus."[2] But leaving the irony aside, we have the sober fact, that the man of genius not unfrequently presents a simple *tabula rasa* to his legitimate heir; while the grace-abounding elder, the man *par excellence,* has often no counterpart except in his thoroughly graceless son. It is not the right thing perhaps to write slightingly of the Caucasian race, for ethnographers tell us that it holds the first place among the great branches of the human family, and a good number take a pride in allying themselves to its dignity and elegant proportions; but it is a painful confession that this privilege has to be conceded to millions who, from their physical appearance, ought to have the humility to hunt for their ancestors among the troglodytes and chimpanzees, or among some animated forms of the kippered herring, rather than of the Indo-Germanic type. At other times, the benighted student, in dealing with the contradictions of language, is almost tempted to wish himself in the position of Rousseau's hypothetical savage; for where are we to stop when honest John Bull is said, wickedly we believe, to be so fond of eating as to worship his diet, while in Presbyterian Scotland his spiritual brother Sandy pretends to revel in a diet of worship? We are told by the learned that these are vagaries, eccentricities, freaks, which help to bring out in stronger light the principles which they violate, just as grammarians coolly appropriate an exception to confirm their rules. The information is no doubt satisfactory, and upon their authority we offer it to the reader as an explanation of the mystery how the late Donald, who to all intents and purposes was a shady character, succeeded in begetting a son who stands out in the annals of the times, as well as in the songs of the Clanranald Macdonalds, as the *beau-ideal* of a Highland chief, possessing most of the virtues, yet stained with few or none of the vices, of his ancestors. His name is Allan Dearg, i.e. the Red.[3] At an early age this gallant chief was transferred from Castle Tirrim to the island of Uist, where, with his father's sanction, he was placed under the care of Macdonald of Benbecula. The change was a fortunate one in every respect, for Benbecula was reputed to be a gentleman of large mind, well cultivated as times went, and imbued with thoroughly Christian principles. It was an additional advantage that the tutor was united by the closest family ties to his young ward, being married to the latter's sister. The statutes passed by James I regarding the education of young members connected with the ruling Highland families were still in force; but owing to the political confusion prevailing at the time of which we write, they were easily evaded by those who chose to do so. In some cases a simple barbarous contempt of letters, or hatred of the Lowlander, influenced the defaulters. In others, it was an opportunity to get rid of a tax weighing heavily on the family resources. With the more conscientious among some of the Catholic families, it was a temporary escape from an odious law, aimed at the perversion of those for whose moral training they considered themselves responsible, and whom they had the right, if they chose, to educate in the old faith, a right which no civil laws can touch. There are good reasons for thinking that Allan's sister had a good deal to do with his being brought at this early stage under her husband's immediate supervision. The influence, as might be expected, tended to the best results. In secular knowledge the young chief's training was probably elementary enough; it was necessarily hampered, both by the scantiness of the appliances at hand, and by the isolated circumstances under which it had to be conducted; but his intercourse, later on, with the celebrities who frequented the courts of St Germains and Versailles, made up for much that books failed to convey. The main foundations, however, on which the formation and development of his character rested, were laid with uncommon care. He was drilled into those wholesome steady habits of discipline which crown the freshness of youth with the wisdom and honour of maturer years. Those habits clung to him throughout life. Both at this time and throughout the rest of his career he was reputed to be gentle, courteous even to the humblest of his people, warm-hearted, and filled with a high sense of honour which rose superior to any feelings of egotism or mere self-interest. He was an enthusiastic adherent of the Stuarts. When the "fiery cross" was carried from the mainland to the seas, Allan and his brother-in-law, at the head of five hundred followers raised in Uist, South Morar, Arisaig, and Moidart, joined Claverhouse in the Braes of Lochaber. Writing to Macleod of Macleod from Moy, on the 23rd June 1689, the Royalist leader mentions that "The Captain of Clanranald is near us these severall days,...the Laird of Barra is among them." The Stuarts of Appin, the Macdonalds of Glenco, Keppoch, Glengarry, together with the Camerons, were "all ready." The Cameron leader was the famous Sir Ewen, who on account of his consummate prudence was justly recognised as the Nestor of the Highland chiefs. Dundee adds that he expected to leave Lochaber with a force of at least 3,000 men. To encounter these the Scots Convention had dispatched General M'Kay with 3,000 infantry and 1,000 cavalry under him, but most of these were Dutch auxiliaries. The two armies met at the pass of Killiecrankie, with results which are well-known matters of history. After a short fusillade, Locheil, Clanranald, and Glengarry hurled their men against the centre of the enemy, which, unable to sustain the shock, broke and fled in the wildest disorder. Owing to the narrowness of the pass, the defeated party fell easy victims to their victorious pursuers, great numbers of them being cut down like poppies under the broadswords of the Highlanders. It is estimated that nearly two thousand of M'Kay's force were destroyed or captured on this occasion. But the victory was dearly purchased, for Dundee himself fell mortally wounded in the very moment of triumph, and died on the field of battle. His successor, Colonel Cannon, had none of the qualities to inspire confidence, or to retain the undisciplined clans together, and, as might be expected where so many feuds and jealousies existed, the host broke up, the clans withdrawing to their native districts. Young Clanranald and his brother-in-law returned to Uist. During the following year, however, understanding that General Buchan had come to an agreement with several of the chiefs at a council held at Keppoch, and was about to resume operations in favour of the king, Clanranald commenced once more levying his men. But before this was completed word reached him that Buchan had met with a fatal reverse, and that the prospects of the Royalist party were for the time quite hopeless. Buchan had allowed himself to be surprised by Sir Thomas Livingstone at Cromdale, and was forced to fly from the field utterly routed. As the old song puts it:

"We were in bed, sir, every man
When the English host upon us came,
A bloody battle then began
Upon the haughs of Cromdale."

This disaster checked any further movement on Clanranald's part, and the subsequent treaty entered into by Buchan and the Government compelled him to adopt the same policy which all the influential chiefs who had been lately up in arms were compelled to follow. It was about this time that Breadalbane received £20,000 from Government to be spent among the Highland chiefs, with the avowed object of detaching them from the Stuarts and of disarming their hostility to King William's rule. How far Breadalbane honestly discharged this trust is a matter of speculation. But according to Burton, who quotes the Melville papers, the king mentioned particularly Sir Donald Macdonald, Maclean, Clanranald, Glengarry, Locheil, and the chief of the Mackenzies, authorising Breadalbane, or whoever was conducting the negotiations, to offer £2,000 or a peerage to these or to any chief whose allegiance it might be necessary to buy.[4] The chiefs seem to have been very sceptical of Breadalbane's communications, but during their intercourse with him they became gradually impressed with the truth that Sir John Dalrymple was bent on a policy of extermination against all those who declined to submit, and this evidently put an end to their waverings. After having tendered their submission, the districts under their sway were supposed to go through a process of disarmament; but as the Government had begun to realise the importance of M'Kay's suggestion, garrisons and forts were established among the more refractory clans, and the iron hand began to make itself felt in compelling their obedience to law and Whiggism. A strong company, detached from the regiment stationed at Fort-William, was sent down to Moidart and put in possession of Castle Tirrim. They held this post for many years, until a short time in fact previous to the insurrection of '15, when the gathering of the storm warned the Government leaders to recall their men from the scattered outposts and to concentrate them at the main places of resistance. Clanranald felt the presence of these soldiers in the family stronghold very bitterly, this being the first experience in the history of the district of any real practical subjugation of his people to the rule of the Government. There is no record, however, of the soldiers having conducted themselves with unnecessary harshness towards the natives; and, so far, their behaviour contrasts favourably with that of their successors who in '45 pillaged, burnt, and wasted with such vindictive fury, that the poor people to this day speak of that year as the "year of the great wasting," —bliadhna nan creach mora. The young chief, chafing under the restraint to which he was condemned, and despairing of seeing another opportunity to draw his sword in favour of the legitimate king, determined to forsake his native country and seek employment in France. He acted upon this resolution soon afterwards, was well received at the royal court, and was given a commission under the Duke of Berwick. A very active career for some years now opened up before him, for France was at this period in the throes of a violent struggle, brought on by her claims in reference to the Spanish succession. Her armies had to fight simultaneously all along the line of her frontiers; but in spite of the wonderful talents displayed by such generals as Boufflers, Villars, Villeroi, and Vendome, the number of fearful reverses crowding upon each other, year after year, threatened to overwhelm the country, and at the same time to pull the monarchy of Louis XIV to pieces. In the north and east, Marlborough and Prince Eugene carried all before them. In the south, Peterborough, at the head of an army composed of British, Dutch, and Portuguese, drove the French out of the Peninsula and compelled them to fall back behind the Pyrenees. Berwick, who had previously been fighting in the north, was recalled and told off to meet the invasion from the south. A brilliant campaign followed, which culminated in the victory of Almanza. Either in this, or in one of the earlier engagements under his leader, Clanranald, who throughout had greatly distinguished himself, was left on the field covered with wounds. He would probably have perished, were it not that a search party, stumbling on the spot to which he had dragged himself, transferred him to a country house in the vicinity, whose inmates by their devoted nursing brought him triumphantly through the crisis. During his convalescence he became acquainted, or renewed his acquaintance, with the lady whom he afterwards married, viz., Penelope Mackenzie, daughter of Colonel Mackenzie, at one time governor of Tangiers. Among the Moidart Clanranalds she is said to have been an Italian, although this possibly may have applied to her mother. She accompanied Allan to Uist, where for some years they lived in great retirement. But another insurrection having been planned in favour of the Stuarts, Allan was among the first to be involved in it, although his better judgment must have shown clearly how hopeless and disappointing the result was likely to be; for in addition to previous failures attending similar attempts, failures where the prospects of success were at one time more promising, the chief had a thorough knowledge of the utter incapacity of the leader selected to conduct the present hazardous enterprise, viz., the Earl of Mar. This nobleman, besides being weak and vacillating in character, was narrow-minded, and utterly ignorant of the most elementary military tactics, the very last person to play successfully the dangerous game of insurrection in the presence of the Government generals, who if not of the first class, were at any rate trained soldiers. Such for instance was John, Duke of Argyle, the general selected to oppose the Jacobites and quell their proceedings. He had served for years under Marlborough; had fought at Ramillies, Oudenarde, and Malplaquet; had taken an active part in the sieges of Ostend and Lille; and proved himself, throughout the terrible campaigns of the English leader, one of the trustiest among the higher officers. In presence of this soldier, Mar was little better than a child. There is no doubt that Clanranald had a presentiment of coming disaster, for, after crossing from Uist to Moidart, he gave secret instructions to one of his followers to set Castle Tirrim on fire, insisting that this melancholy and ill-conceived design should be carried out immediately after his departure for the seat of war. The follower was at first extremely loath to perform the task, and ventured to expostulate with the chief; but the latter removed his scruples, by representing that the building was likely to fall into the hands of the Government troops again, who upon their second visit would certainly show little mercy to the district. "Besides," he gloomily added, "I shall never come back again,—cha till mise gu bràth tuilleadh,—and it is better that our old family seat should be given to the flames than forced to give shelter to those who are about to triumph over our ruin." The deed, unfortunately, was carried out with only too much fidelity. Five hundred men had been gathered from the various Clanranald districts, and, when they advanced about a day's journey on the march, their chief prepared to follow.

There is a tradition that, after having left the castle, he took the path leading up through the steep narrow gorge of Scardoish, and on nearing the top sat down for a few minutes at the spot named Aite-suidhe vich ish Ailein, where the spectator, looking towards the west, commands a magnificent view of the valley of Loch Moidart, and beyond this of several isles belonging to the inner and outer group of the Hebrides. Some of these formed part of Clanranald's estates, and from the gloomy forebodings indicated in his orders to burn the castle, he probably enough felt conscious that he was now looking on them for the last time. It was here also that he bade farewell to a few friends who met him at Castle Tirrim, or who had accompanied him so far from the Isles; then, turning his face eastwards, he went resolutely to meet what fortune should send. He had scarcely however reached Glenfinnan when Castle Tirrim was in flames, and became the melancholy ruin which forms such a conspicuous feature in the landscape of Dorlin. About thirty years ago the great-grandson of the follower who had to perform this painful duty died at Scardoish. He was an old man, verging on ninety, and during the latter part of his life was bed-ridden and completely blind; but his memory was an inexhaustible store of the traditions and legends connected with Moidart, and especially with the Clanranald family. Two or three years before his death he was visited by Mr Hope Scott and the late Duke of Norfolk, who were much interested in his history. The chief subject then occupying the old man's thoughts was the fate of Schamyl the famous Circassian chief, and on this subject he plied his visitors with questions showing the liveliest interest and sympathy.

After reaching Mar's headquarters at Perth, Clanranald and Glengarry mustered nine hundred Macdonalds between them. The other clans were equally well represented; and it is generally asserted that the total force gathered to the standard of the incapable Royalist leader was little short of twelve thousand. At the head of such an army, Montrose or Dundee would certainly have drilled the Whigs to some purpose. As every student of history knows, the two parties met at Sheriffmuir, where, although the action was indecisive, the credit of the day is undoubtedly due to Argyll, who, with inferior numbers, broke Mar's left wing, and would have gained a complete victory if General Witham, commanding the Whig left, had not given way and fled. A contemporary writer makes the following statement regarding the latter:— "Not only all in our view and before us turned their backs, but the five squadrons of dragoons on their left, commanded by General Witham, went to the right about, and never looked back until they had got near Dunblane, almost two miles from us." A touch of comedy accompanied the opening of this battle which was to prove so tragic for the Macdonalds. After placing himself at the head of his clan, Sir John Maclean is said to have addressed them in these terms:—"Gentlemen, this is a day we have long wished to see. Yonder stands MacCailin Mhor for King George. Here stands Maclean for King James. God bless Maclean and King James. Charge, gentlemen."

Clanranald's forebodings proved too true. He had just marshalled his men, and was preparing for the order to charge, when he was hit on the chest by one of the enemy's bullets, and had to be carried away in a dying condition to another part of the field. This sudden disaster almost demoralised his followers. For a moment they wavered, but Glengarry, noticing their consternation, rushed up to where they stood, and, waving his bonnet in the air, cried out: "Revenge! revenge to-day, and mourning to-morrow!" Then, leading them to the attack, plunged with such fury into the fray, that the opposing columns were thrown into confusion, and shortly afterwards compelled to fly. It was the success achieved in this part of the field which saved the day from being a complete triumph to the duke. The chief's body was carried to Drummond Castle, which was not far from the scene of battle, and there, amid the lamentations of his devoted adherents, was consigned to its last resting-place.

"The loss of the Earl of Strathmore and young Clanranald was," writes Sir Walter Scott, "a great blow to the insurrection. The last was a complete soldier, trained in the French guards, and full of zeal for the cause of James." "My family," he replied to Mar's summons to join him, "have been on such occasions ever wont to be the first on the field, and the last to leave it."

Another writer refers to him in these terms:—"This clan (the Macdonalds) did act the part of men that are resolute and brave, under the command of their chief, who, for his good parts and genteel accomplishments, was looked upon as the most gallant and generous young gentleman among the clans,—maintaining a splendid equipage, keeping a just deference to the people of all sorts, void of pride or ill humour. He performed the part of one that knew the part of a complete soldier."

The loss of their chief was felt so severely by his followers, that it seems to have deprived them of all stomach for any more fighting; but in truth Mar was already concerting measures how to escape from the kingdom, leaving the disorganised Royalists to their fate. The Macdonalds returned to their native hills, utterly disheartened at the calamity which had overtaken them. The evil news having preceded them, filled their friends among the Isles and in the Rough Bounds with the deepest sorrow. Perhaps the gloom weighed heavier on Moidart than anywhere else, for the blackened ruined walls of Castle Tirrim, and the sad circumstances under which they became so, impressed more vividly on the natives the irreparable loss which had come upon the whole clan by the death of their brave and gallant chief. He left no issue, and with him terminated the direct line of the Clanranald succession. The estates passed to his sister's husband, Macdonald of Benbecula.[5]

Thirty years afterwards the Macdonalds were up again in favour of the Stuarts; but before proceeding to that part of our narrative, the present seems the proper place to treat of certain other matters of some interest connected with the district.

Notes

1   "Yes, Madame, that is true; but you must admit that it is a fallen angel".

2   "The mountains are in labour, and there is born... an absurd mouse" — Horace, *The Art of Poetry*, 139, after a Greek proverb.

3   He was also known as 'Little Allan of the Big Heart', on account of his short but broad stature and generous nature.

4   Burton, J Hill, *History of Scotland, from Agricola's Invasion to the revolution of 1688*, 7 volumes (Edinburgh, 1867-70). In the 1897 edition the reference is volume vii, pp 396f.

5   On Allan's death in 1715 the estate passed to his brother Ranald. The latter never married, and upon his death in 1725 the estate then passed to Donald MacDonald of Benbecula, husband of their sister Janet (see Clanranald Genealogy, p. 242).

Chapter 7

Traditions regarding St Finnan—And the Island on Loch Sheil which bears his Name—The Island Church, said to have been built by Allan MacRuari —The Bell on the Altar Stone—The Title Rector of Eilean-Fhionnan— Neil Mor-an-eilean—Craig-an-t-Shagart—Camustroloman— Sandy Point—Annat— Highland and Irish Priests from 1652 until after the beginning of the Eighteenth Century—Colin Campbell— His Conversion—Joins the Army of the Prince —Is killed at Culloden

S T COLUMBA, as we have already shown, had visited more than once this neighbourhood, and no doubt had done something towards the conversion of its natives. But after his death there came from Iona a missionary who has always been regarded as the real instrument of bringing the district within the pale of Christianity. His memory has come down through eleven centuries, honoured and cherished by the descendants of those who first received his teachings. His name was Finnan, or St Finnan, as he is better and more appropriately known to most people. Unfortunately little, almost nothing, is known of his personal history, nor has any record been preserved of the labours which he faced when carrying out the noble purpose which brought him to these parts. A few fragments of tradition give the information that he landed at Kilchoan in Ardnamurchan, that he afterwards came on to Moidart, and that he established himself in the little green island at the western end of Lochshiel, called after himself Eilean Fhionnan[1]; and that from this quiet retreat he spread the light of Christianity among the rude natives living on the northern and southern banks of the lake. When his labours had been so far crowned with success he proceeded eastwards, teaching with undiminished zeal in the districts of Lochaber, and finishing his missionary career near

Invergarry. There was a church dedicated to his memory, at a very early period, near the head of Loch Lochy, and called Kilfinnan. After his departure a succession of other holy men from Iona perpetuated the work in the neighbourhood of Lochshiel, down to the eleventh or twelfth century, in spite of many interruptions due to the ravages of the Norsemen. The best evidence of their zeal, and of those who came after them, is to be found in the fact that the faith which they communicated, and which they strove to uphold, sunk so deeply into the hearts of the natives belonging to Moidart and some of the next districts, that throughout the many centuries which have lapsed since that time the people have resolutely clung to it and resisted any idea of change. The Suinart and Ardnamurchan people—weaker, we must confess, in this respect, but no doubt pressed under the reforming influence of the Campbells—gave way, the result being that Lochshiel and the river flowing from it mark the boundaries between the Presbyterians on the south side and the Catholic districts on the north as far as Loch Hourn.

The earlier missionaries, probably after the saint's example, resided on the island. In a short time the island itself, owing to its associations, became a kind of consecrated ground. It was chosen as the chief burying-place for Moidart, Suinart, the east end of Ardnamurchan, part of Morven, and even the head of Locheil. Penitents condemned to do penance for graver offences were frequently enjoined to make pilgrimages to it; and if, as sometimes happened, the storminess of the weather or other causes prevented them from crossing the narrow channels separating it from the mainland, they were ordered to kneel on the shores opposite, and perform within sight of the island the religious exercises which they should have performed on the island itself. This last practice survived among the Moidart Catholics until after the beginning of the present century. About the thirteenth century a large portion of the Western Highlands was detached from the diocese of Dunkeld and went to form the diocese of Argyll, the bishop's residence being at first on the banks of Loch Etive, and afterwards on the island of

Lismore. In consequence of this change, the present parish of Ardnamurchan was divided into three parts, each part forming a separate parish, viz., Ardnamurchan, Suinart, and Arisaig. The component parts of Arisaig were South Morar, Arisaig proper, and Moidart, including Eilean-Shona. The chief church was in Arisaig, and known later on as Kilmhorie. The chief church of Ardnamurchan was at Kilchoan. But the parish church of Suinart took its title from Eilean-Fhionnan (*Orig. Paroch.*). Its priest was termed rector of Eilean-Fhionnan, or Island Finnan. The teinds for his support were levied principally if not totally on lands in Suinart. How Eilean-Fhionnan, in spite of this, came to be reckoned within the parish Arisaig, and to form part of the Clanranald estates in Moidart, is explained in this way:—The whole of Suinart at one time belonged to the Clanranalds. They possessed it in the time of John of Isla, who gave it, as well as the advowson of the church of Suinart, to his son Reginald. The latter was confirmed in these rights by King Robert III in 1392. In course of time however the family lost this portion of their inheritance; and when the separation took place, the dividing march was drawn along the southern channel of the loch between the island and the Suinart shore, the island thus going to the north or the Moidart side of Lochsheil.

The lands of Modworth (Moidart), together with the patronage of the church of Arisaig, were granted by King Robert Bruce to Roderick the son of Allan in 1309. They passed from him to John of Isla, and were confirmed to his son Reginald in 1372 (*Orig. Paroch.*).

It is not easy to give any precise or even approximate date to the erection of the church now lying in ruins on Eilean-Fhionnan. In the popular imagination of course it must be referred to Allan-nan-Creach, a celebrated freebooter of the Cameron clan, who if he were the founder of only one-half of the churches ascribed to him, must have been the most extensive ecclesiastical builder ever produced in the Highlands. This gentleman had laid many districts waste in the noble pursuit of plundering his neighbours and enriching himself, but being at length seized by an illness which threatened to shorten his career, and being smitten with a due sense of remorse for his past misdeeds, he vowed to build seven churches as a reparation of the evil done and as a solace to his troubled conscience. These seven churches, or, if the popular story is true, about double that number, immediately sprung into existence. But before the good work was completed, the chief, contrary to expectation, recovered,— rather an unfortunate circumstance, except perhaps for himself, for such of the churches as were not already roofed were ordered to be left as they were, the pious builder declaring that the roofing of them formed no part of the contract entered into between prospective honesty and past robbery. It was the misfortune of Eilean-Fhionnan that its church was not sufficiently advanced before Allan recovered his health, and with it his appetite for more plunder. In consequence it was never roofed. Such is the legend. As a matter of fact the church was in existence long before Allan's time, and, although there is no positive certainty, the presumption is that it was built by one of the Clanranald chiefs, viz., Allan Mac Ruari, who, like Allan-nan-Creach, was one of the most accomplished plunderers of his day. This wild chief, among other crimes, is accused of having murdered some of the clergy, and of having burnt St Finnan's Church at Invergarry to the ground. In reparation of the insult thus offered to religion and of the outrage upon the memory of Moidart's tutelary saint, it is not improbable that he was urged to build another church dedicated to St Finnan, on the saint's own isle. It was not much to boast of, being a plain stone building, absolutely free from any sign of ornament, but no doubt an improvement upon the wooden structures existing at one time or other on the same spot before it. The one roof covered both nave and chancel, the internal length being seventy feet by seventeen. The altar was of the roughest kind, being formed of an undressed slab, cut probably from the rocks on the northern shore. About fourteen yards distant from the church, on the south side, there is another small building similar in style of build and in material, the original purpose of which is uncertain. It is used at present as the burial-place of the Kinlochmoidart family; but there is a tradition that it is as old as the larger edifice, and some affirm that the MacIans of Ardnamurchan erected it as their own family vault. This supposition is not improbable, for Allan Mac Ruari was married to a daughter of the MacIan chief who was visited by James IV at Mingarry Castle. The internal measurements do not exceed eleven feet by seven. The bell which in olden times belonged to the church is still preserved. It is angular in shape, and tapers moderately towards the top, the height not exceeding seven or eight inches. Its notes are remarkably sweet, and when rung out on a calm day during those moments when the surface of the loch is undisturbed by a passing breath of wind, they waken within the breast of the listener a feeling of sadness, which is not inappropriate in a spot where so many generations are quietly sleeping around. It has been left exposed on the altar for more than two hundred years, nothing saving it from desecration or from being carried away except that deep feeling of reverence which Catholics and Presbyterians alike entertain for the place with which it has been so long associated. There is only one instance on record in which it has ever been unduly meddled with, and that was when a party of soldiers passing from Castle Tirrim to Fort-William landed on the island and carried the bell away with them. They were pursued, however, and overtaken at Glenfinnan, where they received the chastisement which they so richly deserved. The chief delinquent was tied to a tree and soundly flogged by Neil Mòr-an-Eilean. But during the few hours it had been in their possession the tongue was wrenched off and thrown away, the present clumsy substitute having been affixed at a later period by one of the Kinlochmoidart family. Among other rectors of Eilean-Fhionnan, mention is made of Sir Andrew MacEachern, who died in 1515. He was succeeded by Sir Roderick MacAlasdair, brother of John of Moidart, and at one time Dean of Morven. He became implicated in the political troubles caused by Henry VIII., but afterwards got a full pardon under Mary of Guise. He was buried at Ardchattan Priory, where his tombstone is said to bear this inscription, "Hic jacet Reverendus et egregius vir Rodericus Alexandri, rector quondam Finani insulae" *(Orig Paroch.).* A nephew of his, viz., Ian Og, is the ancestor of the present bishop of Argyll and the Isles, Dr Angus Macdonald.[2]

After the expulsion of the MacIans, Suinart went to Sir Donald Campbell, whose oldest son received from the Protestant bishop Andrew Knox a lease of the bishop's quarter of the teinds of Island Finan, 1623 *(Orig.. Paroch.).*

In 1630, John Clanranald gave Allan-Mac-Raonuill, "parson" of Islandfinnan, in life-rent, certain lands situated in Moidart,—viz., Dalelea, Langal, and other parts,—and after him to his brother's son, also in liferent, then to his nearest representative, for nineteen years. This "parson" was a native of Uist, and is supposed to have been connected, more or less closely, with the chief's family. In spite of the most diligent research no trace can be found of his having ever resided in this district, and the conclusion naturally suggests itself that he consumed the rents in his native island, that is to say if he ever got them. The Dalelea and Langal farms were a little after this in the possession of a tenant called Donald Gorm, who probably was the parson's brother's son referred to in the lease. Donald lived and died a bachelor at Dalelea. He had two sisters living with him, one of whom predeceased him at Dalelea, but of the other nothing is known. It was probably owing to the next clause in the lease—"to his representative, for nineteen years,"— that Maighstear Alasdair, the Episcopal minister of Ardnamurchan, came to be established at Dalelea after Donald Gorm's death.

In 1667, a new grant, made to Archibald, Earl of Argyll, by Charles II, included the patronage of Ilanfinnan *(Orig. Paroch.).*

In 1695, a son of the above Archibald was served heir to the patronage of the same church (*Orig Paroch.).*[3]

Towards 1700, or perhaps a little later, a family of the name of M'Gillivray was stationed in the island. Their duty was to act as sextons, and for this purpose a "càin," or tax, was levied on both sides of Lochsheil, which contributed to their support. They were succeeded by Neil Mòr-an-Eilean, who, marrying one of

M'Gillivray's daughters, spent most of his life on the same spot. This
Neil Mor is always spoken of in the district as a person combining
with great bodily strength the most thorough fearlessness and
courage. We have alluded already to the vigorous manner in which
he recovered the bell from the English soldiers, but on another
occasion some of his own countrymen tried his nerves in a way
which few Highlanders, or indeed any person, would relish. It was
a practical joke which nearly ended in a very different manner from
that anticipated by those who conceived it. A funeral party from
Morven had arrived at the island during a winter night long after
Neil had retired to rest, and it occurred to one of them—a young
man suffering from an overdose of mountain-dew—that they
should test for themselves whether Neil's absence of fear was as
genuine as commonly reputed to be. Proceeding quietly to Neil's
hut, and cautiously opening the door, they began pushing the coffin
towards Neil's bed, at the same time uttering certain lugubrious
sounds to waken Neil from his sleep. Neil in starting up was at first
a little taken aback at the dismal object so close to him, but quickly
realising the state of matters, seized his sword, and issuing from the
house gave chase to his foolish visitors. In a very few minutes he
overtook one of them, the young man who originated the idea, and
was about to bring down the sword on his head, when the young
man, frightened out of his senses, cried out, "A ghoistidh, a
ghoistidh, cum air do lamh,"—"Godfather, godfather, hurt me not."
It was a very narrow squeak, for Neil, from all accounts, was not
nice in his appreciation of fun at the best of times, certainly not
when played upon his own person or under such improper
circumstances. He was the last living resident on the island; but
towards the end of his life he withdrew to the opposite shore on the
Moidart side, where he had a croft, and where his family were
accustomed to give the ferry to parties visiting the island, or to
travellers going to Strontian by the Polloch route. One of Neil's
descendants, the father of Raoul a' Phuirt, got the lease of this croft
renewed by Clanranald for many years; but long before it expired
he was cheated out of it by a very unscrupulous person, who was

the tenant of Dalelea, and who was very anxious to attach this small holding to the rest of his land. Under the pretence of ascertaining their boundaries more correctly, the tenant invited the old man to bring his lease down to Dalelea, where they both could comfortably discuss it. The old man complied, but the tenant, after getting the document into his hands and glancing at it for a few minutes, suddenly chucked it into the fire, remarking that the lease was not worth the paper on which it was written. Clanranald himself died shortly before this happened, and his son being quite a minor no redress could be obtained. The old man died the following year, and Raoul a' Phuirt with his family had to clear out, the tenant getting what he coveted.

There was another descendant of Neil Mor, who, at an early age migrated to Skye, where for forty years he wandered about as a fox-hunter. His name was Ewen M'Innes, but in Moidart he was commonly called the "Brocair Sgiathanach." He was a very determined customer, even in his old age, and when roused it was not difficult to get a glimpse of the rough and fiery side of his character.

The rude stone crosses studded over one corner of the island were hewn by Donald Mor MacVarish, a native of Mingarry. He died about fifty years ago.

In some of Alasdair MacMhaighstir Alasdair's poems allusion is made more than once to the "giuthas," or fir trees, of Eilean Fhionnan. Possibly there might have been a few of that kind to be seen in the poet's time, but all traces of their existence have long since vanished, the island at present showing nothing but the broom and a few hawthorns and hollies on its eastern and southern slopes.[4] Not far off, however, is the islet of Camustroloman, where there are some venerable firs, which the herons from time immemorial have claimed as their own. On this small island the poet actually dwelt for some time, and possibly the memory of its trees may have haunted him in after-life, but, by poetical license, he transferred them to Eilean Fhionnan.

The island church was allowed to fall into ruin, so far as can be ascertained, between the beginning and the middle of the seventeenth century, and this regrettable event was undoubtedly due to the indifference or hostility of Sir Donald Macdonald and his son John, who, compelled to adopt the policy of James VI, professed an outward adherence to the Protestant religion. They are not accused of having ever used any forcible means to make the rest of the clan follow them in their new belief, but they withdrew all direct encouragement to uphold the old form, and indirectly tried to help a change by countenancing in a marked manner such as followed their own example. The places of worship were, of course, neglected by them, and the Catholic clergy deprived of any support except what the poor people gave them. No doubt their position, in face of the severe laws passed regarding the profession of the Catholic religion, was a difficult one, and their conduct so far contrasts favourably with that of those vile little tyrants who—like the laird of Coll, and, later on, like Boisdale—used violent methods in detaching the people from the Catholic church and in driving away their clergy. But the fact remains, that Sir Donald and John starved religion, and would have been quite content if it fared no better in any part of Inverness-shire than it did in the neighbourhood of Inverary. John's son, Donald, who died at Canna, was a rough soldier. He troubled himself very little about priests or ministers of any kind. These three Clanranalds are the only chiefs of the race who renounced the Catholic church, until at any rate we come to very recent times.

When the districts south of the Sheil adopted Presbyterianism, they naturally enough still claimed their right to burial in Eilean Fhionnan; but either by a tacit or explicit understanding, an imaginary line was drawn from east to west through the island, one side of which marked off the portion for the Presbyterians, the other for the Catholics. The church went to the latter, as the line was drawn to the south of it. It is probable, however, that some division of this kind existed long before the change in religion took place, as a measure necessary to prevent disputes, and to obviate the risk of one family trespassing on the prescriptive rights of another.

It was a very ancient custom too in Catholic times to make an annual pilgrimage to the island, in which the natives of both sides of Lochsheil took part. This took place on the feast of the patron saint, St Finnan. But it has long since died out, so much so that it is difficult to fix, with any degree of certainty, either the day or the month in which it used to occur.[5]

About a mile and a half higher up the loch there is a spot which, according to local tradition, was inhabited by a priest, who evidently found it a convenient centre whence to minister both to the natives on the north side and to such families in Suinart as still clung to the faith. These he could scarcely visit openly, for the Campbells then possessed Suinart; but his residence being at Sandy Point, opposite Polloch, he had opportunities of putting himself in communication with his flock which no other place along the banks of Lochshiel could so conveniently offer. It was probably this priest who was the first to say mass at Craig-an-t-Shagart, on the Suinart side of Lochshiel, a secluded corner not far from Eilean Fhionnan, where the worshippers were not likely to be taken by surprise. Another version of this tradition has it, that a priest used to live occasionally at Sandy Point even before the Reformation, and that it was part of his duty to say mass in the church of Eilean Fhionnan. Four miles still farther up the loch there is another spot, viz., at Annat, where certain ecclesiastics are said to have resided in olden times; but whether they were seculars or regulars is uncertain. There are faint traces of an old cemetery having existed there, and the natives have preserved the name of a Bishop Macdougald who was buried in it. About the middle of the seventeenth century the number of priests in Scotland became so reduced, that their co-religionists may be said to have been almost bereft of spiritual assistance, the few priests serving at the time being compelled to wander from place to place, and to distribute themselves in such a manner as to be unable to visit the same district or locality more than once or twice in the course of the year. Our earliest register gives only the names of five or six as ministering to all the Catholics dispersed throughout Scotland.[6] The late Bishop Kyle, however, who knew more of these matters than anyone else, used to assert that the Highlands were served at this period, and previous to it, by many priests, whose names have not been preserved; and this is quite consistent with what we know of the numbers of adherents prevailing in the districts, both on the mainland and in the isles. These amounted to many thousands, and it is incredible that they could have been left totally destitute of pastors for any length of time. The scarcity, however, was severely felt, and at the representation of some of the Catholic chiefs, St Vincent de Paul, founder of the missionary congregation known as the Lazarists, was induced to send two of his priests to the Western Isles. Their names were Father Francis White and Father Dominic O'Duegan. They landed in Uist on the 25th March 1652, as recorded by one of themselves on the fly-leaf of a copy of 'Tirinus's Commentaries on the Scriptures, still kept in the college library at Blairs. There is also a document among the Clanranald family papers, and quoted by Buchanan in his history of the family, in which a dispensation is granted to Ranald Og Macdonald of Benbecula to marry his cousin, a daughter of Clanranald. The document is signed "Dominicus Duegin, Priest of the Mission," and is dated from Eilean-Raald, 8th June 1653.[7] These priests travelled for years all over the Highlands, visiting every district where their services could be of any use, and no doubt including Moidart, Arisaig, &c., in the number. They were pious zealous men, whose memory is revered to this day among Highland Catholics. Father Francis died on the 28th January 1679.

Two Highland priests, viz., Francis, and Mark Macdonald, appear in 1669. The name of the latter only occurs in the register for this year, but Francis continues down to 1673.

A very remarkable priest came to devote himself to the service of his countrymen in 1671. This was Father Robert Munro, a native of Ross-shire, whose whole career gives evidence of uncommon fortitude and of the most untiring zeal. He was in Knoydart in 1688, but shortly afterwards was seized, tried at Edinburgh, banished from the kingdom, and threatened with the penalty of death if he ventured to return. After reaching the Continent he was seized again, and imprisoned at Ghent as a conspirator against the Prince of Orange. The intervention of some friends procured his liberation. Attempting to re-enter the kingdom he was captured once more, robbed of everything, thrown into prison in London, where he was detained for a year, and finally banished. Nothing daunted he got on board the first vessel leaving Dunkirk, and this time, landing safely on the Scottish coast, he found his way to his old friends among the glens, AD 1698, to whose service he consecrated himself with more fervour than ever. In 1704, while lying prostrate with fever in a miserable hut in Glengarry, he was discovered by some English soldiers, who carried him off to the castle, where he was thrown into the dungeon, and where, after receiving the vilest treatment, he was allowed to perish. This brave priest, not including the years spent in prison or in banishment, laboured for thirty years among the Highland Catholic districts. During a great part of his life he had the active co-operation of three famous Irish priests, viz., Cahassy, Ryan, and Devoir, who came over in 1680. Among the Catholic clergy who have succeeded them, these three missionaries stand in the highest rank as perfect models of self-devotion, and of fortitude in upholding the faith amid the difficulties which were then crushing it. Ryan was captured in 1696, and died the same year in prison; Devoir survived him two years; Cahassy died in 1704, shortly after Munro. Many other Irish names occur from 1687 during the next thirty years. Thus we have O'Shiels, O'Byrnes, Logans, Carolans, Coans, Hackeens, and others. Coan, or Colgan, was in Moidart in the early part of 1688; he is shortly afterwards mentioned as being in the island of Lewis with Carolan.

The hostility of the chiefs outside the Catholic clans, and the presence of the soldiery, who were gradually increasing in various parts of the Highlands, made the journeys of the priests from one part of the country to another occasions of the greatest peril. They had to adopt every form of disguise, and to take refuge in the most solitary corries, or in caverns when these could be found. In Moidart, during the years that the soldiers were at Castle Tirrim, the priest's chief hiding place was a small cave, more like a fox's den, on the side of a hill between Dorlin and Port-a-bhata. Its entrance is so thoroughly concealed that a stranger might stand within two or three feet without suspecting its existence. It is only about eight or nine feet long by six or seven broad; but the complete sense of security to any one forced to live inside it, is considerably counter-balanced by a sense of extreme discomfort, owing to the lowness of the roof, which is not more than five feet high. An opening between the rocks on the south-west side admits both air and light. Some years ago a small vial, not unlike one of the wine-cruets used at the altar, was discovered below a mass of leaves heaped up in one of the corners, but it was unfortunately broken by some careless person who was unaware of the interest attached to its discovery. In 1700 Bishop Nicholson made a visit to the Highland districts, during the course of which he confirmed three thousand persons.

In 1707 we have the record of a most interesting journey made to the same places by his successor, Bishop Gordon.[8] This visit extended over several months. It began at Glengarry, was continued through Glenquoich, and, after a good many hardships, brought the travellers to the head of Loch Hourn, where they were duly entertained by Glengarry's brother. After some time spent in instructing and confirming the natives of Knoydart, Morar, and Arisaig, the bishop was sent in one of Clanranald's boats to the outer islands, but owing to a storm he was obliged to run for shelter into the island of Eigg, where they remained two days. When the weather moderated they set sail again, and reached Uist on the 27th June. The next fortnight was spent in preaching, preparing for confirmation, hearing confessions, and in other religious duties, at such places as Benbecula, South Uist proper, Vatersay, and Barra. On the 12th July the bishop landed at Canna, remaining among the natives of that beautiful little island for a day or so. After leaving, the boat was nearly lost in a gale which suddenly sprang up during the night; but one of the priests, who from long residence seems to have been familiar with those stormy seas, took the helm, and guided the party in safety to Eigg. After crossing to the mainland, the bishop was extremely anxious to visit the Moidart people; but his friends prevented him, representing that any attempt of the kind, owing to the Government troops stationed at Castle Tirrim, would be attended with serious peril. Unwilling however to abandon his purpose, measures were concerted by which a large number of the Moidart natives were brought within his reach. The bishop came as far as the Point of Ardnish, while the people, crossing over the hills and descending to the sea-coast at Roshven, were ferried over the bay to the place where he was ready to receive them. He preached, said mass, and confirmed those among them who had been prepared for that rite. The event is commemorated by Port-na-h-aifrinne, *ie.,* "harbour of the mass," a name still clinging to the locality. This good bishop repeated the visit several times, and at length became so attached to the Highland people that he longed for the day when he might be allowed to settle down permanently among them. Writing to Rome, he in one of his letters expresses himself thus: "I never had more comfort every way than among these poor people. So far from wearying of them, I long to shut myself up for ever with them. I do not question that I should do greater service there than anywhere else." During each of these visits the bishop usually spent a few days on a very small island at the foot of Loch Morar. On this picturesque spot a house had been built about 1705 with the intention of making it serve as a preparatory school for young subjects destined for the priesthood, but in the meantime it was solely occupied by the priest who ministered to Morar and other parts. When the original purpose came to be carried out, one of its earliest masters was Father George Innes, afterwards Principal of the Scots College in Paris; and one of its earliest pupils was Hugh Macdonald, of the house of Morar, who became Bishop of the Highlands in 1731, and who became involved, much against his will, in the affair of '45.[9]

The ecclesiastical affairs of the Highland Catholics were gradually settling down into some definite form of regular organisation, and no doubt would have gone on improving were it not that the rising in '45 threw everything into confusion again, and made the condition of the priests for a few years as bad almost as ever it had been. During the interval of progress an attempt was made to assign resident pastors to local congregations,[10] and it was in this manner that Moidart became more intimately acquainted with the three following clergymen, Colin Campbell, Neil M'Phee, and William Harrison.

Campbell was stationed in Moidart in 1728. He was a younger brother of Sir Duncan Campbell of Lochnell, and was brought up in the tenets of the reform. Having completed his studies at one of the Scotch universities, he was appointed to a commission in the Argyll regiment of Militia or Fencibles, and while holding this rank was ordered on a certain occasion to make a raid on the Skipnish family, who were reported to be giving shelter to a Catholic priest. An accusation of this kind was of course not a thing to be easily overlooked in Argyllshire, or indeed in any other of the ultra-Protestant parts of the kingdom at the period. Campbell discharged his duty so promptly that the Skipnish family were completely taken by surprise. The house was surrounded by soldiers, and the priest, who was actually with the family, had barely time to fly from the parlour and dive into some secret recess in one of the rooms adjoining. In the hurry, however, of his flight, he left behind him his stole and breviary, which were lying on the table at the moment of Campbell's entry. A glance convinced the officer that the priest was within reach, so, without any ceremony, he challenged Skipnish to deliver him up at once. The latter however positively declined, and told Campbell that if he wished to make a prisoner of a very inoffensive person, who happened to be his guest, he had better go and arrest him for himself Not wishing to be unnecessarily harsh in discharging a duty which at best must have been very disagreeable, Campbell gave Skipnish a few minutes to deliberate over the matter, whereupon the latter withdrew, while Campbell turned his attention to an examination of the articles found on the table. The breviary interested him very much, just as it interests and charms most readers who, by the aid of a classical education, are able to appreciate the devotional spirit and the many beauties with which its pages are filled.

He became absorbed in its contents for a considerable time, until at length, noticing that Skipnish had returned, he repeated his request that the priest should be brought into his presence, this time however adding that no harm should be done to him. Even then Skipnish hesitated, and only yielded when the officer, rising up and going outside, told his men to march a few miles farther off, and to carry on the search for the priest in another neighbourhood. When this was done, the priest was brought out from his hiding-place and introduced to Campbell. A long conversation ensued, the end of the affair being that Campbell, within a few months, threw up his commission, joined the Catholic Church, and, crossing over to France, entered himself as a student for the priesthood in the Scots College at Paris. He came back, after his ordination, in 1722.

It is not known how many years he remained in Moidart, but in 1735 he visited Rome, where he remained until 1738. In 1739 he was again in the Highlands, and during the next five years lived principally with Bishop Macdonald on the island at the foot of Loch Morar. When the Highlands began ringing with preparations for war in '45, and when it was clear that the Catholics almost to a man would take part in it, Campbell asked permission to accompany the Prince's army as one of the Catholic chaplains. Probably his old military instincts prompted him to take this step, although other priests followed the clansmen in the same capacity, viz., Allan Macdonald, a native of the Isles; John Tyrie, from Aberdeenshire; and Æneas MacGilis, from Lochaber. They wore the kilt, and were armed like officers. Campbell fell on the field of Culloden, the news of his death reaching Moidart through Clanranald's men, many of whom were personally acquainted with him owing to his connection with their district, and who were not likely to be mistaken regarding his fate. The writer adds this, because recently some credit seems to be attached to a rumour that Campbell was seen, after Culloden, furtively visiting his brother the Laird of

Lochnell. But a careful examination has stripped this story of any semblance of truth, leaving it almost certain that the melancholy ending of this priest was as described above, and as traditionally preserved in the Catholic districts of the mainland and the isles.

Neil M'Phee had charge of Arisaig and Moidart after Campbell went to Italy, and continued in these districts till 1737. He was arrested by the Government sometime after the '45, and banished from the kingdom.

William Harrison was a native of Strathbogie, was entered as a student in the Scots Benedictine College of Ratisbon, where he had a brother a monk, but after some years was sent to Rome, completing his studies in that city. He returned to Scotland in 1737. He was in charge of Moidart and Arisaig during the '45, winning by his prudence, and abstaining from politics, the approbation of all parties during that trying period, as well as during the next twenty years which he spent among the natives of the same districts.[11]

None of the clergymen had any fixed abode of their own during the time which they served among their parishioners, nor did the Church possess a single acre of land. When ministering to the spiritual wants of their people, the clergy, much after the fashion of apostolic times, were hospitably entertained from house to house, sometimes spending a week or fortnight or longer in this or that family, according to the circumstances of the latter. The same hospitality was extended to the clerk who invariably accompanied them. But the system had too many drawbacks attached to it to be continued by the ecclesiastical authorities a day longer than they could help, and when their circumstances improved it was gladly abolished.

Notes

1   Eilean Fhìonain is known locally as 'The Green Island' (or 'Isle') and is always called by this name in English speech.

2   "Here lies the Reverend and Accomplished man Rodericus Alexandri, one time Rector of Island Finnan". *Rodericus Alexandri*, ie, Roderick Son of Alexander or *Ruairidh mac Alasdair.*

3   *Origines Parochiales Scotiae* (Bannatyne Club, Edinburgh, 1854), Diocese of Argyle, Deanery of Morvern, Elanfinan; volume 2, part 1, p.199.

4   Today there are again two groves of large evergreens on the island, as well as smaller trees of rowan and elder, rhododendron, and masses of bramble.

5   According to Butler's *Lives of the Saints,* St Finnan's day falls on 17 February. On the other hand, *Origines Parochiales* has 16 March, while a tradition in Moidart itself, which must have developed after the author's time, celebrated a day in late August.

6   The earliest register is a Manuscript list for 1653, which names four secular priests plus William Ballantyne, Prefect of the Mission. The list does not include regulars, such as Benedictines and Jesuits, a few of whom were serving in Scotland at the time, several as chaplains in the few remaining Catholic great houses.

7   The author has given us the wrong source here. The history of Clanranald referred to is not by Buchanan; the author is anonymous, and is very possibly Ranald MacDonald of Staffa. The book, printed by Duncan Stevenson and Co of Edinburgh in 1819, is entitled *Historical and Genealogical Account of the Clan or Family of MacDonald from Somerlett, King of the Isles, Lord of Argyll and Kintyre, to the Present Period; more particularly as relating to the senior branch of that family, viz The Clan Ranald.* This is the same history referred to by the author on page 145 as having been written "about seventy years ago" — which would be exactly 1819. The dispensation to Ranald Òg to marry Ann, daughter of John MacDonald of Clanranald, signed at 'Ellan Raald' by Dominicus Duigin, is printed in Appendix XXXII, pp 32f, the text reference to

the marriage being on page 156.

8   This record of Bishop Gordon's 1707 itinerary forms a part of the Scottish Mission Papers (ref SM 3/9/3-4) in the Scottish Catholic Archives, Columba House, Edinburgh.

9   The island is *Eilean Bàn*. The house on it in fact dated from before 1700. It is known that Bishop Gordon had thoughts of a seminary for Scotland even before his consecration in 1706. Visiting the island for the first time in 1707 he may well have noted it as a possible site then. By 1712 he was definitely planning a seminary there, and in the spring of 1714 he set it up. In the summer he brought in George Innes as the first master. There were seven students. As well as Hugh MacDonald they included Allan MacDonald of South Uist, who later served as chaplain in the Jacobite army of 1745-6, accompanied the fugitive Prince to the Hebrides, and suffered imprisonment. The author refers to Allan again on pp 112, 160 and 177; he writes further on Hugh on page 178, and on the seminary and its successors on page 204f. The school on *Eilean Bàn* closed in 1716, it being thought too dangerous to keep it open after the failure of the '15.

10   The author's account is misleading. Bishop Hugh's appointment certainly greatly helped the development and organisation of the Church in the Highlands — indeed, it allowed the successful establishment of a separate Highland District to serve the Gaelic speaking areas of Scotland. But the Church had been settling down into some definite form of regular organisation for some decades already, notably following the appointment of Thomas Nicolson as Scotland's first post-Reformation bishop in 1694. He had divided the Catholic areas into fixed Stations, assigning a priest to each, and in 1700 made the first of several apostolic visits to the Highlands, and also published his *Statutes* which provided guidelines on the role of the clergy, the celebration of the sacraments, and pastoral duties.

11   For a while after 1746 William Harrison was probably the only priest active in the Rough Bounds, the rest being either in prison, fugitive, or dead. He served Morar and then Arisaig for nearly thirty more years until his death at Keppoch in 1773.

Chapter 8

Maighstear Alas-dair—Minister of Ardamurchan—His Force of Character—Is deposed—Kilchoan Church declared vacant by Colin Campbell of Ardchattan— Macdonald established at Dalelea— Misunderstandings with the Natives—Traditions—Short Sketch of his Descendants—Angus Beg of Dalelea—The Bard and his Family.

THE tenant who succeeded Donald Gorm at Dalelea was, as we said in the course of the preceding chapter, the Rev. Alexander Macdonald, Episcopal minister of Ardnamurchan, better known as Maighstear Alasdair, and father of the celebrated Jacobite bard Alasdair MacMhaighstir Alasdair. He was a native of Uist, and was related, although somewhat distantly, to Clanranald himself Having made his studies in Glasgow, he graduated at the university of that city in July 1674, and some years afterwards was appointed to the parish of Ardnamurchan. He was married to a Morven lady of the name of Maclachlan, and came to reside at Dalelea about the end of the seventeenth century. It is he, and his descendants through this lady, who are meant when, in the "Rough Bounds" or in other parts familiar with the Macdonalds, mention is made of the Dalelea family,— a necessary distinction, because after Clanranald sold his Moidart estates Dalelea became the residence of another branch of Macdonalds, who had no connection whatsoever with the minister's descendants. This other family is sometimes called the Macdonalds of Lochsheil, but the proper term is the Macdonalds of Rhu, in Arisaig, the place of their origin. After his arrival in the country the minister must have found himself in a very anomalous position. On the one hand, he was hemmed in for miles by the Catholics; while on the other, the Protestant flock to which he was appointed was spread over the whole extent of Ardnamurchan, with the parish church at Kilchoan, nearly thirty miles from Dalelea. Under the circumstances one would think that the pulpit of Kilchoan stood a pretty fair chance, as the Sundays recurred, of being found frequently and not inexcusably vacant, or that the Presbyterians and Episcopalians who formed the congregation would feel themselves compelled to hunt up and secure some other clergyman within easier access. But such seems not to have happened in either case. Maighsteir Alasdair, with an energy which tells highly in his favour, used to travel the whole distance on foot to his remote church, and seemingly with wonderful punctuality all things considered.

It is one of the commonest traditions discussed at the firesides in Moidart, as illustrative of Maighsteir Alasdair's power of enduring fatigue, that leaving Dalelea at an early hour on Sunday morning he would reach Kilchoan before mid-day, preach, and perform the rest of the service for his congregation, and then travel back on foot to Dalelea, which he generally reached before midnight, covering the whole distance of between fifty and sixty miles in one day. The feat of course could scarcely have been possible except in the summer months; but that this was the minister's regular habit during that season seems indubitable, if the slightest faith can be attached to a tradition preserved among those who had no special reasons for inventing it. On such occasions the minister used to ford the river Shiel opposite the present manse of Aharacle, seldom troubling the boatman who gave the ferry, except when the water was too high to be crossed on foot without risk or too much inconvenience. After reaching Gorten, Ockle, and Kilmory, he was generally joined by small knots of his parishioners, in whose company he made the rest of the journey to Kilchoan church. It is stated that among the few adherents whom he had in Moidart, one, a daughter of one of the tenants living in the strath of Mingarry, and called Iseabal nighean Ian Mhòr, used also sometimes to go down to Kilchoan, and return the same day to attend divine service when the minister officiated in Ardnamurchan, a journey which very few of her sex would undertake to-day. When, after the Revolution Settlement,[1]

Presbyterianism became the established form of church government in the land, Maighsteir Alasdair refused to conform to the change, and was in consequence deposed by the synod. This deposition, however, except in so far as the stipend was concerned, was merely nominal; for, owing to his great popularity, Maighsteir Alasdair maintained his hold of the congregation, and there is no clear evidence that during his lifetime the Presbytery of Lorn succeeded in establishing another in the parish of Ardnamurchan. It was not an easy matter even to declare the church vacant; and were it not that the presbytery happened to reckon among its members at the time a certain person of no ordinary intrepidity, the ceremony would probably have been indefinitely postponed, or omitted altogether. It is told of Colin Campbell, minister of Ardchattan, the person in question, that having volunteered to undertake the task, he was met at the door of Kilchoan church, and angrily denied admittance by Maighsteir Alasdair's friends. But Campbell, dressed in the kilt, and armed with a sword in one hand and a cocked pistol in the other, set his back against the wall, and resolutely defied the stormy audience in front of him. He delivered his message, and *ministeir na-cuigse,* or Whig minister, though he was, got out of the parish none the worse of the adventure.

As to the relations existing between Maighsteir Alasdair and his Catholic neighbours, they were for a considerable time what in modern phraseology might be termed *strained,* and at one period came to an *open rupture.* This arose not from questions about faith, but from questions about marches and fences in which morals were implicated. It seems that the Drum-a-laoigh tenants, who were Maighsteir Alasdair's next neighbours, had an inconvenient habit of allowing their cattle to stray over the minister's pastures. Whenever the case was too flagrant to be denied, the minister's remonstrances were generally met by assurances on the part of the tenants that the whole evil was due to the negligence of their herd, an unenlightened individual, apparently possessing one idea, but that a very fixed one, that the cattle whose welfare he was appointed to watch over throve better on the minister's grass than anywhere else, and that on reasonable principles it would be a pity to restrain them. Maighsteir Alasdair, however, with his usual energy, took decisive steps towards infusing more light into the dark chamber of the herd's mind. On a repetition of the offence he seized the delinquent, gave him a sound flogging, and then tied him to the trunk of a birch tree, near the edge of the wood above Druim-a-laoigh, leaving it to the discretion of Providence to keep him there or relieve him, as the merits of the case might require. The minister's energy almost infused too much light, for the chastised herd nearly came to enjoy the full vision of another world with all its secrets. The tenants were very indignant, and threatened to retaliate; but none showed such wrath as Ian Caol MacDhunnachaidh vich Aonghais, a native of Annat, and from all accounts a formidable opponent of his reverence. This individual, with one or two others, surprised Maighsteir Alasdair near Dalelea, and, if the story is true, handled him, notwithstanding his great personal strength, so severely that he had to be carried home in a blanket. Some time afterwards Maighsteir Alasdair hurriedly removed his family from Dalelea to the little island of Camustroloman on Lochsheil. Various reasons have been assigned for this flight. Some say that it was to escape from a combined attack which some of the natives were meditating against him. But this, on the face of it, is absurd, for Camustroloman is only a few yards removed from the northern shore, and to a determined enemy easily accessible. Moreover, flying to it for refuge must be very much like flying for protection into the jaws of the lion, for Camustroloman is immediately close to the hamlet of Druim-a-laoigh, that is to say, where the angry tenants chiefly resided. It is more probable that the little feud had been amicably settled, and that Maighsteir Alasdair's motive for retreating here was due to a sudden outbreak of fever or smallpox, which at that time was beginning to scourge the district, and which had already carried off two of his daughters at Dalelea.[2] The origin of its being due to the fear of an attack can be traced to some idle boasting on the part of Ian Caol. Happening to pass the way when the family were on the island, and seeing the minister's wife standing outside their temporary hut, Ian Caol, with a good deal of Indian swagger, pointed his gun at a bird perched on some prominent rock close to the islet and knocked it over, then drawing the lady's attention to the feat, remarked that he was waiting for an opportunity to do as much on her husband. When the epidemic ceased, Ian Caol must have found many opportunities of carrying out his evil intentions, if he really entertained such, for the family returned to Dalelea, and Maighsteir Alasdair, in visiting his friend Macdonald of Glenaladale, frequently passed through Annat, in front almost of Ian Caol's door; but we hear of no more attempts at violence, either on the part of Ian or anybody else. The truth is that the minister was not a person to be trifled with. Of great determination, and possessing great bodily strength, he, when fairly roused, had no scruples about using the arm of the flesh when more legitimate arguments failed to keep his neighbours in order. It is reported that on one occasion he met near Lochshiel side a native belonging to a class of people whom he cordially detested, viz., persons who enter into a bargain and fail to keep it. This specimen had purchased a valuable cow from Maighsteir Alasdair, but on one pretext or other eluded payment, until the minister's patience was exhausted. On meeting him so opportunely, Maighsteir Alasdair seized him by the neck, and dragging him to the foot of a precipice not far off, squeezed him into a hole or crevice among the fallen rocks. He was busy covering the prisoner's head with a broad heavy slab, when he was surprised by Macdonald of Glenaladale, who upon inquiring as to the nature of the man's offence, was told by his reverence that it was merely a case of imprisonment for debt. "The punishment," said Glen, "is no doubt effective, but the payment of the debt is likely to be farther off than ever." "Very true," replied the minister, "but we are reasonable. The prisoner can always get out at the demand of any substantial friend who will kindly become security for what is due." The laird smiled, and, taking the hint, undertook to compel payment or indemnify his reverence for the loss. The prisoner was forthwith liberated. It was evidently not inconsistent with the ideas of those rough times that the clergy, when able to do so, should execute a little retributive justice on their own behalf, or on the behalf of injured mortals. It is a story told by the late Bishop Kyle, that a Lochaber priest, who seems to have been a contemporary of Maighsteir Alasdair, or perhaps a little later, once rebuked a notorious thief in presence of the congregation, who had assembled for mass, either in the Braes of Lochaber or about Badenoch. The thief, however, instead of being humbled, showed himself rude and impertinent. This was too much for the pastor, so divesting himself of part of his sacerdotal garments, he advanced to where the thief was sitting, and dragging him outside the building administered such a severe castigation that the wretch had to howl for mercy. When the punishment was done to his satisfaction, the priest returned to the altar, resumed his vestments, and proceeded with the service. Two days afterwards he found himself at Glengarry Castle, and on casually mentioning the incident of Sunday, was much startled to hear the chief indignantly declare that the punishment inflicted was ridiculously inadequate, but that the omission should be promptly rectified. That very night a band of his armed retainers was sent out by Glengarry with instructions to scour the country in search of the offender, and not to re-appear without having him in their company. This was done, and the prisoner, after a summary trial, was condemned to be *starved to death*. He was thrown into the dungeon, and there is little doubt that the sentence would have been remorselessly carried out, if the priest, becoming alarmed at the severity of the judgment, had not used the most fervent entreaties with the jailer, and prevailed upon him to supply a little bread and water, sufficient to keep the prisoner in life for a few days. A few personal friends happened to call upon Glengarry about the same time, and the priest, taking advantage of a certain amount of merriment going on while these men were being entertained, implored the chief to commute the sentence or to remit it altogether. He obtained his request after some difficulty, the chief however impressing upon him, that whatever thieving was abroad, it was utterly intolerable within one's own district, and must be rigorously kept down; and that a low saucy thief was a creature to be exterminated at all times without the slightest compunction.

It is not known how Maighsteir Alasdair fared at the hands of the garrison stationed at Castle Tirrim, but it is a pretty fair assumption that he must have been looked upon, owing to his abhorrence of Whig principles, with considerable suspicion. His sons when they grew up became ardent Jacobites. Two of them were among the leaders of the Moidart people in the insurrection of '45.

There are no means of ascertaining accurately when the minister died, but it is surmised that the event took place between 1720 and 1725.[3] He was buried in St Finnan's island, on the south side of the ruined chapel, a very unpretending monument, with a hideous skeleton sculptured on it, marking the exact site. The remains of his wife were placed near the same spot. This is the common tradition, and it derives a good deal of support from the opinion of the late Miss Bell Macdonald, a lineal descendant of Maighsteir Alasdair, a person who had a wide and most accurate knowledge not only of things connected with her own family but of matters relating to the whole district. The rest of the minister's family, however, were buried on the north side of the church, close to Banker Macdonald's grave.

About the time of his death a valuation was made of the different lands in Ardnamurchan and Suinart by Sir Alexander Murray of Stanhope, who was then owner of these two properties, and who was the first seriously to commence the working of the lead-mines at Strontian. This valuation is reproduced by Cosmo Innes in his *Origines Parochiales,*[4] and may interest the present Ardnamurchan natives who would like to know the rate put upon their holdings a hundred and sixty-six years ago. But unfortunately, although the enumeration of the different farms and homesteads is very complete, the estimate is made in pennylands, a measure or unit which it is extremely difficult to define. Mr Skene, who is the best living authority on such matters, takes the pennyland to be the twentieth part of a davoch, and seems inclined to follow an old tradition according to which the davoch is a measure of land equivalent to the grazing of 320 cows. This would make the pennyland equal to 16 cows. How far this tallies with the valuation referred to is left to the judgment of the Ardnamurchan reader, it being kept in mind that the boundaries are supposed to have remained unaltered, and that in some parts the woods were more abundant than now.

Terbart	=	3 pennylands
Glenborradale	=	5 pennylands
Glenbeg	=	4 pennylands
Glenmore	=	5 pennylands
Ardslignish	=	5 pennylands
Camusangall	=	6 pennylands
Tómamonay	=	4 pennylands
Buorbloige	=	5 pennylands
Skinad	=	5 pennylands
Corrivulline	=	6 pennylands
Mingarry	=	6 pennylands
Kilchoan	=	5 pennylands
Ormsaig Mór	=	4 pennylands
Ormsaig Beg	=	5 pennylands
Grigadale	=	5 pennylands
Achachosnich	=	9 pennylands
Achnaha	=	5 pennylands
Glenduin	=	5 pennylands
Fascadale	=	3 pennylands
Achateny	=	6 pennylands
Braynanault	=	5 pennylands
Kilmorrie	=	4 pennylands
Swardilchorach	=	5 pennylands
Swardil Mór	=	5 pennylands
Swardilcheul	=	8 pennylands
Gortonfern	=	1 pennyland
Lehick (?)	=	1 pennyland
Clash and Ardrimnish	=	2 pennylands

Daal and Gorteneorna	=	6 pennylands
Ardtoe and Waterfoot	=	4 pennylands
Acharacle	=	5 pennylands

It is probable that one cow was estimated as equivalent to two two-year-olds. Thus, according to the Duke of Argyll, the "soum," a small division of land prevailing in the Isles, was the grazing of one cow, or two two-year-olds, or five sheep (*Crofts and farms in the Hebrides,* 1883).[5] In the absence of documentary evidence, it is almost impossible to get at the rent of a pennyland in 1723, unless of course one could reach it indirectly through a knowledge of the teinds.

The minister was succeeded at Dalelea by his oldest son, Angus Beg. This person, although short in stature, was like his father of extraordinary strength, and from the many stories current regarding him has become associated in the popular mind with the figure of a small Hercules. The Moidart people have a curious idea that his thorax, instead of being formed of ribs like that of an ordinary mortal, was composed of one undivided mass of bone, a sort of steel cuirass supplied by nature, and that to this phenomenon must be ascribed his extraordinary power. How far this theory is consistent with anatomy we leave to the specialists to decide. On his first introduction to Macdonald, Boisdale, the latter, who had heard much regarding him, could scarcely convince himself that fame had not exaggerated the strength of the Dalelea athlete. To his mind it was not possible that so much force could be concentrated within such a low frame. By way of solving his doubts, he suggested to Angus that they should have a wrestling bout, and upon the latter giving his consent Boisdale commenced to divest himself of his coat and waistcoat.

Angus, however, declined throwing off even his plaid. At the very first struggle, Boisdale, although a remarkably tall and muscular man, was lifted off the ground with the greatest ease and laid sprawling on the ground, to his own intense astonishment, and to the merriment of some gentlemen who were witnesses of the scene. On another occasion, when returning from a visit made to the outer islands, Angus Beg was driven through stress of weather into some creek or obscure harbour at the back of Mull. During this detention he and his companions experienced some inconvenience, owing to the supply of fuel on board running short. Angus thereupon sent one of the party on shore, with the recommendation that he should help himself to a creelful of peats wherever he could find them. After a certain interval the messenger returned, with information that there was a stack of peats not far off, but that in making towards it he was driven away by a rough churlish individual, who, calling himself the owner, brandished a stick over his head and threatened personal violence. Much disgusted, Angus sent out another messenger, a person reputed to carry a stout heart and a powerful arm; but this one fared no better, in fact worse, for in addition to an empty creel he brought back a bloody pate. After this mishap he deemed it advisable to make a personal reconnoitre, so, leaving the vessel, he sauntered leisurely towards the spot where the warlike Mullman was mounting guard. When near enough to be challenged, he explained to the native the nature of his wants, adding that if the slight favour was not courteously given he would help himself to it by force, and give himself the further pleasure of damaging the native's person. In a moment the islander flew at him, deeply resenting such insulting language from a man whom he had no doubt of being thoroughly able to chastise; but before his cudgel could be properly brought into play, Angus slipped in, and seizing him by the waist, gave him one of those famous hugs which are said to have resembled the hugs of a bear. The Mullman was thrown heavily to the ground, and for a short time was deprived of all consciousness. When he recovered, Angus had filled his creel, and was about to take his departure; but the fallen foe, blinking and staring somewhat like a bewildered owl, cried to him to stop, and then commenced an interrogatory which, as customary in popular stories of this kind, tended to ascertain if the victor was the d—l himself or one of his angels. Upon being solemnly assured that there was no identity, or even the remotest connection with any such objectionable individuals, the Mullman is said to have shouted out: "Then you must be Angus Beg of Dalelea, for there is no other in the west of Scotland who can give that ugly squeeze in which you nearly smothered me." He proved a better man than appearances first warranted, for during the rest of the time spent in his neighbourhood he had Angus and his companions frequently at his house, and entertained them with the heartiest hospitality.

Shortly after his father's death, Angus married Margaret Cameron, daughter of the tenant of Achadhuan, in Lochaber. She is represented to have been a lady of singular piety, and of a gentleness of manners which was well calculated to have a beneficial effect on the fiery characters surrounding Dalelea. The natives still point out a certain spot on the top of the knoll behind Dalelea House, where this estimable person used to spend many of the summer evenings in reading and in devotional exercises. It was here too that she used to withdraw on Sundays to pray, when circumstances prevented her from going to church.

In '45 Angus was appointed one of the captains over the Moidart men in Clanranald's regiment. He followed his chief through the whole business, and after Culloden made his escape in safety to his native district; but he had to lurk among the hills and woods, only occasionally visiting his family, for two years. When the act of indemnity was passed, he settled down quietly at Dalelea, where he finished his days in peace. He joined the Catholic Church many years before the '45.

One of his daughters, Marcella, married young Ranald Macdonald of Kinlochmoidart, the person who is said to have tossed his bonnet in the air on board the "Doutelle," and whose ill-directed enthusiasm decided the wavering chiefs in taking up arms for the Prince, and in plunging themselves and their countrymen into ruin.

He was succeeded at Dalelea by his oldest surviving son, Allan, who married a Macdonald lady from Arisaig. There were several children born of this marriage, the better known being—Alexander, called the banker; Angus, Cinn-a'chreagan; and a daughter married to Donald Macdonald, Lochans, father of Miss Bell.

It was Alexander who built the present house of Dalelea, about the beginning of the present or the end of the last century. He was a person of great energy, and, possessing undoubted talents for business, received a lucrative appointment in the bank at Callander, which he held for many years. He bought Lochans from Clanranald about 1814. He was married to a sister of John Macdonald, Borrodale, and by her had four daughters, viz.:—Flora, married to Major Macdonald of the 42nd, and living for some years at the Wilderness in Arisaig (one of the daughters died at Manchester not long ago); Jessie, married to a Mr Campbell,—further history not known; Joanna, died unmarried; Marjory, or Mysie, married, but died without leaving any issue.

Shortly after its erection, Dalelea House was let for some years to a Dr Maclaren, who lived there with his sisters. They were succeeded by the banker's brother-in-law, Macdonald, Lochans, so called from his having been for a long time tenant of Lochans in Glenmoidart. His daughter, Miss Bell, subsequently lived at Dorlin, whence she removed to Fort-William, where she died.

The second son of the minister, Alasdair MacMhaighsteir Alasdair, who shares with Duncan Bàn M'Intyre the distinction of holding the foremost place in the ranks of Celtic poets, was born at Dalelea about the beginning of the eighteenth century. It is said that one time he was destined for the ministry, and with this view was sent to Glasgow to attend the usual course of lectures at the university. But this project had to be abandoned, owing apparently to pecuniary embarrassments. Later on, he opened a small school at Kilchoan, in Ardnamurchan, under the patronage of the Society for the Propagation of Christian Knowledge, supplementing the living from this source by becoming tenant of the farm of Corrie-mhullen in the same neighbourhood. This situation he held for several years; but the same causes which checked his university career interfered with his useful work among the youth of Ardnamurchan. The funds of the society ran short, and the teacher had to relinquish his post.[6] Before, however, this took place, he compiled his Gaelic and

*The memorial cross to Father Charles on Eilean Fhionain,
looking to the North East*

Father Charles MacDonald

Thatched cottage at Kinlochmoidart c.1890, woman at door not identified

Father Charles, school mistress and School Board outside Mingary School, presenting bureau to the son of Lord Howard of Glossop and his wife, 1887.

Roshven House at the time of its building, 1857–8

Eilean Shona House, 1893

Ardtoe, looking to Eigg and Rum, c.1890

Castle Tioram, from the gardens of Dorlin House, c.1890

English vocabulary, the first contribution of the kind to Celtic literature. It was published by the society, and circulated through the Highlands to facilitate the progress of the scholars under their care.[7] When the chiefs decided upon taking up the Prince's cause, the bard threw himself into the movement with the whole energy of his vigorous yet restless nature. Some of his finest pieces were written under the excitement of this period. The address to the Prince, under the guise of Morag, with its chorus,—

> "Agus ho Mhorag, ho ro,
> 'S na ho ro gheallaidh,"[8]

together with several stirring appeals to the clans, urging them in bold fiery strains to rally round the Prince and to chase King George across the seas, are sung at almost every fireside in the Jacobite districts to this day. In a memoir prefixed to a recent edition of this bard's works, the writer makes the remark:—"It is very characteristic of his reckless courage, that he published these poems, breathing rebellion in every line, and pouring the vials of his wrath upon the whole race of the Georges, five years after the battle of Culloden." The justness of this remark will strike anyone with sufficient knowledge of Gaelic to understand the following lines:—

> "O'n cullach sin righ Deorsa
> Mac na cráine Gearmailtich
> 'S a chàirdeas riunn, 's a dhàimh
> Gaol fithich air a' chùaimh.
>
> …a righ nan dùl,
> Tog dhinn a'mhuc, 's a cuing,
> 'S a-h-àl breac, brothach, uircuineach,
> Le 'n cuid chrom-shoc-thar thuinn."[9]

In other passages he devoutly prays that the "Butcher" may have a rope tied round his neck, and may be made to swing from it,—a blessing to which, if it could do any good, many a Highlander to-day would respond with a hearty amen.

His choicest offering to the king is the Scottish Maiden—i.e. the Guillotine—and so on. But these were extravagant forms of *lese majesté,* and of course not at all to be approved of, even in a poet. They were the effusions, perhaps, of the melancholy madness of poetry, without the inspiration, as Junius would say. He was, as we remarked before, one of the captains or leaders among the Clanranalds in '45.

When the country became more settled after that disastrous business, the bard received the farm of Eignaig, on the Glenuig estate, from Clanranald. one of the most charming and picturesque spots in Moidart; and there is no reason why this place should not have continued to be his home for the rest of his days, if he had regulated his conduct upon ordinary principles of prudence and decency. But unfortunately the bard was unable to restrain his hatred of the Government, and caused serious alarm among those who were interested in the welfare of the district, by his indiscreet publication of those poems in which the royal family were so grossly handled. The country had suffered intensely already, and nothing was more likely, in the opinion of the leading families, to renew or to continue the miserable state of matters through which they had just passed, than this open defiance and contempt of the victorious party. It has to be added, too, that some of the poet's productions were extremely gross and immoral; and if these were composed during his residence at Eignaig, it is not to be wondered at that Clanranald or his agents should be prevailed upon to banish him from the district. He was accordingly deprived of Eignaig, and compelled to migrate to Knoydart. He felt the blow very bitterly, and by way of retaliation composed the celebrated song, "Imrich, Alasdair, a Eignaig,"[10] in which he reviles Eignaig, heaping on it every disqualification which could make any place repulsive and objectionable. But the bard's indignant description is utterly at variance with the true features and attractiveness of the spot. The Moidart people are unanimous in the opinion, that the last five stanzas of the poem referred to were levelled at Father Harrison, who was priest of the district at the time. Rightly or wrongly the poet suspected this gentleman of being one of the chief instigators of the movement against him; and to those who are acquainted with Father Harrison's character for prudence, and his abhorrence as a clergyman of the filthy songs circulating from the poet among the natives, those suspicions will not appear unfounded. At Inverey the bard composed another song in praise of Morar, the exaggeration here also being quite as absurd as it was in the opposite sense in reference to Eignaig. This effusion was written, it is believed, partly out of compliment to the Catholic ecclesiastical authorities then residing at Buorblach, some of whom were inclined to judge the poet less harshly than their subordinate in Moidart. "Thionndaidh riumsa, caoin gach ascaoin," as the poet himself observes, "bhon thàinig mi dh' Ionbhar-Aoidhe."[11] Clanranald subsequently gave him a piece of land in Arisaig, at first near the strath at Camus-an-talmhuinn, later on at Sanndaig, a hamlet overlooking that arm of the sea separating Arisaig from Moidart. Here he lived long enough to win back a large share of that esteem which his objectionable pieces had lost him. In his last illness he was carefully nursed by his Arisaig friends, two of whom, on the night of his decease, finding the hours rather monotonous, and thinking that he was asleep, began to recite in an undertone some verses of their own composition. To their astonishment, however, the bard raised himself up, and, smiling at their inexperienced efforts, pointed out how the ideas might be improved, and the verses made to run in another and a smoother form, at the same time giving an illustration in a few original measures of his own. He then sunk back on the pillow, and immediately expired. It was proposed at first to carry his remains over to Eilean-Fhionnan, but this project, owing to a severe gale then raging along the coast, had to be abandoned. The Arisaig people thereupon got their own way, and Alasdair MacMhaigsteir Alasdair was buried in the cemetery of Kilmhoree, close to the present Catholic church of Arisaig. Dr Scott's statement that he took excessively to the use of *opium,* and died in a *lunatic asylum,* is a wild fiction founded upon absolute error or ignorance.[12] There is an old man living close to the writer whose grandfather obtained the house and lands which became vacant after the bard's death. Reid's unpleasant description ought also to be taken with a considerable allowance of salt. Those who ought to be good judges of his personal appearance and habits know nothing of such objectionable details. At any rate all memory of them has vanished, if it ever existed.

Macdonald was undoubtedly a person of high poetical genius, and although critics may differ as to the exact merits of some of his productions, not one will deny that there are certain poems—for instance, the "Galley of Clanranald"—which will be read and relished so long as the Gaelic language lives. As to his religious opinions, Macdonald was first an Episcopalian, then a Presbyterian, and finally a Catholic. The Mull satirist, among many other sharp things flung at the Moidart bard, reproached him with joining the Catholic Church, not from motives of serious conviction, but from a desire to curry favour with the leaders of the Jacobite party at the court of St Germains:

> "Cha b'e 'n creideamh ach am brosgul
> Chuir a 'ghiulan crois a' Phàp thu."[13]

The best answer to this is, that Macdonald continued a Catholic when it might have been to his temporal advantage to have gone back to either of the former denominations. In Moidart it is generally understood that it was the influence of his brother Angus and of the latter's wife that helped in bringing him over. His children and their descendants were noted for being staunch Catholics.

It is a tradition that the bard while living at Dalelea planted with his own hands a few trees near the house, and these, one is happy to note, still flourish. One of them, a venerable oak, is in front of Dalelea kitchen, the others are near the garden. When the Bunawe Smelting Company were busy cutting down the Lochsheil woods they wished to level these trees with the rest, but the natives, out of respect for Macdonald's memory, resisted, and partly by threats, partly by friendly representations, induced the workmen to abandon their intention. Some years afterwards certain persons possessing something of that low tone of morality which Lord Wolseley discovers in British secretaries for war, tried to persuade the late Lochsheil's father to cut down the oak tree as excellent timber for the "Diamond," a vessel which he was then building; but old Rhu, gentleman and Highlander to the backbone, declared that he would rather forfeit a hundred pounds than lay sacrilegious hands on such an interesting memorial of the Moidart poet.

Macdonald's oldest son Ranald was for some years tenant of the inn at Strath Arisaig, but removing to Eigg he became tenant of the farm of Laig in that island. This farm remained in the family until the poet's great-grandson Angus emigrated to the United States about forty years ago.

Ranald's death was very tragic. In his old age his mind began to give way, and he had to be watched more or less carefully; but escaping from the house one night, he wandered away towards the sea-shore, where he was found lying dead the following morning, apparently shot with his own gun. His aged sister missing him soon after his departure from the house, became alarmed, and ventured out in search of him, but losing her way in the dark, and becoming exhausted, she sunk down and all but perished. She was discovered at daylight quite insensible. She recovered, however, and lived for a year or two longer.

In Allan the son of Ranald, the muscular development so characteristic of all the Dalelea family was reproduced in a very marked manner. Like Angus Beg, his granduncle, he was reckoned to be one of the most powerful men of his time in the Western Highlands. A famous encounter which once took place between himself and one of the M'Gregors of Glen Gyle, at Doune market, is still remembered in the small isles and in parts of the opposite mainland, and often forms a topic of conversation among the natives at their festive gatherings, or when at the fireside on a wintry night their thoughts wander back to the days when Highland gentlemen of the class to which Allan belonged were more plentiful than they are now. This M'Gregor had the name of being a rough customer,— bold, strong, ready to pick a quarrel on slight provocation,—and in consequence was rather shunned by the more peacefully inclined classes in his neighbourhood. Among most of the other M'Gregors he was treated as their favourite champion, being regarded as more than a match for the best man in Perthshire. At the market in question, an altercation took place between him and a native of Eigg, which ended in the islesman receiving a severe pommelling. One of the bystanders, however, who bore M'Gregor some grudge, cried out that after treating the islander in this fashion he would do wisely in keeping out of Allan Laig's way, who would certainly retaliate for the injury done to his countryman. This taunt roused M'Gregor to seek an opportunity of quarrelling with Macdonald; but the latter, after having transacted his business, had left the market and withdrawn to his inn, where he retired to rest at an early hour. He was roused out of his slumbers by a violent dispute going on between the landlord's family and some tipsy intruders who were forcing their way upstairs. In a few minutes the door of his bedroom was burst open, and M'Gregor, gloriously drunk, rolled in, holding a glass in one hand and a bottle of whisky in the other. Approaching Allan's bedside, he hiccoughed out, "You must fight with me, Macdonald, or drink with me—one or the other." Not relishing this form of address, Macdonald, springing out of bed, seized his unwelcome visitor by the neck and pushed him down stairs, on reaching the lower steps of which he was pounced upon by the people of the house and ejected from the premises.

The following morning Macdonald commenced his journey homeward, the previous night's adventure occupying no more of his attention than any other trivial incident coming in his way. But in Perthshire the case was otherwise. A highly coloured story was industriously and rather maliciously circulated that M'Gregor had been soundly drubbed by a stranger, and several hints were thrown out to his friends that henceforth they ought in decency to pitch the praises of their hero on a lower key. This roused the M'Gregors, and especially their favourite, to the highest pitch of indignation. The party chiefly interested determined to settle the business in such a way that at the earliest opportunity the gossips should be compelled to give another and a more creditable version of his prowess. When the next market came round, there was not a soberer or quieter person among the crowd than M'Gregor. But when Macdonald had finished his business, and according to custom had withdrawn to the inn, he was closely followed by M'Gregor, who, entering the room, boldly put his challenge in the very same terms which he had used some months previously, "You must fight with me or drink with me." The aggressive manner in which this was uttered left no doubt in the mind of Allan as to the manner in which he was expected to accept it. A space was cleared in the room, and a desperate struggle between the two combatants took place, which, whether fought *secundum artem* or not, was none the less a genuine bruising business, not unworthy of the sledgehammers brought into play. But M'Gregor sober, according to the Moidart version, was no more a match for Allan than M'Gregor drunk. He was completely disabled, and had to be carried off the field by his disappointed friends. Some of these were inclined to take an active part in the engagement, but a party of Macdonald's west country friends hurrying to the scene awed them into that respect for fairness which is apt at times to be forgotten on such occasions.

At another time Allan, while travelling in a certain part of the Lowlands with which he was not familiar, was wilfully sent astray by a jocose toll-keeper, who to Allan's inquiries as to the proper direction to follow, insisted most particularly that after coming to a certain cross road he should keep religiously to the right, and not upon any account wander to the left. Allan obeyed these instructions; but after riding several miles he met an old woman, who with much sympathy informed him that he was completely wrong, and that he should have taken the turn to the left. Boiling over with indignation, Macdonald rode straight back to the toll-bar with the resolute intention of improving the toll-keeper's morals. The offender however, spying the traveller from some distance, made a hasty retreat into his castle, which he proceeded to barricade in such a manner as to defy an attack. Not being able to get at his person, Macdonald unhinged the gates, which he proceeded deliberately to smash to pieces, and then piling up the wreck in the middle of the road as food for reflection to a knave, continued his journey.

The late Dr Maclachlan, Rahoy, used to relate another anecdote regarding Allan, in which the doctor himself, who was then a medical student, figured prominently. The two Highland gentlemen had met at one of the Edinburgh hotels, and while conversing in Gaelic overheard some sneering remarks passed by a party of young bears at Celts in general, and the barbarity of their language in particular. They resented this, of course, and a rough scrimmage followed, during which the waiters fled from the room, leaving the combatants to themselves. The civilians got their heads broken and had to retreat, but the damage to the crystal and furniture was much greater, everything in the room being a complete wreck. This scene the victors contemplated with some dismay, for visions of heavy bills for damages began to rise up unpleasantly before them. The landlord himself then appeared, who, after grimly surveying the desolation among his household gods, advanced towards the two, but instead of storming at them or suggesting compensation for his loss, cheerfully congratulated them on the excellent lesson bestowed upon their adversaries. He was a Highlander himself, and had often writhed under the insulting pleasantries of the latter.

Allan however was naturally quiet and inoffensive, and among his personal friends none was better liked or more popular; but he never could brook an insult, or endure those who, like conceited Cockneys, sometimes venture to talk in disparaging terms of his countrymen. He died in Eigg, and is buried in that island.

His son Angus, after carrying on the farm for some time, emigrated with his mother to America. When the Civil War broke out, he was appointed to a commission in the 11th Wisconsin Regiment, and distinguished himself by his gallantry during the operations of the Federal army in Alabama and Mississippi. The following notice regarding his conduct is extracted from an American journal published at the time:— "Lieutenant Angus R. Macdonald and Sergeant Moore fell into their (Confederate) hands, and there followed a desperate struggle. Five or six attacked Macdonald with bayonets, and he fought them with the sword, killing two. He received two bayonet thrusts in the breast and a musket-ball in the thigh. When he fell a Confederate fell over him, whom he used as a shield to protect himself from a further thrust of the bayonet. Then Sergeant Moore, who had also received a bayonet wound, picked up a Confederate musket and shot Macdonald's assailant dead." Angus partly recovered from his wounds, and after the war was over received another appointment in the civil service, which he held till his death, an event which took place at Milwaukee about ten years ago. He was never married, and in him the direct line of the bard became extinct.

Notes

1   The Revolution Settlement of 1689.

2   Smallpox was, with consumption, the most common cause of infant mortality. So feared was it that the people of the Highlands would not refer to it by name.

3   The date is thought to be 25 February 1724.

4   The first lead mine was opened in the hills above Strontian in 1724 by a partnership of which Murray was a member. Having run at a loss, it was leased in 1730 to the York Buildings Company, who developed it by sinking new shafts into a recently discovered vein claimed to be the largest in the world at that time. Financial difficulties persisted and after workers' disputes the mines were closed in 1740. They were later re-opened and continued in operation until about 1815.

The valuation was carried out in 1723: the reference is *Origines Parochiales Scotiae* (Bannatyne Club, Edinburgh, 1854) volume 2, part 1, p. 196.

5   Campbell, George D. Duke of Argyll, *Crofts and Farms in the Hebrides, being an account of the management of an island estate for 130 years* (Edinburgh 1883), p. 8. Argyll also states that 4 soums = 1 Mail Land. Thus:

> 4 Soums = 1 Mail Land
> 4 Mail lands = 1 Pennyland
> 20 Pennylands = 1 Davoch

6   Alasdair mac Mhaighstir Alasdair was employed by the SSPCK in a number of schools from 1729, including Kilchoan, latterly with successively reduced salaries. His last post was at Corryvullin, Ardnamurchan, where he worked from 1739, and where he came under increased suspicion due to his Jacobite sympathies and the fact that at some stage he privately converted to Catholicism. He left Corryvullin in Spring 1745, just days before the landing of the Prince, and at a time when he was almost certainly in any case about to be dismissed.

7   *A Galick and English Vocabulary* was published in 1741. The SSPCK, founded in 1709, had as one of its original aims the eradication of Gaelic in Scotland, to which end all teaching in its Highland schools was to be conducted in English. The ineffectiveness of such a policy becoming apparent the Society adopted a more sympathetic approach, and recommended bilingual teaching and learning. It was for this purpose that the *Vocabulary* was commissioned — not for the promotion of Gaelic but for the better promotion of English among Gaelic speaking children.

8   This is the chorus of the poem *Morag*. Composed after the defeat at Culloden, the poem is in fact addressed to the Prince, but in the guise of a lover. It is written as a 'waulking song', to be sung by women waulking cloth, its strong rhythm being an aid to team work in unison. The chorus of Gaelic songs was often composed of syllables with little meaning, and this is probably the case here. But the phrase *'ho ro gheallaidh'* has taken on a meaning in more recent Gaelic songs following *Morag*, and now means something like 'a hoolie'.

9   Oh that hog King George,
           Son of the German sow,
           And his kindness to us, and his generosity —
           Like the raven's love for its bone.

           Oh King of Hope
           Take the pig from us, and his yoke,
           And his spotted litter, scabby, swinish,
           Take the whole crooked-snouted collection away over the sea.

(*chùaimh* is a misprint in the original text for *chnaimh*).

10   *Imrich Alasdair a Eigneig* — Alexander's flitting from Eignaig. The commas in the original destroy the meaning.

11   "Every roughness was made smooth for me, since I came to Inverie", from the last stanza of *Imrich Alasdair*. Buorblach farm lies on the north side of the Morar estuary and was for some years the residence and base of Bishop John MacDonald, and also for most of the 1770s the seminary of the Highland

District. It was held in tack from Lord Lovat (who had purchased the whole of North Morar from Glengarry in 1768) but was lost when Lovat sold it, contrary to an agreement made with the Bishop (see also chapter xii, note 2).

12   Scott, Hew, *Fasti Ecclesiae Scoticanae* (Edinburgh and London 1872), volume 111, part 1, p. 81.

13   "It was not faith but flattery that prompted you to carry the Pope's cross" — *Verses between the Bard and the Mull Herdsman*. There is a slightly different version in MacDonald, A. and A. (eds), *The Poems of Alexander MacDonald* (Inverness, 1924), p. 282; and at least one other version exists.

14   The Bunawe Iron Smelting works were opened at Taynuilt in 1753 by the Lancashire firm of Richard Ford & Co. Several such works were set up by English firms in the Highlands because of the timber available for charcoal smelting, it being cheaper to transport the ore to the timber than vice versa. Local timber met the need at first but the company later went as far as Moidart, Morvern and Lochaber for supplies.

Chapter 9

NEXT to Clanranald's, the two most influential families in Moidart were the Macdonalds of Glenaladale and the Macdonalds of Kinlochmoidart. They were both descended from minor branches of the same stock. The Glenaladales trace their genealogy to Ian Og, a younger son of John of Moidart; the Kinlochmoidarts derive from a grandson of the same chief. It is a tradition that at the time of receiving their estates, the Glenaladales had the condition imposed upon them of guarding the eastern end of Moidart from the encroachments of the Camerons, who at all times displayed a wonderful relish and dexterity in uplifting cattle. Nothing however of any particular interest attaches to the history of either family until we approach the '45, when they both come much more prominently into view.

At an early age there was a small property cutting like a wedge into the Kinlochmoidart estate, and reserved by Clanranald for his Moidart bailiff or "maor." It is called Lochans, and was held for several generations by the same family of M'Isaacs. All minor disputes among the natives were referred to the bailiff for settlement, and all questions connected with land, such as disposal of vacant farms, or payment of rent, came under his cognisance. At stated intervals he held court in the open air, sometimes near Leadnacloiche, but more frequently at Torr-na-breith, a spot situated midway between Brunery and Dalelea. When the office of bailiff ceased to be hereditary in the same family Lochans reverted to the Clanranalds, and, after many changes, became latterly incorporated with the rest of the Kinlochmoidart estate, to which it should geographically belong.

During the thirty years which followed the insurrection of Mar, pretty regular communications were kept up between the Highland Jacobite chiefs at home and the exiled family abroad. The Highlanders were still not unwilling to risk life and property on behalf of the latter; but the bitter experience of past failures had at last firmly impressed this conviction on the minds of most of them, that any further risings, unless well backed up by foreign gold, arms, and men, would be sheer acts of madness, and doomed from the outset to certain ruin. It was then with a feeling akin to consternation that old Clanranald heard of Prince Charles landing at Eriskay, a small island between South Uist and Barra, attended only by half-a-dozen gentlemen, unsupplied with any resources for conducting a campaign, yet bent on winning back his ancestors' throne.[1] The chief resolutely declined countenancing anything apparently so insane, and his example was followed with equal determination by his relative Macdonald of Boisdale. Indeed the replies of the latter to the entreaties and expostulations of the Prince are said to have been almost rude in their bluntness, Boisdale not only repudiating any idea of co-operation on his own part, but affirming that not a single chief of any note would be fool enough to put the halter round his own neck in the deliberate manner suggested by his Highness. In this however he was mistaken, and, like other prophets who take to foretelling the future without being well supplied with positive knowledge beforehand, came to see his vaticinations prove utterly false, in fact much more quickly so than either anticipated or desired. Charles seeing the futility of arguing with these two, ordered the ship's captain to steer for Lochnan-uamh on the Arisaig coast. After casting anchor in front of Borrodale, he despatched a messenger in quest of young Clanranald, who, he expected, would be much more easily dealt with and gained to his cause. Clanranald was at the time in Moidart, and on receiving the message hurried at once, together with Kinlochmoidart and several other gentlemen belonging to the district, to meet the Prince on board the French vessel. But when the project was laid before him, he recoiled, without any hesitation, affirming that without help from abroad the actual circumstances of the country rendered the idea of a rising utterly impracticable. This was the judgment of Kinloch too, and the Prince was as near being baffled by the younger heads as he was already by the older ones in Uist. But during the exciting debates which were taking place among the principals, Kinloch's younger brother, Ranald, settled the whole business, by giving way to one of those sudden bursts of enthusiasm which, although creditable undoubtedly to the generous feelings of the actor, are not always complimentary to his commonsense. In this instance the triumphant waving of Ranald's bonnet in the air was as good as a death-warrant to many of his countrymen, and among them to his own brother. The chiefs, forgetting the wise arguments which they had hitherto opposed to the Prince's advances, allowed themselves to be carried away by the excitement of the moment, and, before leaving the "Doutelle," bound themselves to take part in the enterprise and to help it forward at all hazards. One of them felt conscious that in taking this course he was putting the seal to his own doom. It is stated in the correspondence of Bishop Hugh Macdonald, that Kinlochmoidart, while carrying secret despatches to some of the chiefs, met his lordship in Argyleshire, and, in communicating the startling news of the Prince's arrival, was strongly advised by the bishop to have nothing to do with the business. But to this Kinloch replied that he had already gone too far, and that having staked all, he was bound to see the end of the affair whatever it might be. He then told the bishop that during the night following his promise to fight for the

Prince he had a dream, in which he saw himself captured, led to the scaffold, and hanged by the enemy. This a few months afterwards turned out to be his doom.

Clanranald was sent to Skye with Allan, a younger brother of Kinloch, to solicit the aid of Sir Alexander Macdonald of Sleat and of the chief of the Macleods, but these two gentlemen were very obdurate. So far from complying with what was asked of them, they forwarded a communication to President Forbes of Culloden, in which they gave full information of the Prince's doings, and a list of those chiefs who had joined him:—"You may believe, my Lord, our spirits are in a great deal of agitation, and that we are much at a loss how to behave in so extraordinary an occurrence. That we will have no connection with these madmen is certain, but we are bewildered in every other respect till we hear from you," &c.

This was no doubt very edifying, but these two worthies had sometime previously promised to rise with the Prince, if he brought a foreign force with him strong enough to give a probability of success. When the tide was turning against the Prince they formed two independent companies from among their people to assist his enemies. Locheil's participation in the insurrection was brought about much in the same way as that of the Moidart chiefs. He was at first totally opposed to the movement, and had no intention of joining; but instead of contenting himself with a written communication, in which he might have given reasons for refusing, he decided on having a personal interview as likely to prove more satisfactory. The interview took place, but the satisfactory part of it was mostly appreciated by the Prince. The brave Locheil, moved by the passionate appeals made to his loyalty, and by the Prince's taunts contrasting the chief's opposition with the oft-tried fidelity of his family to the Stuart cause in days gone by, was shaken out of his good resolutions and surrendered at discretion. It is said that the likelihood of this being the result was foretold by his brother Fassifern, at whose house the chief called on his way down to Arisaig. His example contributed more than any other cause in influencing several other prominent chiefs to take up arms against the Government, such for instance as Macdonald of Glengarry, Macdonald of Keppoch, Macpherson of Cluny, the Macintoshes, and others.

Once committed to an enterprise so desperate, these daring men set themselves to the task of pushing it forward with an energy and determination which, judged apart from political bias, are certainly entitled to admiration; and the amazing part is, that in spite of the insurmountable difficulties before them they came so very near realising what they aimed at. In a short time Locheil rallied to the standard of the Prince almost every able-bodied man in his clan, about 1,200 or more, as some affirm; Glengarry brought 700; Cluny, 600; the Macintoshes, under Col. M'Gillivray of Dunmaglass, 700. But Clanranald's contingent was a weak one. This was due to the opposition of his father, and of Boisdale, who refused to allow any of the island followers to obey the call. Most of those who followed the chief belonged to Moidart, Arisaig, and South Morar, with a few from Eigg and Canna. Their total number did not exceed 300. There is a very interesting roll, unfortunately not complete, still preserved in the Clanranald family, giving the names of the Moidart men who had to "rise," their places of residence, and the armour, if any, which they could produce. This roll was published about seventy years ago, in a small history of the family;[2] but as it has been long out of print, the present writer reproduces it as likely perhaps to interest some of his readers. The pleasure of perusing it will be increased when one knows that the descendants of some of those mentioned in it still flourish in the district. In one or two instances the families dwell in the same hamlet, holding the same crofts, or part thereof, which the generation preceding their great grandfathers held, when thus summoned to draw the sword for Prince Charlie:—

"Part of a roll of men upon Clanranald's Mainland Estates—with their arms—made up in the year 1745.

Ranald Macdonald -
Donald Macdonald - gun
Allan MacCallane - sword
Donald MacMylan - sword
Donald Macpherson - sword
Donald Bain - wants
Angus Cameron - wants
Donald Macdonald - gun, sword and terge
John his brother - gun, sword, terge
Allan his brother - gun and sword
Sandy Macdonald - gun and sword
John Macdonald - gun
John MacFinla vic Ean Roy - gun and sword
John MacInnes vic Ean vic Creul - wants
Ian Mac Yonill vic Ean vic Yonill Oig - gun, sword
John MacIsaac the Violer - gun

Hugh MacVoddich - sword
John MacLean - wants

John Macdonald - gun, sword, terge
Ewan Bàn - sword
John Macdonald - gun

John Mac Neill Mor - gun and sword
Ruari Mac Innish Mòir - gun

Duncan Mac Isaak - gun and sword
John Macdonald - sword

Donald Maclean - gun and sword
Angus Maclean - gun

Duncan Cameron - wanting
Donald Mac Neill Mòr - sword
Ewan Mac Vorrich - sword
John Cameron - gun, sword, terge
Donald Cameron his brother - gun
Dan. Cameron - gun, sword

Kinloch-Moidart

Glenforslan

Ulgary

Caolas

Lochan

Leadnacloiche

Irinn
(i.e. Roshven)

Glenuig

John MacLean - sword
Donald his brother - gun
John Mac Yonill vic Creul - sword
Donald Macdonald - gun and sword
Mac vic Yonill vic Creul - gun

Smerissary

Samalaman

John Macdonald - gun and sword
Angus Macdonald - gun and sword

John Mac Isaak - gun and sword
Angus Mac Isaak - gun and sword
Dugald Macdonald - gun

Eignaig

Angus Maclean - gun and sword
Donald Maclean - wanting
John Maclean - gun

Eilean Shona

Aryean Bailly

Ian Og vic Ruari - gun, sword, terge
Donald Macdonald - gun and sword

Dugald Macdonald - gun and sword
Rory Macpherson - gun and sword

Tongue **Tongoi**

Angus Mac Vorrich - sword
John Macleod - gun and sword

Donald Macdonald - gun and sword
Calum Mac Gawry - wanting

Scardoish

John Mac Leasback - gun and sword
Patrick Mac Gillendrich - sword
William Patterson - wanting

Langwell

Donald Mac Eachen - wanting
Allan Macdonald - sword

Dalelea

Angus Macdonald - gun, sword, terge
Alexander his brother - gun and pistol
Angus Bàn - gun, sword, terge

Glenaladale

Rorie Macdonald - wanting
Mac In vic Ean - gun
Donald Mac Vorrich - sword
John Macdonald - wanting
Sandie Macdonald - gun and sword
Allan his brother - gun and sword

Alt-an-Doran

Annat

John Mac Vorrich - gun and sword
John Bain - gun and sword

Downcan Mac Innish vich Ian - gun

Glenfinnan

Alexander Macdonald - gun and sword
Ranald his brother - wanting
Allan Du - wanting
Allan Mac Allister vic Murdo - gun and sword
Ewan Mac Myllan - gun
John his brother - wants
Angus More - gun
Angus Macpherson—tailor – sword
Angus M'Isaak - wants

OFFICERS

Colonel Clanranald
Major Macdonald, Glenaladale
Captain Donald Macdonald, brother of Clanranald
Captain Ranald Macdonald of Balfinlay
Captain Angus Macdonald, Dalelea
Captain Alexander his brother
Captain Alexander his oldest son
Captain John Macdonald of Guidale, brother to Macdonald, Morar
Captain John Macdonald, brother of Glenaladale
Captain Ranald and
Captain Allan - Brothers of Kinlochmoidart
Captain John Macdonald, Laig (in Eigg)"

From various causes most of the families directly connected with this list have disappeared, some having emigrated to the colonies, others having left Moidart to settle in other districts, and some having died out. The M'Isaacs however, of Smerissary, are in the same hamlet still. The Macleans are at Glenuig.[3] The family of Alt-an-dobhran is represented by Hugh Macdougald, stationed at Glenforslan. The present family at Port-a-bhata represents, in the collateral branch, one of the Kinloch followers. One of the Annat families still exists about Langal; and the William Patterson of Scardoish is found, in the female line, at Langal also. Of the officers' descendants, only Col. Macdonald of Glenaladale retains his connection with the country, the family estates still remaining undiminished. The Macdonalds of Kinlochmoidart are represented in the collateral line by Admiral David Robertson Macdonald, but the family estates have recently passed to other hands.

If certain stories whispered through the country deserve any belief, some of the inferior followers, especially the married men, would have much preferred remaining at home, in spite of the ardent zeal displayed by their leaders. But the fear of offending these, as well as the greater fear of being stigmatised as cowards, helped them to overcome their unwillingness, and, although rather ruefully, to bid adieu to their families with as much dogged determination as any of their younger companions. While the clans were busily mustering throughout the various districts, Charles crossed by boat from Borrodale to the Moidart shore. On landing at Glenuig he was met by a crowd of natives, some of the older ones of whom, in the exuberance of their joy, danced a reel in his presence, and a very excellent spirited reel it is, known for years afterwards as the "Eight men of Moidart." Threading his way on foot through Glenuig, he and his suite took boat again at Caolas, and made their way to Kinlochmoidart. Here he remained for a few days. The retired sheltered avenue near the house, called the "Prince's Walk," is named so in commemoration of this visit. When news came that the clans were about to assemble at Glenfinnan, Charles crossed from Kinloch to Dalelea, and, finding a boat ready, sailed up Lochsheil as far as Glenaladale, where he spent the night. In this lonely glen he met that sturdy old Jacobite, Captain Gordon of

Glenbucket, who, having been out in '15 was still bent, in spite of his years, on striking another blow for the royal cause. Glenbucket brought a prisoner in the person of Captain Sweetenham, who had been captured by Macdonald of Keppoch in the Braes of Lochaber. Next morning the party continued their journey by boat to Glenfinnan, making a short stay midway at a spot called Torr-a-phrionsa. The story of the Prince's disappointment at only finding a few of Clanranald's men waiting to receive him is too well known to be repeated; but this short period of gloom gave way to unbounded joy, when several hundreds of the Camerons were seen to descend the opposite hill, to be followed a few hours afterwards by many of the Keppochs. The royal standard, which had been blessed by Bishop Hugh Macdonald, was unfurled to the breeze, the proclamation was read, and the famous advance towards England commenced.

It is a problem, still unsolved, whether the leaders of the expedition acted wisely or not in halting at Derby without making a forced march on the capital. On the one hand, the presence of Marshal Wade's army at Newcastle, and the rapidly gathering army under Cumberland,—a host when compared to the small numbers on the Prince's side,—would imply that to retreat was the only course compatible with an escape from utter annihilation; on the other, Lord Mahon, who is believed to have had a deeper and a more accurate knowledge of that period than any other historian, after weighing carefully all that can be urged for or against either view, has given it as his decided opinion that the advance on London should have been continued, and that if this had been done the British throne would undoubtedly have been recovered to the Stuarts.[4] Whether this opinion be correct or not, most readers will be inclined to condemn the sudden awaking to any calculations founded on wisdom or prudence at a supreme moment like that. For if prudence had anything to do with the adventure, the latter should never have been conceived; or, if conceived, should have been abandoned at the head of Lochsheil. But having risked heavily, and won so far, the leader should have risked a little longer when the stakes were almost within reach. It seems probable too, that even if unsuccessful better terms or terms of some sort could be made in the neighbourhood of London for the Prince and his followers than anywhere else, whereas after Culloden no terms of any sort could be entertained. The old law in its fullest application of "Vae victis" had then to be felt, not only by themselves, but by their friends at home among whom the soldiers were let loose.

At Falkirk Clanranald found himself in imminent peril. He and his men having made a furious attack on the enemy, got mixed up with a regiment of dragoons. In the hand-to-hand struggle which followed, the Highlanders stabbed the horses in order to get more readily at the riders. Clanranald, during the confusion, was knocked down, and a wounded horse fell on the top of him, pinning him so closely to the ground that he could scarcely move. None of his followers noticed his predicament except one, who however was unable to give assistance, being too busy at the moment in a desperate affair of his own with one of the dismounted troopers. The latter, however, having succumbed to the Highlander's claymore, the victor was left free to give his attention to the chief, whom he proceeded at once to relieve from his unpleasant predicament

Before this battle took place Macdonald of Kinlochmoidart was safely shut up in Edinburgh Castle, having had the misfortune to be captured by some of the Government partisans. He was one of the most chivalrous among the undaunted gentlemen who accompanied the Prince on this desperate enterprise. Moreover, he showed abilities which singularly marked him out as a person fit to carry on negotiations requiring tact and shrewdness, and was entrusted more than any one else with the secret correspondence passing between the Prince and his Jacobite adherents, or others whom it was of importance to win over to the Prince's side. "He was exceedingly cool-headed," says Bishop Forbes, "fit for either the cabinet or the field." It is of him that Sir Walter Scott narrates the interesting anecdote given in one of the notes appended to the *Monastery.*—"The gallantry of all times and nations has the same mode of thinking and acting, and it often expresses itself by the same symbols. In the civil wars of 1745-6 a party of Highlanders under a chieftain of rank came to Rose Castle, the seat of the Bishop of Carlisle, but then occupied by the family of Squire Dacre of Cumberland. They demanded quarters, which of course were not to be refused to armed men of a strange attire and unknown language. But the domestic represented to the captain of the mountaineers that the lady of the mansion had just been delivered of a daughter, and expressed a hope that under the circumstances the party would give as little trouble as possible. 'God forbid,' said the gallant chief, 'that I or mine should be the means of adding to a lady's inconvenience at such a time. May I request to see the infant?' The child was brought, and the Highlander, taking his cockade out of his bonnet and pinning it on the child's breast, 'That will be a token,' he said, 'to any of our people who may come hither, that Donald Macdonald of Kinlochmoidart has taken the family of Rose Castle under his protection.'" "The lady," adds Sir Walter, "who received in infancy this gage of Highland protection is now Mary, Lady Clerk of Pennycuik, and on the 10th of June still wears the cockade which was pinned on her breast, with a white rose as a kindred decoration." This lady became acquainted with Kinlochmoidart's eldest son, Colonel Alexander Macdonald, and received from him a silk scarf or plaid of Macdonald tartan, part of which was long in the possession of Mrs Blackburn of Roshven.

This incident at Rose Castle took place on the 8th November 1745. Shortly afterwards Macdonald was sent back to the neighbourhood of Edinburgh on some secret service connected with the Prince's affairs, and it was while engaged in this that he was arrested. Bishop Forbes states that the misadventure occurred on the 12th, *i.e.* four days after he quitted Rose Castle. The greatest obscurity hangs over the circumstances attending his capture. Some say that he was discovered through the indiscretion of his own servant; others affirm that he was recognised near Lesmahagow by a person who, many years before, had been tutor to Macdonald and to some of his brothers, and who instantly denounced him to the nearest magistrate. Bishop Forbes's version is: "He and his servant were taken by some country people, and sent to the castle of Edinburgh." He was kept in the castle until the Prince's army had retreated to the north. He was then transferred to Carlisle, where, along with several others, he was to take his trial. One of his companions was Major Macdonald of Tirendrish, an officer in Keppoch's regiment, and a near relative of the Lochaber chief. At the battle of Falkirk he carried the pursuit too far, and having by mistake got among some companies of General Huske's regiment, was recognised, and seized amid cries of "Here is a rebel; shoot the dog down." They were tried at Carlisle in the August or September following, and were condemned to death. Before the sentence was carried out, Kinlochmoidart got a secret message conveyed to Bishop Smith, Vicar-Apostolic of the Lowland district of Scotland, then living in Edinburgh, asking him to send a priest, at whose hands he and his companion the major might receive the consolations of religion before leaving this world. As the task was very difficult, and required a person of no ordinary courage and coolness, the bishop referred the matter to Father George Duncan, who at one time had been professor in the small Highland seminary on Loch Morar, and who was probably personally acquainted with Kinloch. At this time Father Duncan was in charge of a small congregation in Banffshire, and had no connection with the Highland district, but, undeterred by the dangers of the enterprise, he wrote to the bishop that he was quite willing to make the attempt, and to face the risks.[5] He succeeded so well that he was introduced to the prisoners, without the slightest suspicion of his true character being entertained by either the governor or any of the jailers, and was able to hear his friends' confessions and give holy communion. He then re-crossed the border, but had not gone far when his secret became divulged, and a party of dragoons were sent in hot haste after him. He was too quick for them, however, and got back to the north in safety. The two Highland gentlemen were led forth to the place of execution on the 18th October 1746, and met their doom with the greatest fortitude. The sentence was carried out with all the barbarous inhumanity characteristic of the English law at the time, such as cutting down the victim and disembowelling him before life was extinct. Kinloch's head was stuck up over one of the Carlisle gates, and remained there bleaching under rain and sunshine for many a year afterwards. Few Highlanders passed the way without reverently saluting it. At length Allan Macdonald, a connection of the present family owning Glenuig, was threatened with arrest, and with being brought before the governor of Carlisle, for having climbed up to where the head was nailed and kissed it. This was construed into an open act of sympathy with rebellion. But the governor, a member of the Lennox family, on hearing the story, was so touched by the Highlander's attachment to his chief, that he gave orders to have the head taken down and decently buried. Some of the old people in Moidart, however, have a tradition that the head was taken down for fear of the sight giving offence to a Highland regiment which came to be quartered at Carlisle, many of the soldiers in this regiment belonging to the Jacobite clans which had fought on the same side as Kinlochmoidart during the '45.

At Culloden the Macdonalds behaved very badly. It was extremely short-sighted policy of course on the part of Lord George Murray to dispute their traditional claim to fight on the right wing, and to drive them to the left, at a supreme crisis like this when unanimity was a matter of the most vital importance. Nothing could have touched their pride more keenly than to see a rival clan stationed at the post which they looked upon as their own, and with which their honour, as they imagined, was peculiarly associated. But they carried their resentment to the most unreasonable lengths. They refused to fight, or, if a few fired a volley at all, not one could be induced to move forward to the charge. The Duke of Perth attempted over and over again to lead them in person, assuring them that by their valour they would make the left wing as honourable and glorious as the right. He went the length of promising to call himself for ever a Macdonald, if they would but obey him on this occasion and do their duty. But they seem to have treated his words with sullen contempt. Their own favourite chief Keppoch made a frantic appeal to their better sense, reminding them of their past deeds, and of the terrible disgrace which would cling to the whole clan if, at a supreme moment like this, they kept aloof while the rest of their countrymen were nobly dying within a few hundred yards of them. But all these appeals were made in vain. Keppoch, bareheaded, and with drawn sword in hand, turned from them in despair, exclaiming, "My God, I never thought to see the day when my children could abandon me thus." He set his face to the English regiments, and, advancing all alone, was shot down under the very eyes of his shameless followers. Captain Donald Macdonald, called Roy or Gorm, and probably a brother of Clanranald, on seeing him fall rushed forward to his assistance. The wound apparently was not mortal, and Keppoch was implored by his friend to rejoin the ranks of the clan; but the brave chief, scouting the suggestion as an insult, declared his resolution still to move forwards. He was in the act of doing so when, another bullet hitting him with more fatal precision, he dropped down dead, almost in the arms of his friend. When the day was lost, the Macdonalds withdrew to the hills, and by keeping well together, and by having their flanks partly covered by the Prince's cavalry, they were not much molested by the dragoons. The losses among Clanranald's men were trivial, and of the officers not one save Kinlochmoidart was amissing. Some of them, however, had been severely wounded. No one has ever questioned the personal bravery of the men who behaved so badly on this occasion; but their case is an instructive one, as illustrating in a striking manner the extraordinary callousness to every right feeling that can sometimes be induced, by giving way to a pride which is not more intense than it is childish and contemptible. The other clans fought like heroes, notably so the Macintoshes, the Athole men, the Frasers, the Stuarts of Appin, the Maclachlans, and the Macleans. Their losses were terrible, whole ranks having been mowed down by the fire of the enemy, and more than one-half of their officers having been destroyed. It is computed that twelve hundred

Highlanders were left dead on the field.

About a fortnight after their return to Moidart, and before the Government troops came down in pursuit, the district witnessed a naval engagement between two French and three English frigates, which took place on the arm of the sea dividing Moidart from Arisaig. The largest of the English ships was commanded by Captain, afterwards Lord, Howe. The action lasted for twelve hours, and was a very stiffly-contested affair. It is still well remembered in the district. The larger of the French vessels was crippled at an early part of the day, so that the brunt of the fight had to be borne by its consort. The English attempted to board the latter several times, but they were successfully beaten off. At length Howe's ammunition ran short, and he was compelled to withdraw in the direction of the Point of Ardnamurchan. The French heaved their dead overboard, fifteen of the bodies being washed ashore a day or two afterwards. The losses of the English were never ascertained, but they are supposed to have been nearly equal to those of their adversaries. The natives on each side of the loch stationed themselves on knolls and on the slopes of the hills, whence they had a complete view of what was going on before them. During the hottest part of the fight, one of them, an old man belonging to Gaotal, was heard to offer up the most fervent supplications to Heaven for the preservation, not of the French, less so of the English, but of some goats belonging to himself, and which at the time were grazing on an island within close range of the combatants' guns.

Notes

1   The date of the landing was 23 July 1745.

2   This is the *Historical and Genealogical Account* referred to on page 107, details of which are given in chapter vii, note 7. The roll is printed in Appendix XXXVI, pp 37-41. It contains the same eighty names as printed by the author, but excludes the officers and also differs in name order and grouping, some spellings and the particulars of farms.

3   There are still MacIsaacs living in Smerissary today (1995), and until very recently MacLeans were living in Glenuig.

4   Stanhope, Philip Henry, 5th Earl *'The Forty Five'* — *being the narrative of the insurrection of 1745, extracted from Lord Mahon's History of England* (London, 1851; 2nd edition London, 1869), p. 89.

5   George Duncan was trained at Scalan and the Scots College Paris, and was ordained in 1732. He was serving at Angus from 1734 at the latest, and seems to have been there (not in Banffshire) in 1746. After his adventure at Carlisle he became chaplain at Traquair House (1747-52) and later Master at his old seminary Scalan, leaving that post after a year to become the missionary for Glenlivet in 1759.

Alexander Smith was consecrated bishop in 1735 and for eleven years acted as Co-adjutor to Bishop Gordon in the Lowland District. On the latter's death in 1746 he became Vicar Apostolic, a post he held until his own death in 1767.

Chapter 10

Return of Charles to Borrodale—His Flight to the Outer Isles—Descent of the Government Troops upon Moidart—Their Cruelties—The Argyllshire Militia Officers more Humane—Bishop Hugh Macdonald and Lord Lovat compelled to fly from their Hiding Place at the Foot of Loch Morar—The Bishop's Residence burnt to the Ground by a Naval Party —Surrender of Lovat—Escape of Clanranald— Career of his Brother Donald— Adventures of the Prince after his Return to the Mainland, as described in the Journal of John Macdonald, one of his guides—Final Escape of the Prince—Seizure of Barrisdale and his Son by the Chiefs—Imprisonment in France— Continuation of John Macdonald's Life—Adventures of his relative Ronald Mor-a-Chrolen—Severities of the Government upon the Highland Priests

IMMEDIATELY after the battle of Culloden, Charles hurried to the west coast, in the expectation of finding a French ship to take him away from the country. The first night he spent at Inverary; the second was passed in the house of Cameron of Glenpean; and the third at Meoble. He then came down to the neighbourhood of Borrodale, but not finding what he wanted, he insisted upon being sent on to the outer islands. Clanranald and some of the Moidart gentlemen were greatly averse to this plan, representing truly that many Government vessels were prowling about these parts, that in a short time they would be much more numerous, and that the means of escape, if he came to be hemmed within the isles, would be almost cut off. But the persuasions of his Irish companions induced the Prince to slight the advice, and he pressed more eagerly for a boat and crew to remove him from the mainland. A large boat belonging to a son of Angus Borrodale was then placed at his service, and under the guidance of Donald Macleod, together with a competent crew, Charles, O'Sullivan, O'Neil, Burke, and Father Allan Macdonald, one of the chaplains, set sail. The Prince was so impatient of any delay that he refused to listen to Macleod's warning regarding the state of the weather, the experienced seaman being unwilling to commence the journey in the face of a violent storm which he foresaw was about to burst upon them. It came on shortly after their leaving land, and raged with such violence that Macleod had to run the vessel before the gale, having lost during the darkness of the night all calculations as to his true course. By the merest chance they found themselves close to the island of Benbecula at daybreak the following morning. While the Prince was giving himself up to an experience of the exciting adventures among the outer isles, his Moidart friends were beginning to feel the full vengeance of the Government for the part which they had taken in the late insurrection. The troops were let loose upon their district, and immediately commenced to enact those scenes in which pillage, burnings, and slaughter of the natives filled up the principal parts,—as they did in every other locality which had the privilege of being visited by the cowardly ruffians. The houses, after being first plundered, were burnt to the ground, the cattle were driven away or wantonly destroyed. Shooting parties ranged over the hills, chasing the unfortunate people, and hunting them down like wild beasts. Those that escaped from their hands had to suffer from famine and exposure, and these privations told heavily upon the miserable people, especially the women and children. When Kinloch House was burnt down,[1] the chief's mother, a lady far advanced in years, had to be carried out in a dying state to the garden, and placed near that group of old yew trees which form such a conspicuous feature of the locality. She died there, before the last embers of the burnt house had yet cooled. The rest of the family fled to Glenforslan. The only person who showed any humanity was a Captain Duncan Campbell, in command of one of the Argyllshire companies of militia. It is said that his forbearance was most honourable, and that few had ever reason to complain of his contributing any share to the general misery prevailing around. The high terms in which Macdonald the poet writes of him, leave little doubt that this gallant soldier and gentleman was one of the best friends the district could have had in its hour of need:—

"Tha 'n Saighdear agus an Criostaidh
An aon phearsa ghrìnn a chaiptin:

Beannachd nochd a's bhochd sin Mhùideart
Beannachd gach dùthcha ad chuideachd;
A bhrìgh nach do chuir thu le dòlas
Sean no og dhiubh chum na-h-uidil."[2]

But he was a solitary exception, although some of the other Argyllshire officers were at times not indisposed to be kind, as the following cases would imply. A party of militia having landed at Glenuig, and seized a considerable number of cattle, were about to slaughter these at Ardeannach, when an old man, who had lost every hoof, unable to bear the thought of his misfortune descended from the hill, and advancing to the officer in command boldly addressed him in these terms:— "Your work is not the friendly turn that one kinsman expects from another!" The officer, rather puzzled at this form of address, asked the old fellow if he belonged to Argyllshire, or if he was a Campbell. "Not to Argyllshire," replied the native; "but I am a Campbell, nevertheless, to the backbone." "In that case," said the other, "pick out your beasts, and be off with them before their throats are cut." No time was lost in following this recommendation, and the old man, who was in reality a reprobate M'Isaac or Maclean, went away rejoicing. His wife, on hearing his story, satirised his apostasy in the following verses:—

"Is bodachan nam briogaisean a rinn a chinnidh àicheadh
Cha Chaimbeulach e–cha Shiosolach e
Cha-n-eil fios co as dh'bhas e."[3]

Perhaps it was the same party who landed at Bailly in Eilean-Shona, Captain Swineburne's present residence, with the intention of burning the house and plundering the neighbourhood. They were met, however, by the tenant's wife, who by a timely present of milk, bread, and cheese induced them to forego their evil intentions and to spare her property. The regulars who ravished the country belonged, according to Brown, to the regiment commanded by Lord George Sackville,—rather an ominous name for a district open to plunder. Some of the worst visitors were landing parties detached from the men-of-war cruising along the coast. Bishop Hugh Macdonald and Lord Lovat had taken refuge on the island at the foot of Loch Morar, and for a short time thought themselves in comparative security, especially as all the boats in the neighbourhood had been brought over and anchored near the island. But the commander of one of the cruising ships having been informed of their hiding-place, landed some of his sailors, who dragging one of the long boats from the coast inland launched it on Loch Morar and rowed towards the island. This compelled the bishop and his companions to take immediate flight. They were able to gain the Arisaig side of the loch, and landed hurriedly at Ceann-Camuis-Ruaidh. The thick birch woods of the vicinity sheltered them from further pursuit. In the hurry of departure, one of the bishop's servants was unwittingly left behind, but he, with great presence of mind, jumping into the loch, swam to one of the nearest islets, the banks of which were fringed with long wavy heather. Creeping under this, he hid himself so securely that the sailors, although passing and repassing several times within a few yards, failed to notice him. After their departure he swam to the Morar shore. The bishop's correspondence, and every article of any value, were seized and carried away. The house was burnt to the ground. The island has never been inhabited since. The garden attached to the humble residence is said to have been cultivated with the greatest care, and to have been a productive one. Lord Lovat, owing to his great age and infirmities, was utterly unfit to endure the hardships which the hunted life to which he was now condemned naturally entailed. After living for some days at Meoble, he sent a message to the officer commanding at Arisaig offering to surrender himself. He was accordingly apprehended, and soon afterwards taken away to London. Perhaps nothing gives a truer idea of the abject contemptible terror prevailing among the ruling authorities of the time, and of their keenness for revenge, than the eagerness with which they proceeded to cut off the head of this nobleman, who was broken down with gout and asthma, and who was over eighty years of age. The esteem which one feels at the calm courage which he displayed when undergoing his sentence, obliterates the memory of some of those crooked ways which his Whig enemies seem never weary of parading before the public. In these, however, he was not a worse offender than several of his contemporaries, whose reputations stand higher, because their sins, moral and political, have been better masked, or not dragged with the same persistence to the glare of day. Bands of fugitives lurked among the woods, and in the more inaccessible solitudes of Moidart, Arisaig, and Morar, waiting for an opportunity to make their escape abroad, or until the soldiers would withdraw, when they might rejoin their families. Some of the former were fortunate enough to get on board the French frigates after the engagement with Lord Howe and reach the Continent in safety. Of this number were the Duke of Perth, Lord John Drummond, Lockhart of Carnwath, and probably Bishop Macdonald, with several others. Clanranald missed the opportunity. In a family history it is stated that his hiding-place was betrayed by a false kinsman, and that on this occasion he only escaped by throwing himself down a precipice, at the imminent risk of being dashed to pieces. He was near enough to hear one of the soldiers exclaim, "The nest is warm, but the bird is flown." The "false kinsman" probably refers to Macdonald, Barrisdale, who, rightly or wrongly, was accused of giving information to the Government, and putting its emissaries on the track of the unhappy men whose lives were already in sufficient jeopardy. The chief was too popular among his own people of Moidart or Arisaig to have such an evil turn served upon him, or if any among them attempted anything of the kind the traitors could never have remained another day in the country. The only approach to treachery in Moidart was that of a native who, under pressure, was induced to give information regarding the spot where the Kinloch title-deeds and some family plate were hidden, viz., at Craig-an-Dùn, close to Loch Moidart; but the wretched creature became in consequence such an object of hatred and loathing to the rest of his countrymen, that he and his family were compelled to leave the district, never to return. Despairing of getting away by the west coast, Clanranald made his way to the east side of Scotland, and through the help of some relatives living at Brahan Castle got on board a Scotch ship about to sail from Cromarty to London. He reached the capital without any suspicions being wakened as to his identity, and a few days afterwards got over to Paris. His name, however, was on the list of those who were excluded from the Act of Indemnity, so that he was compelled to remain abroad for several years. He got employment for a short time on the staff of Marshal Saxe, but after the latter's death had to live a good deal, like many others, on the bounty of the French Government, or on the slender resources of the Chevalier de St George. His estates, however, were not confiscated, and so far he and his family were much more fortunate than his friends of Kinlochmoidart. His escape was due to the fact that old Clanranald, his father, was the real owner, and to the other significant circumstance that this gentleman had steadily refused to participate in the insurrection. When the clouds began to drift away, Clanranald was allowed quietly to enter into possession; while his brother Donald, from an ardent Jacobite, was converted into a sedate Whig. Donald joined the army, and rose to distinction during the American war. He was killed at the siege of Quebec. "Captain Macdonald," writes General Stewart, "was an accomplished high-spirited officer. He was a second son of Clanranald. He entered early in life into the French service, and following Prince Charles Edward into Scotland in 1745, he was taken prisoner, and along with O'Neil, afterwards a lieutenant-general in the service of Spain, and commander of the expedition against Algiers in 1775, was confined in the castle of Edinburgh; but being liberated without trial he returned to France, where he remained till 1756, when he came back to Scotland, and was appointed to a company in Fraser's Highlanders. On the expedition against Louisburg and Quebec he was much in the confidence of Generals Amherst, Wolfe, and Murray, by whom he was employed on all duties when more than usual difficulty and danger had to be encountered, and where more than common talent, address, and spirited example were required. Of this several instances occurred at Louisburg and Quebec." The O'Neil referred to above was one of the gentlemen who accompanied Charles from Borrodale to the outer isles. He was captured in Uist, and was exposed at one time to the risk of certain personal indignities from an over-zealous officer who wished to extort information regarding the movements of the Prince. But O'Neil found a champion in another officer of the Scotch Fusileers, who quickly and rather sternly put an end to this sort of treatment (*Brown's High.*).

The adventures of the Prince among the outer isles were of the most exciting kind, and are too well known to be repeated here. Driven back from Stornoway to Uist, he was so thoroughly hemmed in by his enemies that his capture would have been certain were it not for the heroism of Flora Macdonald. Through her efforts he got over to Skye, whence, by the devotion and courage of Kingsburgh, Raasay, and Mackinnon, he was safely transferred to the care of the Macdonalds of Arisaig and Moidart. In handing him over to the staunch old laird of Borrodale, Mackinnon is reported to have said, "I have done my duty, do you yours." "I am glad of it," replied Angus Macdonald, "I shall lodge him so securely that all the forces in Britain shall not find him out." Considering that at this time the laird's house had been burnt down, his cattle swept away, and his family reduced to the most miserable straits by the Government troops, for the part which he had already taken in behalf of the Prince, one experiences an instinctive feeling of admiration at his readiness to make fresh sacrifices and to face new perils in sheltering the unfortunate fugitive from the pursuit of his enemies. But his generosity was only a type of that of hundreds of others throughout the Highlands, who would rather have died than let the Prince fall into the hands of the British Government. Holding out a bribe of £30,000 to men like these, was about as idle a process as dancing jigs to a milestone, as an Irish orator once put it. The woods and fastnesses in the vicinity of Borrodale, and the loyalty of its neighbours, no doubt confirmed the old laird in the belief that Charles would be perfectly safe beside him; but, after a few days, Macdonald got private information that the troops had tracked the Prince to this part of the country, and that they were about to make a thorough exploration of it. In this dilemma he deemed it advisable to guide the Prince farther inland, and to find a retreat for him in those districts where, his presence not being suspected, the search would not be so active. An extraordinary series of adventures, in consequence of this determination, followed during the next two months, which are graphically described by Borrodale's second son, John, who was one of the Prince's companions during that eventful period. This young man, better known in his own country as Ian Fràingeach, had been destined for the priesthood, and with this view had been sent to make his studies at Ratisbon; but on the breaking out of the civil war he hurried home, and joining the Prince's army at Perth, accompanied it to England, and was afterwards present with it at Falkirk and Culloden. He wrote an account of the Prince's wanderings, embracing principally the period between the Prince's return from Skye under the guidance of Mackinnon, and the meeting of Charles with Lochiel and Cluny in Lochaber about a fortnight before the Prince achieved his escape from the kingdom.[4] The manuscript was left among John's descendants, and was for many years an object of great interest to the many visitors who used to frequent Dalelea House during the lifetime of the late Lochshiel, and of his sisters the Misses Joanna and Jane Macdonald. The latter, after her brother's death, communicated it to Messrs Blackwood, who published it in their well-known magazine in October 1873, with a very interesting introduction and appendix from the pen of the distinguished writer Mr George Skene. The only correction which one feels tempted to suggest, is in reference to the true character of the "dug-out" in which Charles is supposed by Mr Skene to have been ferried across Lochshiel, which was afterwards sunk in the loch, and which is now to be seen somewhere about Kinlochmoidart. The present writer was often assured by the best informed among the older Moidart gentlemen, now gone, that the vessel in question belonged to a kind used for domestic purposes alone, and was quite common at one time in almost every Highland household of the better class. General Ross himself became convinced of the truth of this, and latterly relegated its supposed history to the regions of romance. After Culloden Charles never crossed Lochshiel, nor, so far as is known, did he lurk in any part immediately close to its shore, he and his guides, as will be seen from the manuscript, keeping to the high hills about Meoble, Morar, and the Braes of Glenfinnan, when attempting to break through the cordon which intercepted their advance eastwards. Mr Skene of course was to be excused, as he saw no reason at the time for entertaining any doubt regarding the authority of the person who volunteered the information. Having determined to get the Prince away to a safer place, Borrodale sent for his nephew, Alexander Macdonald of Glenaladale, to help him in the effort. It may be remarked that Glenaladale was if anything worse off than his uncle, for he had been stripped of everything, and furthermore was suffering from a severe wound received at Culloden. He came at once, however, accompanied by his brother Captain John Macdonald, who before the insurrection held a commission in the French army. At the consultation which followed, it was decided that Glenaladale, Captain John, and Borrodale's son John, author of the manuscript, should force their way into the land of the Camerons, and place the Prince in safety among that faithful clan; but after reaching Meoble and the Braes of Glenfinnan, they made the alarming discovery that a line of sentinels had been drawn from the head of Lochshiel to the head of Loch Arkaig, and from Loch Arkaig to the head of Loch Hourn, that is to say along a distance of thirty miles. This line was so tightly drawn that no one could pass without being immediately challenged; and to prevent any attempt during the night, large fires were kindled at regular intervals, the glare of which was sufficiently strong to light up the distance which each sentinel had to tread. The strictest watch was kept along Loch Sheil, Loch Hourn, and the seacoast, crowds of vessels constantly sailing backwards and forwards, ready to give chase to any suspicious stranger, and all eager to secure the rich prize of £30,000, the price set on the Prince's head. In addition to these precautions, large bands of military were kept constantly patrolling the hills studded over the three districts which lay within the enclosure. "Between Loch Arkaig and Loch Morar," says Macdonald, "we passed, in the course of three nights, four camps and twenty-five patrols, and some so nigh us that we heard them frequently speaking." At another time, while on the top of a high mountain near the head of Loch Hourn, overcome with hunger and fatigue, they lay down to rest "in a bit hollow ground covered with heather and branches of young birch trees," a company of soldiers with their captain being visible within a short distance, as they were guarding the very hill on which the adventurers were hidden. For many days the party almost despaired of breaking through the line, but at length, under the guidance of Cameron of Glenpean, who came to join them, they took advantage of a dark night, and slipping between two sentinels who had just turned their backs to each other, crossed to the other side of the path, on which escape and security became possible. Travelling all night as best they could, they reached Glenshiel the following day completely exhausted.[5]

There is a story told in Brown's *History of the Highland Clans* to the effect that on the eve of forcing the line Cameron's nose began to itch, a circumstance regarded by the worthy Highlander as of very dangerous portent.[6] When the line was safely passed, the Prince, turning to Donald, said, "Well, how does the nose do now?" "It is better," replied Cameron, "but still it yucks (itches) a little," as if smelling further dangers ahead. At Glenshiel they were helped to some provisions by Macrae, a native of the district, who however, owing to their knowledge of his political leanings, was carefully kept in ignorance of the chief guest whom he was entertaining.

After leaving that neighbourhood, Glenaladale made the awkward discovery that he had lost a purse containing forty guineas, all the money they had to depend upon at the time. This compelled himself and the writer of the memoir to retrace their steps in search of it. With some trouble they found the purse lying on the ground, but the guineas had disappeared. Suspecting a son of Macrae to be the thief, they boldly accosted the father, and made him acquainted with the circumstances of the case. Macrae, "without a minute delay, returned to the house, got hold of a rope hinging there, and griped his son by the arm in great passion, and addressed him in the following words:—You damned scoundrel, this instant get these poor gentlemen's money, or, by the heavens, I'll hing you to that very tree you see this moment. The boy, shivering with fear, went instantly for the money, which he had buried under ground about thirty yards from his father's house." Whilst Charles was waiting for their return, an officer with three men passed quite close to him. 'This excited great apprehensions regarding the safety of his companions, who he was certain would be brought face to face with the soldiers; but, fortunately for the Macdonalds, they returned by one side of the river, whilst the enemy went down by the other, each party being screened from the view of the other by the banks of the river. Disappointed in his hopes of getting away by any foreign vessel calling at the coast of the Mackenzie territory, Charles committed himself, with the consent of his guides, to a Macdonald from Glengarry, who offered to conduct the party to the Braes of Glenmorrison. At the time of their meeting, this Glengarry man was flying from a party of soldiers who had just murdered his father. The journey was made under the most trying difficulties, arising chiefly from wet, hunger, and fatigue. Towards its close they fell in with a party of four Macdonalds and one Grant, who to escape from the soldiers were condemned to live among the hills, and in supporting themselves to seize whatever came in their way, without troubling themselves about the permission of the owners. One of them recognised the Prince at the first glance, but so far from dreaming of betraying him, he and his companions swore on their naked dirks to give him all the protection in their power. They conducted him to an extraordinary cave, the entrance to which was concealed by a large stone. According to the manuscript, "Under that stone, said one of the Macdonalds, fourty men can accommodate themselves, and the best water in the Highland runnen throu it, and a large void heather bed already made in it for your reception." The party entered into this welcome shelter, a bullock was slaughtered for their entertainment, and for three days, as the writer remarks, "we found ourselves as comfortably lodged as we had been in a royal pallace." Observing that the Prince was almost in rags, the freebooters, we learn from other sources, determined to supply him with at least some clean linen. Having ascertained that some of the Fort-Augustus troops were about to cross over to Strathglass, the friendly outlaws watched their opportunity, and making a sudden rush on those in charge of the luggage, seized some trunks belonging to the officers and scampered off with them. Charles had more than enough to pick and choose from. From this pleasant retreat however they were soon forced to fly. A party of militia came to encamp in the neighbourhood, so that "we thought advisable to proceed to the Chisholm's firr woods, where we and our party spent near a month in pace and plentie. At the root of one large tree we build for the Prince, Glenaladale, and me one tent of firr branches. At the other side of the tree another one of a larger size. Two of our party was always employed in providing provisions, other two as outpost, inquiring for information. One honest tenant of the name of Chisholm, at the distance of a few miles from us, affoarded us with meal, butter, and flesh weekly; neither did we want for aqua vitae and tobacco, which commodity we all made use of." They afterwards removed westwards, and finding some of the leading men among the Camerons, two of the Macdonalds returned to their own country, while Charles was consigned to the care of Locheil and Cluny. On reaching home, Macdonald remarks, "We found all left behind us in the greatest distress for want of all necessaries of life, or houses to shelter us from the inclemency of the weather." It had been arranged that they should send information to Lochaber whenever any French vessel came to the coast to assist the Prince; and about a fortnight afterwards, two frigates appearing off Borrodale with English colours flying at the masthead, "my father and brother Ranald and I immediately had recourse to the muirs to avoid being apprehended." Finding however that they were French, they sent notice at once to the Prince, who without loss of time came down to Borrodale with Locheil and several others. More than a hundred gentlemen, many of whom were lurking in the two districts of Moidart and Arisaig, availed themselves of this opportunity of getting away to France. There was one person however whom the leaders, especially the Camerons, were determined to bring along with them,—this not from love, but from a deep feeling of animosity, and from a desire to have him sternly dealt with according to his deserts. This was Coll Bàn Macdonald of Barrisdale. By a little stratagem he and his son were enticed over to Borrodale, when being pounced upon they were put on board the French vessels, and carried away to France. On reaching that country they were thrown into prison, where they were kept for nearly a year. A formal indictment, charging them with several specific acts of treachery, was drawn out against them, but whether this was ever argued before the French courts is uncertain. Probably it was not. They saved the prosecutors further trouble by breaking out of jail and making their escape to Scotland. These charges, it must be confessed, appeared to have no better foundation than mere suspicion; and in one sense it is a pity that the case was not thoroughly sifted, as the parties might have had their innocence, if such really existed, fully established. But left undecided as it was, the reputation of the family necessarily suffered, many of their countrymen, prejudiced by the accusation, behaving towards them as if they were guilty. The Government, if it ever got any aid from the incriminated parties, took a strange way of showing its gratitude, for Coll's son was arrested, tried, and condemned to death, although the sentence was not carried out, while old Coll himself was flung into prison in Edinburgh, and detained there for the rest of his life. It was a clear case for the unfortunate men of being roasted between two fires. It is not to be wondered at that the next two generations abandoned themselves, so it is said, to a certain vindictive moroseness, which made their house still more unpopular. Towards the conclusion of his narrative, Macdonald makes the remark that the Prince, after bidding farewell to the Highlands, "left us all in a worse state than he found us."

When the agitation throughout the kingdom began to calm down, the author of the memoirs married a daughter of Barrisdale, and having obtained the farm of Rhu in Arisaig from Clanranald, applied himself to agricultural and pastoral matters with so much industry, that he became one of the most successful and independent gentlemen of the district. He was the father of Archibald Macdonald who inherited the estate of Lochshiel from his cousin Alexander Macdonald, son of Alasdair-an-oir.[7]

Macdonald was one of the best scholars in the western Highlands. One of the most frequent visitors at his house in Rhu was Raonull Mor a Chrolen, a half-brother of his wife. This person was noted, from his very youth, for the turbulence and fierceness of his disposition, and these objectionable qualities soon got him into trouble. Happening to get embroiled with one of his neighbours over some grievance real or imaginary, he in a fit of passion drew his sword and ran his opponent through. He was arrested for the crime, and by a mere chance escaped hanging. He was condemned however to a sentence of perpetual banishment to the penal settlement of Barbadoes. During the passage across the Atlantic, the ship in which he and many other prisoners were confined was attacked by a French privateer, carrying much heavier equipment both in men and guns. In the long and stubborn fight which ensued, the British suffered so severely that the enemy were emboldened to make an attempt at boarding; and they were in the act of carrying this out, when one of the officers informed the British captain that the prisoners were clamouring to be let loose, and imploring to be allowed to take part in the fight. To grant this might of course entail very serious consequences, for the prisoners might turn upon the crew, and make the threatened catastrophe to the British complete. In the emergency however of his situation, the captain chose to risk it. He gave permission, and as the captives were let loose they one and all flung themselves into the engagement, doing their duty manfully. They were led on by Ranald, who after coming on deck had armed himself with an iron crow-bar, the most effective weapon within reach. Swinging this about him, he advanced among the French, who were already in possession of part of the ship, and brought it down with so much fury about their heads and ribs, that while the nearest were knocked over bleeding and stunned, those behind began to fall back precipitately, quailing before his terrible blows. This timely assistance so re-animated the courage of the exhausted sailors, that, setting themselves to the struggle with renewed energy, they succeeded in clearing the decks, and making the survivors of the attacking party jump overboard. The fight, however, between the two ships was carried on until night separated them, when the British captain, after some hasty repairs, was able to take his vessel away and reach his port without further molestation. He and the rest of the officers were so pleased with Ranald's behaviour on this occasion, that they interested the favour of the authorities in his case, and after a short delay obtained a full remission of his sentence. He was sent back in one of the Government ships, and landed by it on the west coast of Skye. The amazement of his friends and relations in Knoydart may well be imagined, when Ranald, without the slightest warning, one day burst in among them, free and happy, like a deer regaining its native hills. He joined the party of the Prince in '45, and fought among the ranks of the Glengarry Macdonalds. He was present at Preston or Gladsmuir, Falkirk, and Culloden, and during the occupation of his district by the militia and other Government troops had to hide closely among the wilds of Knoydart. He subsequently settled down quietly as tenant of the farm of Crolen. It is said that during a certain period of his life Ranald's morals were very weak; and there is a story going that the priest being very indignant at several cases of illegitimacy which, one after the other, were brought before him, and without exception referred to Ranald, went straight to the supposed delinquent and implored him, sarcastically, to make a diligent search through the country, and if he found any more of his offspring to bring them all together, so that they might be baptized with the least possible trouble. But Ranald blandly declined, on the plea that every hussy in Knoydart who had left the proper path, was known to be cursed with a defective imagination,-the consequences being very unpleasant to an innocent person like himself. During his visits to Rhu, Ranald could scarcely talk of anything except of the Prince, his adventures, and of the great regret which all right-minded persons ought to feel at the failure of the Stuarts to regain their throne. These topics pre-occupied his mind, even when far advanced in years, viz., when he was over eighty. In his enthusiasm he used to raise his trembling arms, and, in a weak quavering voice, call all to witness that he was still ready to draw the sword and fight for the right cause. On such occasions his sister, losing all patience, used to retort that an army of such warlike veterans as himself would no doubt perform prodigies of valour, but that any general, Whig or Jacobite, would give thanks to heaven that he was not called upon to win victories with them. Nothing brought the old boy's fury to a quicker climax than a remark like this. The veins in his forehead would swell, his lips would tremble, and his features would assume such a ferocious vindictive look, that the late Miss Joanna Macdonald, who in her youth was a frequent witness of such scenes, used to fly from his presence in sheer terror. In his prime Big Ranald was a tall powerfully built man, but his countenance had at all times a harsh and sinister cast about it. It was perhaps rather in keeping that a stormy life like this should, in its close, involve the nearest friends in something of a family disaster. It was while on his way to attend Ranald's funeral that the late Lochshiel was nearly lost off the coast of Morar. The boat was struck by a sudden squall, capsized, and filling rapidly went down—the whole crew, three in number, going down with it. It was almost by a miracle that the survivor, after a hard struggle, reached the shore; but throughout the rest of his life, which was a long one, he never fully recovered from the effects of the shock received on this lamentable occasion.

The old warrior's sword, a true Andrea Ferrara, was suspended for years among other interesting memorials at Dalelea House. It was sold at the dispersion of the late Miss Jane Macdonald's effects a few years ago; but as to where it went, or what became of it since, the writer has been unable to ascertain.

Macdonald died at Rhu, his oldest son Archibald succeeding him in the farm. A younger son, James, became a priest, and for some years was in charge of the Catholics in the island of Barra. He was unfortunately drowned in the Sound of Sleat, together with the crew of the vessel in which he was sailing.

With the exception of Ranald, all the other members of the Kinlochmoidart family sailed with the Prince to France, and none of them ever returned. Two or three years after their departure, Ranald married a daughter of Angus Beg, Dalelea, and settled down at Roshven, which he received from Clanranald for his lifetime. After his death the widow withdrew to Innis-a-Rudha, a small promontory close to the boundaries between the Dorlin and Kinlochmoidart properties, and projecting into Loch Moidart. One of her sons, Eoin, became a priest, but owing to a serious illness contracted abroad was unable to perform any active duties. He resided for some years at Innis-a-Rudha, when his complaint assuming a more complicated form he finally succumbed. He was buried at Eilean-Fhionnan. The old lady was subsequently taken over to Langal, near Lochshiel, where her nephew, Banker Macdonald, Dalelea, provided her with a house, and attended to her wants for the rest of her days. In Sir John Sinclair's "Statistical Account," mention is made of a Moidart lady who had twenty-one of a family, and it is supposed that this refers to Ranald's wife; but if so, most of them must have died at an early age, or gone abroad, for, with the exception of the priest, every trace of their existence has disappeared from the memory of the district.

While running down the "rebels," and crushing them under its iron heel when caught, the Government was quite as unmerciful towards the Highland priests. No doubt these, as a body, sympathised with the Prince, and some of them, as we have seen, acted as chaplains to his Catholic followers; but many of them, beyond sympathising, had taken no part in the movement, yet these were made to suffer as severely as those more deeply implicated. In an account left by Bishop Geddes,[8] we have a very strong picture of what Father James Grant, priest of Barra, was made to undergo after his apprehension:—"Early in the spring of 1746, some ships of war came to the coast of the isle of Barra and landed some men, who threatened they would lay desolate the whole island if the priest was not delivered up to them. Father James Grant, who was missionary then, and afterwards bishop, being informed of the threats in a safe retreat in which he was in a little island, surrendered himself, and was carried prisoner to Mingarry Castle on the western coast (*i.e.*, Ardnamurchan), where he was detained for some weeks. He was then conveyed to Inverness, and thrown into the common prison, where there were about forty prisoners in the same room with him. Here he was for several weeks chained by the leg to Mr MacMahon, an Irish officer in the service of Spain, who had come over to be of use to the Prince. In this situation they could not in the night time turn from one side to the other without the one passing over the other. The people of the town, out of humanity, furnished them with some little conveniences, and among other things gave to each a bottle, which they hung out of the window in the morning and got filled with water. But one morning the sentinels accused the prisoners to the visiting officer of having entered into a conspiracy to knock them on the head with bottles, which they had procured for that purpose. Father Grant and the others pleaded the improbability of this ridiculous accusation, but they were not heard, and the bottles were taken away."

Five other priests were shut up in the same prison about the same time. Three of them belonged to the west coast, viz., Father

Alexander Cameron, who was connected with the Lochiel family; Father Alexander Forrester, priest of South Uist; and Father Alan Macdonald. From Inverness they were taken away on board a man-of-war to London; but during the passage Father Cameron, whose health had been completely shattered during his captivity, died, and was thrown overboard.[9] After a long confinement in London, the survivors were brought before the Duke of Newcastle, who informed them that the Government was disposed to deal leniently in their case, and would therefore sentence them to perpetual banishment from the country, provided they could give bail of £1,000 that they would never return. As this was an absurd proposal, these poor priests having neither friends nor money, the duke compromised the matter by asking them to go bail for each other. They got over to Holland, but most of them came back again. Forrester quietly resumed his duties in South Uist, and died in that island. Macdonald got an appointment abroad. It is said that he wrote an account of the Prince's adventures in Scotland, which ought to be a valuable document, as Macdonald was during most of the time a close companion of his highness. The manuscript, or a copy of it, was at one time preserved in the Scots College at Rome, but we believe it has disappeared.

The only priest to whom the authorities showed any consideration was Father Harrison, priest of Moidart. This person, by a sort of happy inspiration, appeared at a seasonable moment before the Sheriff of Inverary, and emitted a declaration to the effect that he took no part in politics, was loyal to the Government as a true patriot should be, and regretted that any of his co-religionists should have allowed themselves to be involved in an enterprise so foolhardy, etc., etc. Probably enough these were his real sentiments, for Father Harrison, from all accounts, devoted himself entirely to his spiritual duties, and cared for nothing else. He got a pass at once from the sheriff, which was of considerable value when presented to any of the Argyllshire officers of militia stationed in this district or visiting it, but his reverence had too wholesome a dread of the other troops to try its efficacy upon them. With commendable discretion he hid himself whenever these came to his neighbourhood.

Another priest, supposed to be Maighstear Alasdair Mor Mac Aonghais vich Alasdair, escaped apprehension by feigning madness. He had taken refuge in a miserable hovel, tenanted by a forlorn old woman, somewhere in the neighbourhood of Borrodale, when a party of soldiers were suddenly perceived approaching towards the dwelling. Unable to escape without being fired at, the priest was advised by the old woman to remain where he was, and to assume the character which he immediately afterwards played to such perfection. Upon the soldiers inquiring roughly who and what he was, the old woman interposed by replying that he was a son of hers, a poor fool, and one who had always been so from his childhood. The incoherent mutterings of the lunatic, as well as the vacant idiotic stare with which he contemplated the visitors, and other acts quite worthy of a genuine fool, confirmed the soldiers in the impression that the old dame was uttering the truth; so, after poking about to make quite sure that no "rebels" were concealed inside the house, they took their departure, leaving the couple in peace.

Bishop Macdonald ventured back to Scotland several years after the '45, but he was apprehended in 1755, and after being tried in Edinburgh was sentenced to perpetual banishment. The Government, however, did not press the sentence.[10] He died at Glengarry, in 1773.

Old Clanranald, Lady Clanranald, Macdonald Boisdale, Flora Macdonald, and many others, were made prisoners and taken away to London for having helped the Prince in his distress. The authorities, however, did not know what to do with them, so after a time they wisely sent them home again.

Notes

1   Kinlochmoidart House was burned by Capt Fergussone, who was responsible for so much destruction and death on the West coast. It is said that Argyll knew of his intention and sent a message of countermand which arrived too late.

2   The soldier and the Christian together
                     Are in one fine man the Captain:
                     A blessing from poor Moidart,
                     The blessing of every community be with you,
                     Because you did not by destruction
                     Put old and young among them into peril.

3   It is rogues in trousers who denied their kin —
                     He is no Campbell, no Chisholm he;
                     You wouldn't know where he grew from.
                     (dh'bhas in the text should read *dh'fhàs).*

The reference to trousers would be recognised as a term of abuse from a Highlander, especially after the Disclothing Act of 1747 which forbade the wearing of the plaid. The implication is exactly that of the English idiom 'turncoat'.

4   Iain Fràingeach's narrative is printed among the eye-witness accounts gathered by Bishop Forbes and published as Forbes, R., ed. H. Paton, *The Lyon in Mourning*, 3 volumes (Edinburgh, 1895-6; new edition, Edinburgh, 1975), volume 3, appendix I, pp 375-83. Volume 2 includes a letter by Iain's cousin Major Alexander MacDonald of Glenaladale (volume 2, pp 362-6), while volume 1 includes a journal partly written by Major Alexander (his part is volume 1, pp 334-40), both treating of some of the same events as Iain's narrative.

5   This is Glenshiel by Kintail, not to be confused with Loch Shiel and the River Shiel in Moidart.

6   This historian is James Browne: Browne, J. *A History of the Highlands and of the Highland Clans*, 4 volumes. (Glasgow 1838). The story of Cameron's nose

is in volume iii, p. 319.

7   See further, chapter xi, pp 182f.

8   Bishop John Geddes, *Some Account of the State of the Catholic Religion in Scotland During the Years 1745, 46 and 47*. A handwritten copy of Geddes's original MS is held in the Scottish Catholic Archives, Edinburgh. It has been printed in full in Leith, W. Forbes, *Memoirs of Scottish Catholics During the xviith and xviiith Centuries*, 2 volumes (London, 1901), volume 2, pp 332ff.

9   Father Cameron in fact survived the sea journey and died on board a prison hulk on the Thames.

10   Bishop Hugh had returned to Scotland in 1749. In 1755 his whereabouts in Edinburgh was betrayed and he was arrested, tried and ordered to reside at Duns. But, as the author implies, Government officials afterwards connived at his return to the North. He was nevertheless not able to move back to the Western Highlands, and resided for many years at Preshome on the Banffshire coast, administering his Highland District from a distance and making Summer visits to the West whenever possible.

Chapter 11

Short Sketch of the Glenaladale Family—Alexander MacNab of Inneshewen—His Defence of Lord George Murray—Col. John Macdonald during the Indian Mutiny—The Kinlochmoidart Family after the Death of Donald Kinloch—Many of the Catholic Gentlemen in the Rough Bounds become Protestants after receiving Commissions in the British Army—Close of the Kinlochmoidart Family—Dangers attending the Formation of large Sheep Farms

THERE is little doubt that it would have gone hard both with the Borrodales and the Glenaladales if the Government had been cognisant of the prominent part which they took in effecting the Prince's escape, after all the trouble which it had given itself in drawing its meshes so tightly around him; but probably the Government was not fully aware of the extent of their complicity, until it was no longer worth its while to prosecute, or the parties themselves were too vigilant and sedulously kept out of its way. They had friends constantly on the watch, and by their means were kept well informed of the movements of the troops, so that on the slightest appearance of danger they invariably retreated to their hiding-places among the woods and in the mountains. Old Angus Borrodale died comfortably in his bed, without having become acquainted with the inside of any of the government jails, or without having made that trip to London which so many of his friends and countrymen had to undertake at the dictation and under the guidance of the ruling powers. His nephew, Alexander of Glenaladale, seems after a time to have recovered from the ruin caused to his property, and to have spent the rest of an honourable life in peace. These two families were closely allied to each other, Angus of Borrodale, and John, father of Glenaladale of '45, being sons of John the fifth laird of Glenaladale. Angus left three sons, viz., Ranald, through whom the family is represented in the direct line to this day; John, progenitor of the Rhu or Lochshiel family; and Alexander, who at an early age went to the West Indies, amassed a considerable fortune, and returned to his native country late in life. He was called Alasdair-an-Òir. It was he who built the house at Keppoch in Arisaig, and it was through him that the estates of Glenaladale and Glenfinnan came into the Borrodale branch of the family. In this way :-John, son of Glenaladale of the '45, being indignant at the ferocious manner in which Macdonald, Boisdale, was persecuting his Catholic tenants, and feeling convinced that these, as well as many of the small tenants in Moidart and other places on the mainland, would do far better as colonists in America, conceived the idea of uniting as many as possible in a wide scheme of emigration. To give effect to this, he resolved to sell his own family estates, and to settle in the new country along with those who should enter into his views. Indeed, prompted by the warmth and generosity of his own nature, he spent a large portion of his money in paying the passage of his poorer companions, and in helping them to make a successful beginning after reaching the American shore. His estates of Glenaladale and Glenfinnan were sold by him to his cousin Alasdair-an-Oir. The new proprietor had married a Miss M'Gregor, sister of Mrs Archibald Macdonald Rhu, and had by her an only surviving son called also Alexander Macdonald. This gentleman succeeded his father, but being unmarried, he, before his death, which happened a few years after he came to the inheritance, disposed of Glenaladale and Glenfinnan in favour of John, son of Ronald, and grandson of old Borrodale. In this manner the direct representatives of the Borrodale branch became the Glenaladales of to-day.

The Glenaladale who emigrated was accompanied among others by many of the tenants living on Lochshiel side, the natives of the hamlet of Druim-a-laoigh almost to a man going away on this occasion. This took place about 1773.[1] The colony prospered so well, that the original two or three hundred have long since developed into many thousands. They are to be found in Prince Edward's Island and other parts of the dominion. During the American war, Glenaladale distinguished himself both by feats of bravery and by unflinching loyalty to the British crown; and it is said of him that he took a leading part in raising the 84th, or Regiment of "Royal Highland Emigrants." In a report forwarded to the British Government by General Small, the following honourable tribute is paid to him:—"The activity and unabating zeal of Captain John Macdonald of Glenaladale, in bringing an excellent company into the field, is his least commendation, being acknowledged by all who know him to be one of the most accomplished men and best officers of his rank in His Majesty's service."

The Government made him an offer of the governorship of Prince Edward's Island, but owing to the objectionable kind of oath which had to be taken in those days, Glenaladale, as a Catholic, felt obliged to decline the honour. He died in 1811.

His brother, Father Hustian Macdonald, was priest in Moidart for many years after Father Harrison's death, and was highly respected by persons of every class, both Catholic and Protestant, who came to form his acquaintance. He lived principally at Altegil, on the Glenuig property. He afterwards went to America, where he settled among the colony founded by his brother Captain John, and died in Prince Edward's Island.

The pipes which belonged to Glenaladale of the '45, and which were borne by his piper on the field of Culloden, are still preserved at Glenfinnan.

John, the grandson of Angus Borrodale, who thus succeeded to the Glenaladale estates, is still spoken of among the natives of Arisaig and Moidart as a person of exceptional probity and abilities. To a thorough knowledge of law he united a wonderful natural shrewdness, which over and over again proved of service in helping his neighbours out of their difficulties, and at times in rescuing them under charges which threatened infallibly to bring them within the clutches of the law. The natives have a saying, that no case if once seriously taken up by John was ever known to fail.

Cool, clear-headed, and persevering, he could work his way through obstacles which most ordinary men would have fled from as insurmountabie. As a consequence he was the adviser and support of all in doubt or trouble, and throughout his lifetime his presence was justly reckoned to inspire with confidence the members of almost every class belonging to the districts with which his family was more intimately associated.

He was married to Jane, daughter of Alexander Macnab of Innishewen, and from this marriage were born several sons, some of whom will come under our notice.

His father-in-law was cousin of Francis, twelfth chief of the Macnabs, a very eccentric personage, of whom all sorts of extraordinary anecdotes are related, and who was noted among other things for his gigantic stature. This laird was frequently reproved by Innishewen for the laxity of his morals; but the invariable retort to these lectures was, that Innishewen, after departing this life, would have the kingdom of heaven entirely to himself if persons like Francis were to be excluded. While the chief sided with the Government, Innishewen threw himself with enthusiasm into the party of the Prince, and his example was followed by Archibald Macnab of Acharne, as well as by the greater part of the clan. They were attached to the Duke of Perth's regiment, and throughout the whole campaign conducted themselves with the greatest gallantry. One of Innishewen's near relatives, while attempting to protect his own or a friend's house from being burnt in Perthshire, brought down seven of the soldiers to his own gun, the stock of which is said to have been fitted so as to contain a supply of bullets. Innishewen was a warm admirer of Lord George Murray, and when the latter was accused by a certain clique of being disloyal to the Prince, wrote a vindication of his character, the manuscript being still preserved in the Glenaladale family. He ascribes the origin of this fiction to the malice of a certain person connected with one of the best known families in Lochaber. As to Lord George's unwillingness to commence the battle on the field of Culloden, he finds grave reasons to justify it, for the greater part of the army had gone to Inverness in search of provisions, the scarcity of which was so great that such of their companions as remained with the chiefs had only the most miserable rations served out to them, viz., a hard sea-biscuit to each man in the twenty four hours. On hearing of Cumberland's advance the absent ones began to hurry up, "each ran with the best speed they could, and so were coming up in different parties without observing order; and, as I was afterwards informed, the Prince sent orders to Lord George to attack immediately with the handful of men that remained, before the enemy had formed, which Lord George had refused to do till the whole would come up from Inverness." The Prince never forgave Lord George this act of disobedience, and from a conversation, said by the writer to have taken place between the former and John Roy Stewart, attributed the failure of the day to his lieutenant's behaviour on this occasion. While giving vent to his displeasure, Charles was told by John Roy that "had it been any other but his highness he would take upon him to vindicate Lord George's conduct. Then the Prince said: Well, John, I am another person, let me hear your vindication. After which John Roy vindicated Lord George. The Prince then asked, Well, John, have you done? John replied, Please his highness he had. Well, says the Prince, before the enemy had formed I sent Lord George an aide-de-camp with orders to attack immediately, in which, if I had been obeyed, I would drive their front in their rear, which order I repeated several times without being obeyed; and by the time the enemy had formed, I sent orders to the Duke of Perth, who immediately obeyed, but it was then too late. I know, continued he, Lord George would make a very good dragoon, but he knows very little of the general." The skilful manner in which Lord George conducted the retreat from Derby, is a sufficient refutation of the low estimate of his abilities so candidly expressed in this last remark of the Prince.

The latter part of Innishewen's life was spent at Borrodale, the residence of his son-in-law. He died there when close upon a hundred years of age. From his youth he is said to have been a person of the most unblemished character, while in his political principles he was consistent to the very last, being a thorough outspoken Jacobite. Like most chivalrous gentlemen of the same stamp, he was popular with all classes, especially so with the young generation growing up around him. Sometimes, however, to test the devotion of his grandchildren, he used to call upon them to make certain sacrifices which, while trying to their palates, were ostensibly very gratifying to his own. But the youngsters invaribly contrived to pull through the crisis with considerable discretion, for while readily offering what was requisitioned, they never failed to remind him that what was good for them was extremely unwholesome for such a dear old gentleman like himself, who had not a tooth left in his gums. They of course got the benefit of such sound logic. The sword which he used at Culloden is preserved at Glenfinnan.

It was in the lifetime of John's successor, viz., the late Angus of Glenaladale, that the family seat was removed from Borrodale to Glenfinnan, close to the head of Lochshiel, and within sight of the Prince's monument. The latter, which is in the form of a tower surmounted by a statue of the Prince, was erected shortly after the beginning of the present century, by Alexander Macdonald of Glenaladale, John's immediate predecessor in the estates. It bears an inscription, written by Dr Donald Maclean, native of Ardnamurchan, a gentleman distinguished by many abilities, and who at one time practised in his native parish. It was approved of by Sir Walter Scott, and was translated into Latin by Dr Gregory of Edinburgh (Stat. Acct.). Angus left three sons, one of whom is the present laird, another is the Catholic bishop of Argyle and the Isles, while the third is superior of a religious order.[2] A younger brother of the late laird, viz., John, was an officer in the East Indian army, and during his many years of service gave proof of those sterling qualities which have distinguished, in so prominent a manner, the men to whom Great Britain owes so much for the rearing-up and maintaining of its dominion in the East. By his daring, promptitude, and decision of character at Umritzir, he quelled the first movements of a Sepoy revolt, and saved the Europeans from a general massacre. In promoting him for his services on this occasion, Sir Charles Napier wrote:—"You have won it, if ever a man deserved well of his chief. But for your decision, we should have had the devil to pay at Umritzir." The same qualities, during the great mutiny, kept in awe his own regiment, and prevented it from going over to the insurgents, while stationed at Rohnee. On this occasion Macdonald, owing to a sudden attack made by some of his own troopers, had a very narrow escape. He, Sir Norman Leslie, and Dr Grant were sitting one evening in front of their tent, when half-a-dozen miscreants, carefully disguised, suddenly sprang upon them. Sir Norman was cut down at once, Macdonald had his scalp shaved off, and Grant received wounds which, although not fatal, were very severe. The major and the doctor however defended themselves as best they could with their camp stools, until they got an opportunity of rushing into the tent for their arms. This frightened the murderers, who immediately took to flight. The regiment was paraded without loss of time, and the weapons of the troopers were subjected to the closest scrutiny, but not a single trace of blood was found on any of them, nor was there a man missing from the ranks. A few days afterwards, however, Macdonald got secret information that the outrage was perpetrated indubitably by some of his own men, who were using every effort to stir their comrades to revolt and to murder their officers. A closer inquiry led to the discovery of these ringleaders. They were at once seized, tried by court-martial, and condemned to be hanged. The danger however became imminent when the sentence had to be carried out. One of the culprits, a person of high caste, made a violent speech to the regiment drawn up to witness the execution, urging them to take courage and to shoot down the Feringhees; but Macdonald, without a moment's hesitation, went up to him, and pointing a revolver at his head swore to blow out his brains if he uttered another word. The murderer trembled like a leaf, and, rather than have his precious skull shattered in the manner threatened, allowed himself to be quietly noosed, mounted on the elephant's back, and an instant afterwards was left dangling to the branch of a tree. In like manner the others got their due, Macdonald standing close by superintending the operation. His own account is that not for one moment did he expect to come through the business alive. But evidently the stern resolution with which he punished the ringleaders had a most sobering effect upon the others, who completely abandoned all thoughts of murder and treason. The colonel's conduct during these critical moments has been highly and deservedly lauded by some of the historians of the Indian mutiny. By a similar display of coolness and decision, he on another occasion rescued a brother officer from the grasp of a wounded bear. While worrying its helpless victim, the infuriated animal shifted its position so constantly that Macdonald was unable to fire without hitting his companion. As the struggle however threatened to be fatal to the latter in a very short time, Macdonald determined to risk a shot, so, taking a steady aim, he sent a bullet through the bear, and *also through the calf of the leg of the officer,* which happened to be in the line of fire. It was pretty much a case of neck or nothing, but fortunately no bones were broken, and the mauled victim soon recovered from this as well as his other injuries. But the story goes that he never quite appreciated the method by which he was thus rescued from certain death. The gallant colonel is still living, and although not indifferent to the loss of his scalp, which he would have preferred to feel remaining on the place where nature first placed it, is quite hale and hearty, to the delight of many friends.

To resume our sketch of the Kinlochmoidart family. After Donald's execution, the property was confiscated by the Government and retained in its possession for forty-one years, the commissioner appointed to superintend it being Butter of Faskally, a gentleman from Perthshire. Donald's widow, together with her young family, had in consequence to face many sad privations, but these were somewhat alleviated by the sympathy of a few friends, notably so of the noble house of Traquair. Two of her sons, Alexander and Charles, were sent to the Scots College in Paris, where they remained until their education was completed. Charles entered the French army, and seems to have proved himself an officer of merit, for he rose to the rank of lieutenant-general. Alexander, having stronger interests binding him to his native country, returned home. He soon afterwards received a commission in one of the many Highland regiments raised by the Government at the time, and sailed with it to North America. During the campaign which followed, it happened that he and Charles had to fight on opposite sides; but during a short cessation of hostilities the two brothers, by a singular coincidence, were deputed to make arrangements about an exchange of prisoners. It was their first meeting since leaving college, and their last for many a year to come. Charles ultimately perished during the French Revolution. He fell into the hands of the Reds, and was guillotined in 1792, a fate which also overtook his uncle Æneas, banker in Paris, and brother of Donald, Kinloch. Alexander married a daughter of Campbell of Airds, and by her had two sons, John and Donald, and one daughter, Margaret. He visited Moidart several times, whenever in fact his military engagements allowed his doing so, for although the family property was in the hands of strangers, his very happiness seems to have been wrapped up in it. It was during one of those visits that, arriving on a Sunday morning, he made straight for the church, knowing that most of his friends and acquaintances would be found there. But the congregation had just entered before his arrival, and Alexander hovered outside waiting until the service would finish. His uncle Ranald happened to be present on this occasion, and on learning that Alexander had neglected to enter and assist at mass was deeply hurt. It was whilst remonstrating with his nephew on this subject that Alexander broke the news that he no longer belonged to the Catholic Church, but for various reasons had given it up in exchange for the Church of England. This confession gave great offence not only to his nearest relatives but to the whole country, and it is stated that Alexander was never afterwards treated with the same warmth and cordiality. The information seems to have excited the greater surprise, as many of the good country people could scarcely bring themselves to believe that the son of their gallant and staunch chief Donald, could have been guilty of such a grievous falling away in the one thing worth a man's serious consideration in this life. The popular explanation to this day is, that he renounced his faith and married a Campbell lady at the instigation of the head of the Argyll family, who is supposed to have assured him that by this course he would win the favour of the Government, and get back more speedily the forfeited family estates. There may be some truth in this; but it is far more likely that the atrocious penal laws then in force against Catholics, and the utter ostracism to which a Catholic officer would find himself exposed in the army, had far more to do with modulating Alexander's conscience in a way so agreeable to British prejudices than any other cause. It is certain at any rate that most of the young Catholic gentlemen from these districts, after joining the army, behaved much in the same way as Alexander did. Besides the isolation to which in those days their religion would probably condemn them, the prospects of promotion would either completely vanish, or seem very faint and dim.[3] Thus Simon Macdonald of Morar, a nephew of Bishop Hugh, after joining the 76th, joined also the Protestant Church, the tenets of which he held to his death, which took place in his native district, after he had attained the rank of major in the 92nd. His example was imitated by his brother Coll, a captain in another of the Highland regiments, and who fought in Egypt under Abercrombie. Colonel Gillis, Kinloch Morar, acted in a similar manner, and several others. This Colonel Gillis, although latterly rather eccentric in some ways, is allowed to have been an excellent soldier, and by sheer merit to have worked his way up from the ranks to the position which he held towards the close of his career. Born of very poor parents, he left home with all his worldly chattels wrapped up in a cotton handkerchief, which he carried on his back as he made his way to the south in search of employment. For some time he worked as an ordinary navvy; but happening to see a recruiting party with fife and drums pass one day near the canal at which he was toiling, he flung down his pickaxe, declaring to his companions that henceforth he would shoulder a musket and fight for the king. He enlisted that same day, and as the times were lively soon found plenty of employment of a kind much more congenial to his taste. He went through a good deal of fighting both in the West Indies and in Europe, and was fortunate enough to come under the favourable notice of the Duke of York, who, recognising his merits, took care to have them duly rewarded. In one of his last battles Gillis was hit near the shoulder by a ball, which penetrated so deeply that the surgeons were unable to extract it. He had to carry this inconvenient memento of French politeness for several years, long after his retirement to Kinlochmorar. But one winter it caused him so much uneasiness, that on going up to Fort-William, he consulted Dr Smith, who informed him that by a very slight operation the enemy could be dislodged. He submitted at once to what the doctor suggested, and to his great surprise the ball was extracted with comparative ease. Shortly after his promotion to the rank of commissioned officer, Gillis was sent to raise recruits in the neighbourhood of Inverness, and for this purpose was entrusted with a considerable sum of Government money. The money went, but a large number of the recruits, who had enlisted while attending a feeing-market, never turned up, and no one seemed able or willing to tell where they could be found. As he could not account for the men, he had at any rate to account for and to make good the money spent upon them. But the officer, owing to the slenderness of his personal means, had a great difficulty in doing this, and he would probably have found himself in a serious plight at the headquarters of his regiment, if he had not accidentally met with Mr Fraser, Gorthleck, who hearing from his own lips the trick played upon him by the young men, and being touched at the distress which it caused, advanced the sum out of his own pocket, although Gillis was an entire stranger to him. His confidence, however, was not misplaced, for Gillis sometime afterwards became entitled to some prize money, and his first act after receiving it was to repay his generous friend. After retiring from active service, he built the present house of Kinlochmorar, and in that remote corner finished the rest of his life. His stories were of the most extraordinary character, being almost all founded on the same solid basis of truth as that of the Arabian Nights and Baron Munchausen; yet the worthy veteran could tell them in the gravest manner, solemnly assuring his hearers that no doubt could be thrown on their authenticity, since he or some of his military friends, if not actual witnesses, had at any rate seen things quite as extraordinary and hard of belief during the stirring campaigns which they went through. In his last illness he sent for Father Angus Macdonald, priest of Morar, and thus, after an interruption of fifty years, ended where he had begun. He was buried at Meoble. In this digression to Morar, it may be mentioned that Major Simon was very popular with such of the natives as joined the same regiment and fought under him. General Stewart gives a striking instance of this, which took place during the American War:—"At the moment Lord Cornwallis was giving the orders to charge, a Highland soldier rushed forward and placed himself in front of his officer, Lieut. Simon Macdonald of Morar, afterwards major of the 92nd. Macdonald having asked what brought him there, the soldier answered, 'You know that when I engaged to be a soldier, I promised to be faithful to the king and to you. The French are coming, and while I stand here neither bullet nor bayonet shall touch you, except through my body.'" Many years after the major's death, one of these veterans, living on the Morar or adjoining estate, was unfortunate enough to incur the wrath of the factor or agent, and as there was no protection for persons of his class at the time, he was ordered to be summarily evicted at the Whitsunday term. Two or three days before the sentence was carried out, the disconsolate veteran wended his way to the grave of Major Simon, near the church of St Mary's, in Strath Arisaig, and kneeling down began to adjure his old commander in the most passionate terms to intervene and to prevent this injustice to his follower. Occasionally, by way of emphasizing his entreaty, he would vigorously strike with his stick the green sod under which the body lay, and exclaim,

"Simon, Simon, you were ever good to me. Come once more to the help of an old comrade, and save him from being driven forth from hearth and home." This was immediately reported to some of the resident gentry, who by their representations prevailed on the agent to forego his cruel designs. Simon's brother, Captain Coll, married a daughter of Captain Cochrane, Lochaber, and for some years resided at Knock, in the island of Skye. He unhappily became deranged in his mind, and had to be confined for the rest of his life in a lunatic asylum. James, a son of Simon, joined the army, and distinguished himself under Sir John Moore. He was severely wounded at Corunna, and died, soon after coming home, at Edinburgh. Unlike his father, he never hesitated to profess himself a staunch Catholic. A younger son also of Simon, called Sime Og, was accidentally killed at Roshven. The property of Morar then went to their brother John, who became insane, and died at Cross. He was the last in the direct line of the old Morar family. The estate afterwards went to the nearest collateral heir, a son of Dr Macdonald, Gaotal. But he also becoming insane, had to be placed under the care of a certain John Macdonald, tenant of Gascan, near Lochsheil side. After John's death the property was claimed by several heirs, but after a protracted litigation the courts decided in favour of a Macdonald family from Uist. They immediately disposed of it to Mr Æneas Macdonell for £11,000, who in his turn, and after greatly improving it, sold it to the late Francis Astley of Arisaig.

One great cause of anxiety to Alexander during his visits to Moidart, was the condition of his mother, who for many years lived at Briaig behind Dorlin. The sufferings which she had to pass through in '46, and the difficulties which she had to face while the family property was forfeited, caused a strain which was too great for the mind to bear. She had to be confided to the care of some distant relatives living at Briaig, and although carefully nursed by them, and tenderly waited upon by her son and his wife when in the country, seems never to have recovered the full use of her faculties. She was afterwards removed to Kinlochmoidart, where she died. Her body lies buried in Eilean-Fhionnan. The sad fate of her husband, and the cruel reverses which followed, have always won for this lady the deepest sympathy of the Moidart people. She was a daughter of Robert Stewart of Appin, and grand-daughter of Sir Duncan Campbell of Lochnell.

Alexander served in the army until he became colonel of the 71st; but in spite of his gallant conduct during several campaigns, and although wounded in them, and otherwise shattered in health from the effects of privation and climate, he never succeeded in disarming the relentless hostility of the Government to his family. The dogged obstinacy with which the latter withheld the estates is, under the circumstances, very inexplicable. To judge from its behaviour, one would feel inclined to accuse it of persecuting its own children. When his infirmities increased to such an extent that he could no longer visit Moidart, his thoughts kept still travelling towards it, and towards some of the companions of his younger days. There is a well-preserved tradition in Moidart, that during those sad moments he used to express a wish for only three things, viz., a bed of heather from the hillside of Torloisk, a drink of the cool and refreshing water of Samhnuich well, and half an hour's conversation with Father Hustian, Glenaladale's brother.

> "Leaba d'on fhraoch Torloisc;
> Deoch a tobar na samhnuich;
> S'leth uair do Mhaighstear Uisdean."

Torloisk hill is close to Kinlochmoidart house, and Samhnuich is an excellent well of spring water near the Prince's Walk. Father Hustian seems to have been one of his early acquaintances, with whom he formed a friendship which was strengthened during the year that this priest was in charge of Moidart. He came to the diocese, after finishing his studies abroad, in 1769, and remained in it thirty years, most of this period being spent in his native district. He went to America about the beginning of the present century, several years after Alexander's death.

Alexander died at Edinburgh in 1781, leaving two sons and one daughter. John, the oldest, was a captain in the 21st, but was killed in the expedition against the island of Guadaloupe. It was under John, viz., in 1786, that the estate was restored to the family. The second son, Donald, also joined the army, and proved himself in every way worthy of his ancestors. He was among the first to land and storm the French batteries at Aboukir, under General Abercrombie. He rose to the rank of colonel, and subsequently was appointed governor of Tobago. He died while holding this post in 1804. Neither of these sons of Alexander having left any issue, the property devolved on their sister Margaret. This lady was born in 1773, and in 1799 married Lieutenant Colonel Robertson, youngest son of the celebrated historian, Principal William Robertson. She accompanied her husband to India; but after his retiring from the army, they both returned to their native country, and spent the rest of their years at Kinlochmoidart. A small house had been erected near the site of the old building burnt in '46, while the property was in the hands of the Government, and this, after being considerably enlarged by the colonel, was converted into a very comfortable residence. An additional wing was erected under the next laird, William; but the whole has now given way to the handsome mansion recently raised by Robert Stuart of Ingleston. It was under Colonel Robertson that most of the tenants emigrated to America, viz., about the year 1812. The natives of Ulgary, Kinlochuachair, Brunery, and the lower parts of the strath, may be said to have gone away in one body, leaving their lands to be incorporated in one or two large holdings. The ship which was to take them away was brought round to the Moidart coast, and anchored at Camus-a-linne. Their departure seems to have been the deliberate act of the people themselves, who were glad of the opportunity of leaving a poor country in exchange for one where they could live more comfortably, and push their fortunes with a prospect of success. One or two families, who had not the courage or the good sense of the rest, settled in Morven, but after a few years they discovered that this was not the wisest step to have taken. So far as one can judge from stories current in the district, it would appear that the Ulgary tenants, for instance, while living comfortably enough for six months in the year, had to endure other six of something like downright starvation, and there is little doubt that this hamlet was typical of many others in the district. To dissuade people from emigrating to richer lands under circumstances like these is absolute folly. Cases of this kind, of course, are not to be confounded with evictions, or driving the poor people away from their homes against their will,—a policy worthy only of tyrants, and sure some day to tell against its authors and abettors. The relations between the colonel and his people seem to have been of a friendly character. On one occasion the Ulgary tenants having to suffer more or less from the depredations committed by the deer among the crops, and being unwilling to shoot the depredators for fear of giving offence to the colonel, who was a keen sportsman, sent a deputation to the latter, who half in joke advised them to poind the trespassers, and then inform him, so that he might do justice to the case. The tenants quietly took him at his word, and a few days afterwards returned with a polite message that the thieves were caught, and that they would now like to know how they were to be dealt with, and what compensation was to be given to themselves. The colonel, as may be imagined, was very much surprised, but, true to his bargain, duly appeared on the scene to administer justice. The deer when visiting the crops used to come down from the high grounds through a narrow gorge with very steep sides, called Pole-a-bhainne, and the tenants, perfectly aware of their habits, by erecting a rude but effective fence across the lower end of the gorge, and then seizing the upper end and enclosing it in a similar manner after the deer had entered, kept them prisoners as effectively as any sheep in a fank. None enjoyed the joke more than the tenants themselves, who by way of compensation were at once assisted by the proprietor in having their arable ground well fenced against future incursions of their troublesome neighbours. The colonel left a large family of sons and daughters, some of whom are still in life. The oldest of the sons, viz., William, succeeded to the property after his father's death, and for fifty years was the leading man in Moidart. Another son, John, joined the army; he was killed while gallantly leading his men into action in one of our numerous Indian wars. David, a younger son, joined the navy, and won great distinction by his bravery during the troubles with the Maories in New Zealand. He was severely wounded and lamed for life, while storming a Maori stockade; he still carries a bullet in the leg which hit him during the engagement. He received the thanks of Parliament for his services to the country during this war, and was soon afterwards promoted. He is now a retired admiral of the British Navy. The last of the small tenants on this estate, viz., the Caolas people, left in 1852, when nearly one half of the Moidart people were forced to emigrate, many of them against their will, to Australia.

The property towards the close of the late laird's life had to be sold, under circumstances which would not be alluded to here, were it not that they illustrate in a very striking manner the grave peril which accompanies the formation of large sheep farms, both here and elsewhere throughout the Highlands. One of the largest farms on Kinloch estate was suddenly thrown, during the late crisis in sheep-farming, on the proprietor's own hands, and the delivery of the stock necessitated a payment of £10,000. To raise this large sum, the property had to be disentailed at a cost of other £10,000 as compensation to the nearest collateral heir. Unfortunately these transactions had to take place shortly after the fall of the City of Glasgow Bank, when a general panic seemed to come over the country, and when the interest upon money advanced was exceedingly high. The heavy sum thus to be paid annually in the shape of interest, together with the expenses incidental to the management of an estate, was more than the property could meet, especially as markets for wool and stock were almost at their lowest ebb. There was nothing for it but to sell; and thus, to the great grief of all who knew the family, the estates passed away to strange hands, after being three hundred years with the Macdonalds. In this case the danger comes out more prominently, as the Kinloch estate was always said to be carefully managed under the late laird, who resided constantly upon it, and who, while freely dispensing the hospitality of his house to his friends and guests, lived inflexibly within the limits of his income. Those who are acquainted with the real state of the Highlands, are perfectly aware that a very large number of other proprietors have been brought to the verge of ruin from causes precisely similar; and where the blow has not yet fallen, the unhappy victims are in the position of Damocles with the sword suspended above his head. In the face of this, one wonders that instead of struggling on in the hopes of better times, and wishing to perpetuate a vicious theory, or of converting their good lands into deer forests, they do not resolutely grapple, if at all able, with the real difficulty, and cut down their large farms so as to bring the sections within the reach of men of moderate capital. The process may necessarily be slow or bitter, or both, but the result at any rate would relieve the owners of land from the incubus of those cumbersome holdings under which they are at present nearly smothered. Increasing the number of deer forests by clearing away the sheep and putting the land under deer, can scarcely be called an escape from the present difficulty, for deer forests are notoriously expensive luxuries, and in times of commercial strain or panic are apt to be the first to suffer, being prudently shunned or relinquished when possible by the moneyed classes. On the other hand, to restore the sheep, if such a step were deemed advisable, to lands from which they have been once cleared, is pretty sure to involve a frightful waste of capital; for sheep have as a rule to be *bred* on a farm, or a class has to be selected from other farms, which very few farmers, even among the cleverest and most experienced, can tell *a priori* will suit the land to which they are about to be transferred, before they give satisfaction. Strong healthy animals are apt to die like flies when brought to graze on lands to which they are strangers; and it is the melancholy experience of this that induces farmers as a body to stand shoulder to shoulder in insisting upon high valuations, when at deliveries an acclimatised stock is transferred from the outgoing tenant to his successor. In a difficult problem of this kind, experience, which is the true guide, unquestionably points to a bold subdivision of large holdings as the safest and most satisfactory solution.

The Kinlochmoidart family became extinct in the direct line at the death of David William, who survived his father, the late laird, only a few months. The three large cairns near the high road to Kinloch were erected in commemoration of this warm-hearted gentleman, of his brother Captain William, and of their father. A more elaborate monument to the last-named was raised by public subscription, and placed in Eilean Fhionnan.

Notes

1   John Glenaladale bought the land on St John's Island in 1770, and the following summer sent out a small advance party to make preparations. In 1772 some 210 people, about half from Moidart and the rest from South Uist, crossed the Atlantic in the brig *Alexander*, with a priest and a doctor in the party. John joined them in 1773, settling at Tracadie. His plan to have the tenants on his land did not prove satisfactory, and in time many moved away to Nova Scotia where Crown grants of land were available.

It is probable that John did not actually sell the estate to Alasdair an Òir; rather, Alasdair gave him a loan to meet the full costs of the emigration, taking the estate as security should John not repay. John was probably happy that Alasdair retained the estate, since he did not wish to return from America himself and he knew that Glenaladale was in the good hands of his close relative.

2   The oldest son, and heir, was John Andrew. The second, Hugh (whom the author places third), became a Redemptorist and, at the time of writing (1889), was Provincial of the Order; the following year he was consecrated Bishop of Aberdeen. The third son, Angus, had been made Bishop of Argyll and the Isles in 1878 and, as the author states, held that position at the time of writing. In 1892 he became Archbishop of St Andrews and Edinburgh, where he remained until his death in 1900.

3   Alexander was no doubt right in believing that conversion to Protestantism could help the recovery of his estate in that, by the Act of 1700 still in force, inheritance of property at all was in any case forbidden to Catholics unless they renounced their faith. The author's further argument that there was pressure on Catholic recruits to the British Army to convert, through fear of ostracism and the hope of promotion, is only part of the truth; in fact the position was more cut and dried: they were obliged to declare allegiance to the Protestant faith in order to receive a commission. The regulation was later relaxed at a time when officers and men were needed for the American War of Independence.

Chapter 12

Ruin of the Clanranald Family under Reginald George—Sale of the Property—Short Sketch of the Moidart Portions down to the Present Time—Glenuig—Roshven—The College at Samalaman—Fate of the "Little Katie"—Eilean Shona—Andrew Macdonald—Black Ranald of Eigg and his Son—Smuggling—Lochans or Glenmoidart—Lochshiel—Archibald Macdonald of Rhu—Clearances and Voluntary Emigration among the Natives of Moidart—The Population reduced to One-Half—Mr Hope Scott —The late Lord Howard of Glossop

AFTER his return to the country, young Clanranald of the '45 abjured politics, and, settling down quietly among his people in Uist, sedulously devoted his mind to the cultivation and improvement of the family estates. His first wife having died, he married a Miss Mackinnon from the island of Skye, by whom he had two sons and three daughters. John, the oldest son, was yet a minor when his father died, and his education being left in the hands of Protestant relatives, he was brought up in the religious tenets of his instructors. After travelling abroad for some time, he was appointed to a commission in one of the dragoon regiments; but he resigned this about the time of his marriage with Miss Macqueen, daughter of Robert Macqueen of Braxfield, Lord Chief-Justice Clerk of Scotland. It is of the latter, who used to speak the broadest Scotch even on the bench, and was thus sometimes unintelligible to witnesses or others brought before him, that the following anecdote is told:—"Judge to prisoner at the bar: Hae ye ony counsel, my man? Prisoner: No. Judge: Do ye want to hae ony appointit? Prisoner: No; I only want an interpreter to make me understand what your lordship says."

The marriage was not a happy one. John died at the early age of twenty-nine, leaving a son and heir, Reginald George, who in the course of his career ship-wrecked everything. Yet at the beginning no chief ever gave surer promises of doing well than this young representative of the Clanranalds. Clever, polished, and possessing every advantage which the most refined education could bestow, he speedily became a favourite in the most select circles of society, and found himself one of the privileged few who in those days were admitted to Almacks. The family estates at the same period were in a most flourishing condition. The rents came in punctually; and owing to the extraordinary rise in kelp, a very large profit found its way into the pockets of the proprietor. Those are said to have been the golden days of landed property in the west. It is calculated that Clanranald's income for some years averaged from £20,000 to £25,000 per annum, a large sum when the character of most of the land is taken into consideration.[1] But all these opportunities went for nothing. The folly and extravagance of which the Prince Regent is accused of having set the example, brought Clanranald, like many stronger men, to absolute ruin. One after another large slices of the family inheritance were cut off and sent into the market. In this manner not only Eigg, Canna, Eilean-Shona, Glenuig, Roshven, Lochsheil or Dorlin, and Glenmoidart, but Inverailort, Arisaig proper, Benbecula, and South Uist, were steadily got rid of, until at length nothing remained of what was once something like a principality save the little, barren, uninhabited island of Risca, in Loch Moidart, and the roofless walls of Castle Tirrim.

The estates thus disposed of, after being five hundred years in the family, were purchased by the following parties:—The island of Canna, by Mr Macneil, chief tenant and factor on the island; Eigg, by Professor Macpherson, of the Aberdeen University; Lochsheil and Eilean-Shona, by Alexander Macdonald of Glenaladale, about the year 1811; Glenmoidart, by Macdonald, banker, of Dalelea, about 1814; Glenuig, by Major Macdonald of Bail Finlay in Uist, said to be represented to-day by Captain Macdonald of Waternish in Skye; Inverailort, by General Cameron, previously living at Erroch in Lochaber. Arisaig was purchased by Clanranald's second wife, Lady Ashburton, who bequeathed it to Lord Cranstoun; the latter very soon after sold it to Mackay, Big House, who sold it to the late Mr Astley of Duckinfield. South Uist and Benbecula were sold in 1837 to Colonel Gordon of Cluny, an Aberdeenshire gentleman, through whom the property came to the present owner, Lady Gordon Cathcart.

Although thus busy disintegrating what his ancestors had guarded and preserved with so much jealous care, the late chief showed any amount of energy in vindicating his claim to be the real head of the Clanranald. This title, which had hitherto never been disputed either in his own person or in that of his ancestors, was assumed by Glengarry, whose excessive vanity was perpetually leading him into some absurdity or other. A very animated controversy was carried on between the two chiefs in the public prints of the time, and is not devoid of literary merit; but the interest which the reader begins to take in it, is rudely shaken by the bitter reflection that while the disputants are fighting over a title, they were both at the time doing all in their power, by the extravagance of their manner of living, to rob that title of all that could give it any substance or real dignity.

When all was gone, Clanranald had to live more than thirty years regretting, when too late, the miserable causes which brought on his frightful shipwreck.

He was married three times; first, to Lady Caroline Edgecombe; secondly, to Lady Ashburton; and later in life to Miss Newman.

No family throughout its history has ever been more deeply cherished among its tenants and adherents than that of the Clanranalds, and deservedly so, for, independently of the chivalrous qualities which distinguished them as leaders of the clan, they won a name for justice, humanity, and sympathy with their people, which to the very last remained unclouded. Sterling virtues of this character will not easily perish from the memory of those Macdonalds who consider themselves closely or remotely allied to the great branch once ruled by this generous and distinguished house.

The present representative is Sir Reginald Macdonald, K.C.S.I., admiral in the British navy.

As it will help to bring before the reader a fuller view of the district, we shall take up in succession those portions in Moidart that became detached from the Clanranald family, and continue briefly the account of the various changes which have come over them from that time till now.

Glenuig, as already stated, was purchased by Major Allan Macdonald in 1827. It was sold again to Dr Martin in 1834, who also acquired Roshven. After being twenty years in the possession of Martin, Glenuig was purchased by Alexander Stewart, Esq., late tenant of Glenforslan; while Roshven was disposed of to the present owner, Professor Blackburn. The chief residence on Glenuig was the college built at Samalaman by the Highland bishops in 1770. They had, after the burning of the small houses on the island at the foot of Loch Morar, removed to Buorblach nearer the sea coast, and for some years opened a very humble establishment, at which the young students destined for the priesthood were instructed in a preparatory course of Greek and Latin, besides a more comprehensive one of English literature.[2] The aspirants were then sent abroad to the Scots colleges at Paris, Ratisbon, Valladolid, and Rome, where they entered on a fuller course of studies suited to their profession, and seldom returned to their native country until they were ordained priests,—that is to say, ten years or so after they had left it. This custom prevailed also at Scalan in Banffshire,[3] and has been continued among the Catholic clergy of Scotland to this day, although Ratisbon has been given up. Sometimes a few of the students, for certain reasons, commenced and finished the full course at the home establishments, and were among friends called "heather priests"; but in point of attainments they were little or if at all inferior to the others, sometimes indeed, owing to individual character or personal talents, they were far superior. Buorblach was closed under Bishop Alexander Macdonald, who transferred the teachers and the students to his new house at Samalaman. This building has been slightly altered since that time, one of the wings, for instance, which used to be the students' study-room, having been completely removed. The flower-garden also, between the two wings, and facing the porch, has disappeared. Some of the rooms are likewise differently arranged; but in its general outlines the college is very much as it was when Bishop Macdonald, and his successor Bishop John Chisholm, dwelt in it. Among others who studied here were:—The Rev. J. Lamont, who died at Glengarry in 1820. The Rev. Anthony Macdonald, for more than thirty years priest in charge of Eigg and Canna. He was a most worthy clergyman, whose name to this day is fondly remembered among the islanders. Mr Angus Mac Eoin bhàin vich Eachen, who in after years became bishop in North America. The Rev. Charles Macdonald, a native of Moidart, who after becoming priest was appointed to the mission of Knoydart, where he spent the greatest part of his life. He died at Borrodale. One of the earliest teachers at Samalaman was the Rev. Allan Macdonald, who at one time was professor at Valladolid. He died in 1788. The bishops used to officiate in a thatched house, which served as chapel for the congregation, and which was situated near the shore within a few hundred yards of Samalaman. In 1804 the college and the bishop's residence were transferred to the island of Lismore, principally with the view of getting into easier communications with the south; but from all accounts it would have been much wiser to have clung to the arrangement made by Bishop Macdonald, and to have remained at Samalaman. After their departure the house and grounds were let by Clanranald to a Mr Chisholm, father of the late Mrs Macdonald, Tormore, in Skye. This gentleman, during a long life marked by prudence and wise economy, succeeded in amassing a considerable fortune, part of which was sunk in the purchase of Glenmoidart, or Lochans, for the benefit of his son Lachlan. Chisholm was succeeded, as tenant, by a Mr M'Guarry, native of Mull, who laid claim to a valuable estate in that island. The case was tried before Lord Patrick Robertson, but went against M'Guarry, much to the indignation of his friends and many Highlanders, who seemed to think that his right was solid enough to be in justice incontestable.

A good deal of odium has reflected on the judge, who, if the story is to be believed, stated in open court that he attached little weight to the evidence of any Highland witness, for the latter could be got to swear falsely by the bribe of one glass of whisky. The story however sounds apocryphal, in spite of its currency in the western Highlands. M'Guarry, who had hitherto done well in Australia, was ruined by this litigation. After living for some years at Samalaman he removed to Campbeltown, or to some other part of Argyllshire. The next occupier was the new proprietor Mr Stewart, whose family, originally from Lochaber, settled in Moidart about the beginning of the present century, and for a long period were tenants of Glenaladale and Glenforslan farms. It was while Mr Stewart was in possession that the college was struck one winter night by lightning, the building on this occasion being greatly damaged, and the inmates making a most miraculous escape from destruction. When daylight appeared, the house looked as if it had passed through a siege,—roof, windows, and chimney-stalks were completely demolished, while large rents gaped in each of the gables. Parts of the masonry, after being hurled up in the air, seemed to have come down upon the roof, crashing through the upper and lower stories and alighting on the ground floor. The interior was a scene of indescribable confusion, the furniture being overturned in most of the rooms and buried under piles of lath and plaster. The corridors were in some parts blocked up to within two or three feet of the ceiling, while everything in the shape of glass or crystal was shivered to pieces. Had a few shells exploded within the premises, the ruin could scarcely have looked more awful. This took place between midnight and the early morning, the inmates, until so rudely awakened by the thunderbolt, being buried in slumber. Their escape, as stated, was extraordinary, not a single individual being hurt or touched, or having suffered from anything beyond the violent mental shock. A loaded gun, suspended close to the shepherd's bed, and within a few inches of his head, had its barrel twisted and its muzzle fused by the electric fluid, without the charge going off. A large stone built into the wall, and supporting a chimney lintel, was violently detached, flung across the room, and, after grazing the face of one of the maids, alighted between her head and the adjoining wall. In one of the upper rooms a bedstead was crushed to pieces by a fragment of masonry, which penetrated to the room below, its occupant, a niece of the proprietor, having only left the house to rejoin her own family twenty-four hours previously. The lady has since become a nun. It was after a considerable interval, and with much difficulty, that the laird contrived to reach the ground floor and to communicate with the other members of the household, whom he found assembled, pale and almost speechless with consternation, in his mother's room. Satisfied that none of them were injured, he groped his way back to his bedroom, where, as he used to assure his friends, he carefully dressed himself; but on descending sometime afterwards, he made the discovery, or rather it was made for him, that although properly equipped in everything, even to shoes and stockings, he had quite omitted to invest himself in his inexpressibles! In recalling these scenes, this worthy laird never hesitated in affirming his belief that a special Providence seemed to guard the bedroom in which he was sleeping, this being the bedroom formerly used by the bishops, and, singularly enough, the only one that escaped without injury amid the general wreck. The adjoining rooms on each side of it were completely ruined. A small corner cut off in the attics also escaped, but as to the particular kind of genius watching over it he was not so.sure. It contained his whiskey and stores of wine, all quite safe. Probably it was benign. The one person who seemed to retain any presence of mind was his mother, who was then nearly ninety years of age, but she was a remarkable woman in every way. While the confusion was at its height, she gave her orders to the panicstricken servants with a clearness, promptitude, and decision that would have done honour to any general rallying his disordered troops under some sudden disaster, or extricating them from some deplorable mess. It was entirely due to her coolness that something like order and confidence was restored. This lady lived to the age of one hundred and two years, retaining the possession of her faculties to the very last. In her youth she had conversed with many persons who had been out in the '45, and being blessed with a wonderful strength and clearness of judgment, as well as with a most retentive memory, her reference to those times, as well as to the state of the country during the great wars with Napoleon, never failed to create the liveliest interest among her hearers. She was intimately acquainted with the history of almost every family of any note in Lochaber, Moidart, and the surrounding districts, and seemed to have their bewildering genealogies at her finger ends. The laird himself had studied, when a boy, under the bishops in Lismore. He then proceeded to France, where he was a pupil in one of the best educational houses of the time for eight or nine years. Strangers thrown into his company used to stare at finding a sheep farmer quoting Horace and Virgil, and discussing the classics with the ease and familiarity of a scholar. Never having married, he left the estate to the present owner, his nephew. He was one of the warmest-hearted and most hospitable lairds of his time.

After Ranald-Kinloch's death, the tenancy of Roshven seems to have gone to the elder Dr Maceachan, a native of Arisaig, and to have been transmitted after the beginning of the present century to his son John, who was also, although improperly, styled "doctor." A few Cameron families who had holdings in the same place disappear from the scene, their descendants still surviving in the south and about Langal on the Lochshiel estate. Like a good many others in his time, Dr Maceachan is said to have been deeply engaged in smuggling, he being the chief owner of a notorious craft called the "Little Katie," which used to visit the Orkneys, the Baltic, and the Faroe Islands, and to dispose of its cargoes among the isles and along the western mainland of Scotland. After many successful voyages it suddenly disappeared, and for a year or more its fate was wrapped up in mystery, the general impression being that it had been overtaken by some great storm and had foundered. But after a time letters came to the country from the captain and crew, announcing that their vessel had been captured off the Faroe Islands by an Algerine pirate, and that they were at the time of writing languishing in captivity in the Dey's stronghold of Algiers. Knowing that the price of their ransom might not be within the means of the owners, the unfortunate men prayed hard to have their case made known by the latter to the British Government, so as to obtain its intervention. These entreaties were renewed, it is said, more than once; but whatever steps were taken, if any, no assistance could be given, the British Government probably having much more serious business to attend to at the time than the delivery of a few troublesome smugglers. Nothing more was ever heard of the men, and it is surmised that they were either sold as slaves, or that they were carried off by disease during their confinement. But after the bombardment of Algiers by Lord Exmouth, a Scotch merchant ship called at the port, and one of the hands, a Mull man, is credibly asserted to have identified the "Little Katie" drawn up on the beach, slowly decaying from neglect and old age. It was while visiting Dr Maceachan's son John, that Sime Og of Morar met with the accident by which he lost his life, about the year 1807. He breathed his last just as Father Norman Macdonald, who had been hurriedly sent for, was approaching the house. John gave up the farm soon afterwards, and went to the United States, where he came to a considerable accession of property left by his half-brother Allan; but he mysteriously disappeared one Christmas night, without leaving any trace to help his friends in ascertaining what had become of him. The general opinion was that he was waylaid and foully murdered.

The next tenant was a certain Captain Ranald, who was succeeded, although not immediately, by Lachlan Chisholm. The latter gave way to Dr Martin, who, after purchasing from Major Macdonald in 1834, fixed upon Roshven as his place of residence, and continued in it until the acquisition of another estate induced him to remove to the island of Skye. Professor Blackburn bought Roshven in 1855. The great improvements on this property during the last thirty years, being conducted with much taste and judgment, have made Roshven one of the loveliest places in the western Highlands.

In Eilean Shona, one of the best known men, before the end of the last century, was Andrew Macdonald mac Aonghuis vich Ian. He had the farm of Baily, and is still remembered as one of the most daring smugglers who trafficked along the western coast. He was well known to the Government officers, and although often chased was never captured, his coolness and boldness, joined to his excellent skill as a seaman, carrying him safely through every danger. His vessel was as notorious as the "Little Katie." There is a tradition that Andrew having on one occasion taken in a cargo of smuggled goods at the Faroe Islands, proceeded to dispose of it at Loch Boisdale, but shortly after reaching this port his crew were filled with dismay at perceiving a revenue cutter suddenly appear in the offing, its course evidently being directed towards the spot where they were anchored. In their alarm the men wished to land and leave their vessel to its fate, but Andrew, scouting the suggestion, ordered them to busy themselves without any fuss about their usual work on deck, promising them that if they kept cool he would bring them all safely through this disagreeable crisis. Assuming, an air of the utmost unconcern, he leant over the bulwark, and calmly awaited the approach of the cutter. The latter soon came up, and anchored close to the smuggler, when the captain perceiving Macdonald, and identifying him, challenged him as to the kind of cargo, if any, he had on board. To this Andrew promptly replied, that his cargo was of the very best, being made up of silks, gin, brandy, and tobacco, and other goods of a miscellaneous character, not an article of which had paid duty to the king, that the opportunity was a golden one, and that the captain should come over and seize it without a moment's delay. The retort to this was a polite message shouted to Andrew to betake himself to the hottest regions, ending with, " Your saucy tongue will be better bridled when you have something to conceal."

Andrew's family emigrated to America, some of his descendants at this day being among the leading men of business in the Dominion.

Another famous smuggler was Black Ranald, a native of Eigg.

Being once hotly pursued, while engaged in one of his illegal expeditions, he sought refuge in Loch Moidart, on gaining the entrance to which he ran his vessel into a narrow creek opposite Eilean-Shona, on the Ardnamurchan side. By lowering his masts he concealed himself so effectively that the revenue crew swept past, being under the impression that he had gone up the loch towards Risca, where they expected to secure him. Allowing them go some distance on this false move, Ranald rehoisted his masts and sails, and, making for the open sea, was soon scudding away towards the Point of Ardnamurchan. One of his sons was as noted as himself for his boldness and skill in these daring enterprises, and it is a tradition that, being once boarded in a calm off the Ardnamurchan coast by a party of revenue men, he, instead of surrendering, fought them, and, getting the upperhand, deprived them of their arms, which he threw into the sea. He then unceremoniously tumbled his adversaries into their own boat, with the mocking assurance that the Government would comfort them, and, like a tender mother, pour oil into their wounds. He was outlawed for this outrage, and for a long time was eagerly sought after among the isles and along the coast; but he left the country, or was so well kept hid among his friends that the officers of justice never got hold of him. A brother of his, however, who bore a strong personal resemblance to him, was seized at Greenock in his stead, and, by mistake, was made to suffer. He resisted the officers, and during the scuffle received a wound, to which he ultimately succumbed. This pernicious and demoralising habit of defrauding the revenue was carried on to such an extent, that for many years before the end of the last and after the beginning of the present century the Government seemed powerless to cope with it. Directly or indirectly almost every class in the Highlands countenanced it. The more daring imported their smuggled goods from abroad, and found ready customers among the well-to-do farmers and the gentry, while the smaller folks worked at their illicit stills, and carried their whiskey to the merchants in the nearest villages and towns who were in league with them. There is scarcely an estate in some parts of the western

Highlands which is not studded over with the vestiges of those "sma" stills. Vessels used to call at Loch Moidart with cargoes of barley from Uist and Tyree to be converted into malt, and depart with cargoes of wood. The effects on the character of the people may be judged from the fact, that on Sundays, when coming to church, it was not an unusual practice for some of the congregations to bring bottles of whiskey with them, which they drank, in small groups, while sitting outside waiting for the service to begin, or which they discussed when the service was over. At funerals the consumption was excessive, often leading to very disgraceful scenes. Smuggling came to an end in Moidart about fifty years ago, this result being largely brought about by the establishment of excise officers in the district.[4] Two were stationed in succession at Eignaig, and another at Briaig. One of the last smugglers chased by the revenue officers was a native of Langal, while creeping down along the coast of Ardnamurchan with a cargo of whiskey which he was to deliver at Tobermory. He was sighted, and turning back reached the North Channel, where with the assistance of some of the Eilean Shona people he got rid of his dangerous cargo, which was immediately hidden away among the ferns and heather towards the east end of Shona. Before reaching Dorlin he was overhauled by the pursuers; but, to their disappointment, they only found a bag of potatoes, some salt fish, a small supply of meal, and a creel or two of peats in his boat. One of the cleverest and most esteemed clergymen attached for more than thirty years to one of the next districts, and who was well known to every one in Moidart, was in his younger days an uncompromising smuggler, and through smuggling may be said to have made the discovery that his true vocation lay in the direction of the altar. He and some companions, all natives of Deeside in Aberdeenshire, were conveying their smuggled goods on one occasion to the city, when at a certain bend of the road they came suddenly face to face with a party of mounted excise officers, to escape from whom under the circumstances was impossible. The smugglers were on foot, leading the horses which were carrying the kegs of whiskey, and

realising the hopelessness of their position, quietly surrendered,—
all except our friend, who, severing the ropes which tied the kegs,
and letting the latter fall to the ground, sprung on the pony's back
and galloped away as fast as the legs of his hardy animal could take
him. rhe leader of the excise party immediately gave chase, and for
some time steadily gained on the fugitive, the distance between the
two being reduced to a few yards. Not making much of it after this,
and his horse being unequal to a continuation of the wild pace at
which they were going, he twice called on the smuggler to stop, but
the latter paying no heed he drew his pistol and fired. The smuggler
was wounded in the leg, but in spite of this continued his flight,
and after another mile or so struck off into the rough ground
leading to the hills and made his escape. For six months he kept
very quiet; but when his wound was sufficiently healed, he
ventured into Aberdeen at an early hour on a winter morning, with
the intention of communicating once more with some of his
customers regarding the delivery of another supply of smuggled
goods. Not a person seemed stirring in the city, and he was almost
congratulating himself on the success of the journey, when, at the
head of Union Street, he found himself confronted by his late
pursuer. The latter had issued from some close, and casually
glancing at the stranger recognised him at once. Uttering a very
rough oath, he made an instant attempt at seizure; but in doing so
got a vigorous blow on the head from the other's cudgel, which sent
him sprawling and senseless into the gutter. The assailant had to
take to immediate flight, and in consequence of his being outlawed
had soon afterwards to leave his native district. He obtained a
situation in Glasgow, and while in this city signalised himself by
gallantly jumping into the Clyde and, at considerable risk, rescuing
an unfortunate man who was drowning. He then seems to have
entertained the idea of becoming a priest, and on consulting one of
the Catholic bishops was first sent to Lismore, and subsequently to
France, where he spent many years. Although promoted to the
priesthood, it was not judged expedient to bring him back to
Scotland until his former collision with the law was laid before the

Lord Advocate, who without any difficulty promised that it would be completely condoned and forgotten. For the rest of his life he devoted himself to the zealous discharge of his duties, in the exercise of which he particularly proved himself the largehearted and constant friend of the poor, while, as an antithesis to former principles, he steadily upheld not only temperance but total abstinence. This last part of his doctrines provoked some dissenter to make the suggestion that he should be styled the Priest of Castle Tiorm—i.e., the dry castle.[5] The fate of the officer with whom he was brought in conflict was very remarkable, he was the last man hanged in Scotland for trying to defraud an insurance company.

Eilean-Shona was bought from Clanranald by Alexander Macdonald of Glenaladale for £3000, who bequeathed it at his death to Archibald Macdonald of Rhu; but in this disposition the house at Bailly was reserved by Macdonald as a residence for his mother, rent free, during her lifetime. This lady, called Bean-a'ghlinne, came to live in it in 1814, and occupied it till 1840, the date of her death. She was a sister of Rhu's wife, and closely related to the Rev. Mr M'Gregor who about fifty or sixty years ago was minister of the *quoad sacra* parish of Aharacle. She is said to have been a person of the most amiable disposition, gentle, forbearing, and generous almost to a fault. After her death an English gentleman, Mr Easdale, became for several years the tenant. He got a lease of the house, of the salmon fishing on the river Shiel, and of the shootings on the Ardnamurchan property from Kintra to Achnanellan, about six miles in extent, for £140 per annum, a bargain that sportsmen nowadays only meet with in their dreams.

In 1853 the island was sold by the late Lochshiel, son of Rhu, to Captain Swinburne, R.N., for £6,500.

The eastern extremity of the island, called Shona Beg, seems, through some incongruity which is not easily explained, to have always formed part of the Kinloch estate. It was reserved at the sale of the latter for a connection of the family, who has done wonders in improving and beautifying it. Those who knew it a few years ago would have characterised it without a moment's hesitation as a desolate little wilderness. One of the properties in the district which oftener than any other has passed from one owner to another, since it was sold by Clanranald, is that of Lochans, or Glenmoidart. It has been in the hands of Banker Macdonald, Lachlan Chisholm, Captain Grimstone, General Ross, and has finally been acquired by Mr Stuart of Kinloch. Although small in size, it has many attractions, the house, for instance, being picturesquely situated in front of the river Moidart and of a small lake through which the latter flows on its way to the lower end of the glen. This house was enlarged by General Ross, to whom also are due the fine plantations in its vicinity, and which help so much in diversifying the scenery of the place. It is now being pulled down in order to make way for a larger building. This estate seems to have been rather neglected in Banker Macdonald's time, who although possessing it for many years only came to reside on it a short time before his death. As a quiet retreat for an old soldier, glad to rest after an active life and to be finally done with arms and camps, no spot could be imagined more appropriate; and it was in this sense that it was viewed by the late General, who resided most of the year on it, and was extremely attached to it. Being a bachelor, the worthy veteran found full scope for adhering to old habits, and gladly established his government on the principles of a modified military despotism, to the good no doubt, although not always to the comfort, of those under him. Under a stiff and somewhat stern demeanour he concealed a warm and generous heart, to which those in want or in any difficulty could always find easy access. He died at Glenmoidart, regretted by the whole district.

Mr Archibald Macdonald of Rhu, who inherited Lochshiel estate from Alexander Macdonald of Glenaladale, was a son of John Macdonald, the companion of the Prince during part of his wanderings, and the writer of the journal quoted in a former chapter; but although thus made proprietor, he never came over to reside on the estate, owing probably to the house at Dalelea, which was the only suitable one on it, being let with the farm on a long lease to Banker Macdonald, who had installed his brother-in-law,

Donald, Lochans. He continued accordingly to reside at Rhu, much to the delight of his old friends and acquaintances of every class in that part of the country, where Macdonald, owing to the geniality of his disposition, and to the frank unstinted hospitality which he at all times displayed, was extremely popular. His house at Rhu was a sort of recognised resting stage for the gentlemen farmers of the small isles, who on their way to and from the southern markets were able to appreciate to the fullest the advantage of being guests under such a hospitable roof; for towards the end of autumn, when the last markets were over, these gentlemen were not unfrequently prevented for days and weeks, by the storminess of the weather, from venturing out into the wild seas separating them from their own homes. On such occasions their stay used to give rise to a considerable amount of festive conviviality, which helped, to the satisfaction of the host, his family, and their guests, in getting over pleasantly a period of the year which in most places is apt to be dull enough, at any rate in the Highlands. There was a sort of programme which, day after day, suffered little variation. It was something like this, as one of the members of the family used afterwards to describe it:—On coming down to the parlour, each guest was helped by the host to the morning dram, i.e., a small glass of whiskey flavoured with the extract of gentian and camomile. This was, of course, in consonance with a habit which then universally prevailed among the better-to-do classes in the Highlands, to keep out the damp, as they used to say, and which is not altogether extinct yet. One steady upholder of the habit, who was nevertheless not an intemperate man, used to help himself to a double dose; but by way of justification used occasionally to address the bottle, giving it at the same time a slight shake, "You are none the worse of it, while I feel all the better of it,"—"Cha mishde thu-sa e, agus 's fhèirrde mise e." Breakfast was a very solid business, which, in addition to coffee, eggs, meat, with scones of wheat, oat, and barley meal, often comprised potatoes and salt herrings, a dish to which most Highlanders are partial, and which can commend itself at all times to the appetite of any healthy man, be he Celt or Saxon. After breakfast, the guests at Rhu took a stroll outside to have a look at the weather, when their host invariably made the discovery that the sky was not one to tempt any Christian to venture out to sea, or that the sea was too boisterous for any boat to live in, and that his guests, for that day, must obey the will of Providence and stick to the mainland. On re-entering the house, the party betook themselves to reading, or to a game of backgammon, or to any other light amusement which the host could supply, and which suited the taste of his guests. As a rule they all knew how to make themselves comfortable and to pass the time agreeably, especially when the wind was howling outside, and the rain or the hailstones beating against the windows. At midday the bottle appeared a second time, and each was helped to his "meridian," the time for taking this little consolation being announced by the host declaring that "the sun had crossed the mainyard." Dinner was served at two or three o'clock, to be followed by the traditional tumbler or tumblers of toddy. When the candles were lighted, the ladies and gentlemen made up parties for a game of whist, while the host, taking down his fiddle, entertained them with a performance on this difficult instrument, of which he was said to be a perfect master. After supper there was generally a dance, the fiddle being again brought into requisition, or a piper was introduced by way of variation. The merriment was kept up till eleven o'clock at night, or later, until the ladies withdrew to their own quarters, when the gentlemen sat down once more to their toddy, which they continued to imbibe until they were reminded of the poet's warning, "Nunc suadent cadentia sidera somnos."[6] In some years, when the weather was exceptionally bad, this style of living has been known to be kept up at Rhu for weeks together; and in most of the Highland houses, where a few visitors happened to call at the same time, the same method of passing the stormy months was pretty much resorted to.

Macdonald had a wonderful tact in preventing or allaying quarrels. When Glengarry, on a certain occasion, was getting very hot over some dispute with some Skye gentlemen at a public dinner in Portree, and his violence likely to lead to a disgraceful scene, Macdonald mounted on the table, and went through every step of a Highland reel without once touching any of the glasses or dishes spread over it. This, considering that he was not by any means a light weight, put all the guests in good humour, and sent the demon of discord elsewhere. His goodness to the poor is remembered in the district, and draws down the blessing of the more helpless among the crofters to this day; for if a poor man lost his cow, or if a family was-in want of meal, "fear Rhu" was always the first one they applied to for help, and from all accounts never in vain. This excellent gentleman died about sixty years ago, and was buried at Arisaig; but when the rest of the family came over to Moidart and took possession of Dalelea, his remains were raised from their old resting-place and placed in Eilean-Fhionnan. He left a large family of sons and daughters. None of the former ever married except John, who was an officer in the British army, and who went through the whole of the Peninsular war under Wellington, being present at almost all the chief engagements, as well as later on at Waterloo, without receiving a single serious wound. The letters written by him during that period to his family give a good idea of the terrible sufferings which the soldiers had to go through in those campaigns. He died at Gibraltar, without leaving any surviving issue. The property was left to Alexander, who unfortunately had few of the business habits of his father, and under whom from various causes—especially the great failure of the potato crop in 1846, which threatened to involve the western Highlands in a general famine, and which necessitated measures of public relief on the part of Government—the difficulties of management increased to such an extent that it was no longer self-supporting. Various schemes were suggested to retrieve it from this hopeless condition, but the one which found favour, and which was acted upon, was to remove most of the population, and to place their holdings under sheep. In this way Dorlin, Scardoish, Portabhata, Briaig, and Mingarry were swept clean, the majority of the crofters being sent away to Australia, while a few migrated to the south, or got the offer of settling down in less favourable localities of the estate. Some of the Eilean Shona tenants were sent away at the same time, as the island had not yet been sold to Captain Swinburne. They were accompanied by most of the tenants of Glenuig, who, although under no pressure, seemed glad to avail themselves of the opportunity of trying their fortunes in the same colony, and their example was followed by the Caolas tenants. The priest of the district, Father Ranald Rankin, was himself an outspoken advocate in behalf of emigration, and, convinced from his thorough knowledge of the people and the resources of the district that living here could never in the generality of cases be far from the verge of pauperism, did all in his power to get his flock to view the abandonment of their old homes with courage, promising to go forth with them, and to settle in their midst in any part of the world. The bulk of the emigrants reached Port Philip in 1852, their numbers being increased by other bands during the two following years. In July 1855, the priest, having obtained the sanction of his bishop, was able to make good his promise, and rejoined those who had gone away before him. Altogether about five hundred persons left the district, the Catholic congregation of Moidart, which formerly stood at eleven hundred, being reduced to six hundred.[7] One would like to be able to add that these Highlanders, thus cast upon a new world, with opportunities offered of realising a position which they could never have dreamed of at home, did well; and no doubt when the parties were sober and industrious, the exchange led to a material progress, which one takes a pleasure in recalling; but, unfortunately, many of them had not the moral courage to shake off certain habits which the smuggling days had instilled, and continuing to indulge these under the burning climate of Australia proved a deplorable bar to any real improvement. It must however be remembered that several left the old country against their will, and these, in spite of every encouragement, never took kindly to the new one, and utterly failed in accommodating themselves to their altered circumstances. Their children, it is to be hoped, proved wiser. In spite of these clearances, the financial difficulties of the Lochshiel estate continued as they were before, or rather increased, so that it was with the view of obtaining a better price, when the property should be thrown into the market, that a new house was built at Dorlin to serve as the future residence of the purchaser. Towards the end of 1855, Alexander, or Lochsheil as he was more frequently called, was successful in inducing Mr Hope Scott to buy it for £24,000. From this time an era of prosperity set in, which happily has not been seriously interrupted. The good done by Mr Hope Scott is sufficiently recorded, in spite of several blunders, by his biographer, Mr Ornsby.[8] To Mr Hope Scott are due the present large Dorlin mansion, completed in 1864, the excellent roads opening up various parts of the estate, the first attempts at improving the dwellings and the lands of the small tenants, and the erection of the church and school at Mingarry.[9] He was succeeded in 1871 by the late Lord Howard of Glossop, who during the next twelve years took a deep interest in the property, spending large sums of money upon it, and doing all that a wise and enlightened policy could suggest, to overcome the difficulties naturally opposed to the improvement of land like this, and of the condition of the people attached to it. How far he has succeeded only those can fairly judge who, knowing how matters stood before they came under his control, were witnesses of the thorough transformation which came over the whole estate before he died. It was a constant axiom with this energetic and clear-headed nobleman, that on small estates like Dorlin, or on larger ones, the real way to improve the condition of the people was, where not too numerous for the efforts of one man, to enlarge their holdings, and to give them facilities for maintaining an increase of stock. A steady pursuance of this system would, he believed, ultimately tend to convert crofters into a well-to-do class of small farmers, and thus do away with the two great drawbacks telling against crofter estates, viz., a population looking to the proprietor for employment, and brought to the verge of starvation when this is not got, and the perpetuation of a class who are the chronic feeders of the pauper rolls in the parishes where these estates are situated. Although not averse to their emigrating to the colonies, he had a positive horror of Highland families being drafted into the cities, where, as he alleged, they had little chance of escaping contamination both in their health and in their morals. In these views he was so far consistent, that to the very last he strenuously acted up to them.

He died in December 1883 and was succeeded by his only son, the present Lord Howard, who inherited Lochshiel, as well as the English estates belonging to the family.

Notes

1   It has been calculated that landowners' profits on kelp increased nine-fold between the 1720s and the 1780s, while prices paid to the tenants who gathered it only doubled. By far the most abundant sources were in the Hebrides, and the greatest of all on the Clanranald estate of Uist, but some was also harvested on the West coast of the mainland. Kinlochmoidart Estate papers for 1784-5 mention eight tenants who made kelp, five from Kyles Ian Og and three from Kyles Mor. The process involved gathering weed, drying and burning it, after which it was shipped to the Clyde for use in bleaching and the manufacture of glass and soap. Prices peaked during the Napoleonic Wars, but the peace, and a series of Acts favouring alternative methods of manufacture, brought a massive decline in the industry in the 1820s.

2   The author's account implies a direct move to Buorblach after the burning of the school on *Eilean Bàn,* Loch Morar, in 1746. In fact *Eilean Bàn* had not been used after 1737, when the seminary moved to Guidale (or Gaotal) in Arisaig. Both places were destroyed by Government forces in 1746, and there was no seminary in the West until 1768 when one was briefly established at Glenfinnan. The farm at Buorblach was used 1770-79, and the house at Samalaman, Moidart from 1783-1803.

3   Scalan had first opened in 1717, following the closure of the original school on *Eilean Bàn* (see chapter vii, note 9), and until 1732 had served as the junior seminary for the whole Scottish Mission. From then on it became the seminary for the Lowland District, while the schools listed in note 2 served the Highland District. It too was destroyed by Government forces in 1746, but re-opened the following year. Over one hundred priests and six bishops received all or part of their training within its walls. With the abolition of most of the Penal Laws in 1793 the Catholic Church was able to take a more open profile, and Scalan's remoteness, previously a necessity, now became a disadvantage. It was closed in 1799, the scholars moving into much larger and more accessible premises at Aquhorties in Aberdeenshire.

4   Distilling was a domestic industry in the Highlands in the eighteenth century, with many farm towns owning a small pot or still and the tenants sharing the costs and the profits. But legislation passed in the 1780s imposed

a heavy licence on whisky manufacture and defined a minimum size for stills, so effectively putting small-scale Highland distilling beyond the Law. As a result the "sma' stills" went underground, and liquor smuggling became both necessary and profitable. It was the successive relaxation of the Laws after 1815, as well as the more effective deployment of excise officers, that took away the profit and the need.

Funerals, which brought people together from far and wide, were sometimes made the opportunity for settling old scores. After one particularly drunken fight Father Charles imposed a penance on the combatants to spend an hour each alone at night among the gravestones on the Green Isle!

5   The smuggler-turned-priest was William MacIntosh. He was born in Glenmuick near Ballater, Aberdeenshire. After training at the Highland seminary of Lismore and at St Sulpice, Paris, he was ordained in 1831 at the late age of 37. After a spell as teacher at Blairs College and a brief posting to Barra, he was assigned to Arisaig and served there until his death forty years later in 1877.

6   *"Suadentque cadentia sidera somnos"* — and the setting stars counsel sleep — Virgil, *Aeneid*, 4,81.

7   Some Moidart tenants sailed to Port Philip, Victoria, on the ship *Allison* in 1852, and more on the *Hornet* in 1854, but documented numbers were small. The greatest concentration of Catholic Highland settlers was at Little River, thirty miles from Melbourne, and also at Belmont, a suburb of Geelong. Father Ranald Rankin made Little River his home from 1857. Moidart families were still also taking the traditional emigration route to America after the Famine, one group reaching Giants Lake,Guysburgh, Nova Scotia about 1848, and another, which included Lochshiel tenants, sailing in 1850.

8   Ornsby, Robert, *Memoirs of James Hope-Scott of Abbotsford, with selections from his correspondence*, 2 volumes (London, 1884).

9   The previous church was at Dorlin, near Castle Tioram and close to the gardens of Mr Hope-Scott's recently built Dorlin House. Hope-Scott paid for the new church at Mingarry, which was opened in 1862, to give parishioners a more central venue and his own home privacy from the crowds.

Appendix 1
Place Names and Personal Names

This Appendix is included to help readers who may have difficulty with some of the names of places and people referred to in the text.

Nearly all the place names derive originally from Gaelic, or in a few cases from Norse or a combination of both languages. Some of the older ones, particularly, through being handed down by word of mouth, gradually changed from their original form over time. And when, more recently, place names came to be written down, on maps or estate accounts etc, it was English speakers who recorded them, expressing the sounds as best they could according to the rules of English spelling. In most cases the approximation was reasonably close — *Dail an leigh* ('the meadow of the physician') is recognisable in 'Dalilea', for example — but since such names have no obvious meaning for the English speaking reader, s/he has no guide as to their pronunciation and may be trapped even by the innocent looking ones. How would someone without local knowledge pronounce 'Lochaline', for instance? The Gaelic form (*Loch àlainn*) answers the question — the middle syllable carries the stress, and it must be pronounced long. Or again, how should 'Strontian' be pronounced? The Oxford Dictionary gives the false impression that the place is pronounced like the mineral Strontium named after it with the stress on the 'o'. But again the Gaelic (*Sròn an t-Sithein*) gives the clue that it is the 'i' that takes the stress.

Since his book is written in English, Father Charles MacDonald naturally uses those anglicised forms wherever they exist. There are many West Highland place names, on the other hand, which never acquired an anglicised form. Some are so local as not to figure on even the most detailed modern maps. Typically they refer to a notable feature of the terrain, or are associated with a particular person or happening. Many such names occur in the book — *Loch na Fala* ('the lake of blood'), or *Aite suidhe vich ish Ailein* ('the seat of the son of the son of Allan'), the latter illustrating the further complication of the author's spelling, which is often at variance with modern Gaelic (which in this case would be written *Aite suidhe mhic 'ic Ailein*).

The personal names pose similar problems. They are Gaelic, of course, except in the case of incomers, and follow the traditional manner of naming in Gaelic society, in which one is always called by one's first name and identified by the addition of other names. Most commonly the additions are patronymics, naming the person's father, grandfather, etc; so in the present book we meet *Aonghas mac Eòghainn bhàin mhic Eachainn* ('Angus, son of fair haired Ewan, son of Hector'). Sometimes the addition is a sobriquet, perhaps alluding to a personal characteristic, as with fair haired Ewan above, or with 'left handed Col' (*Coll Ciotach*), or to an event with which the person is associated, as in the case of *Ailean nan Creach* ('Allan of the Plunderings').

As with places so with people the author normally uses the anglicised form, at least for the first name. For the additional names he generally uses Gaelic, but again with a spelling often at variance with modern practice and falling somewhere between the two languages. The resulting form — 'Andrew MacDonald mac Aonghuis vich Ian', for example — is something of a hybrid.

The personal names in the Clanranald list for 1745, quoted by the author on pp 146ff, are a special case. Some of the list's eighteenth century spellings are idiosyncratic to say the least, and for this reason the names have been placed separately in this Appendix, and because they do not occur elsewhere in the book only those that present a difficulty have been included.

The main lists below include every place and personal name mentioned in the text. They are arranged in alphabetical order for easy reference, and contain the following information:

the form as in the text;

the page number of its first appearance;

the page number(s) in parenthesis, of alternative form(s) in the
    text;
the pronunciation, in [ ], except where obvious, using the sound
    equivalents given in the Key;
and for the Gaelic parts of names only —
the standard modern Gaelic form, in italics, where different from
    the text;
the English meaning, in ( );
and in the case of place names —
the grid reference for the appropriate map in Appendix II.

A caveat regarding pronunciation: the Key offers the best
approximation that I could make, but it is no more than that. Only
the spoken word — spoken preferably by a *Muideartach!* — would
give the exact sound. The reader would then hear, for instance, the
difficulty of expressing precisely in a key the sound of even so
common a Gaelic word as *beag,* which the Key has as 'bek' but
whose sound really falls somewhere between 'beck' and 'bake'; or
the place name 'Polnish', whose last syllable is nearer to 'niche' than
'nish'. Any Key that aimed to cover every Gaelic sound exactly
would be so complex as to defeat its own purpose. It is hoped,
nonetheless, that the Key provided, along with the lists, will prove
of some help to the reader in recognising, pronouncing and locating
the places and people that appear in the book.

Key to Pronunciation

Consonants

g   hard as in 'girl'
y   as in 'yes'
ɣ   like the y in 'happy'
ch   as in 'church'
<u>ch</u>   as in German 'ich'
gh   between 'g' and 'y'
all others as in English

Vowels

a,e,i,o,u as short vowels in English
ā   as in 'hate'
ē   as in 'feed'
ī   as in 'fire'
ō   as in 'wrote' (but sometimes a little closer to 'wrought')
ū   as in 'brute'
aa   long, as in the second syllable of 'barrage'
au   as in English 'now' or German 'auf'.
aw   as in 'lawn'
ay   as in 'May'
eh   as in the second syllable of 'cortege'
oeu   similar to the French 'oeuf'
oo   as in 'noon'
ə   like the vowel sound in the second syllable of 'constant'
Note   a letter placed in ( ) is barely sounded

Stress

· main stress (placed after vowel of stressed syllable)
: secondary stress (placed after vowel of stressed syllable)

Place Names: Alphabetical List and Gazetteer

Abertarf 39 [a:bər taa·rf]

A'bhrideanach 81 [əvrē·jena<u>ch</u>] iA8

Achadhuan 127 [a:<u>ch</u>əgh oo·ən]

Achnanellan 214 [a:<u>ch</u>nən e·lan] iiF1

Aharacle 15 [aha·rakəl] iiC1

Aite-suidhe vich ish Ailein 93 [aa·chə sū:iə vi<u>ch</u>k i<u>ch</u>k e·līn] *aite suidhe mhic 'ic Ailein* (the seat of the son of the son of Allan) iiC3

Alisary 31 [a·lisərɣ] iiF8

Alt-an-Doran 148 (149) [au:lt ən daw·ran] *allt an dòbhrain* (the otter stream) iiI6

Altegil 183 [au:ltəgi·ly] iiB5

Annat 106 [a·nat] iiG2

Ardeannach 161 [aa:rd je·na<u>ch</u>ɣ (locally)]

Ardnamurchan 1 [aa·rd na mu·rə<u>ch</u>an] iB-D4

Ardnish, Point of 110 [aa:rdnē·sh] iiD9

Ardtoe 59 [aa:rdtō·] iiA2

Ardtornish, Castle [aa:rd to·rnish] iD/E2

Arisaig 2 [a·risayg] iD6

Aros, Castle 50 [a·ros] iD2

Aryean 147 [a:rɣē·en] iiB4

Bail-nan-cailleach 21 [ba·l nan ka·lyə<u>ch</u>] *baile nan cailleach* (the township of the old women)

Bailly 147 (210) [ba·lɣ] iiB4

Balfinlay 148 (202) [balfi·nlɣ]

Barrisdale 171 [ba·rizdel] iF9

Bealach Breac 32 [be·la<u>ch</u> bre·<u>ch</u>k] (the pass of many colours) iiF9

Bloody Bay 28 iC3

Borrodale 143 iD6

Briaig 15 [brē·āik] iiC3

Brunery 37 [broo·nərɣ] iiE3

Bourblach 131 (boo·rbla<u>ch</u>] iD7

Bourbloige 14 [boo·rbloi:g] iC/D4

Camus-a-linne 195 [ka·məs ə lē·ny] iiE8? Location not identified for certain. The name means 'bay of the channel', or — less likely — 'bay of the ship'. Either name makes sense if the location is iiE8, and it is likely that Ulgary people would walk over the hill to this embarkation. A much less likely location is in the Moidart estuary near Risca Island.

Camus-an-talmhuinn 131 [ka·məs ən ta·liny (locally)] iD6. The author's spelling suggests a name derivation of 'bay of the land'; the local pronunciation suggests 'bay of the salt' (*camus an t-salainn*), perhaps a reference to shore-side salt stores dating from the days of the Salt Laws of the eighteenth century.

Camus-nan-Geall 14 [ka·məs nan ge·al] iC3/4

Camustroloman 104 [ka·məs dro·ləman] iiG1

Caolas 146 [koeu·las] (narrow channel) iiC4-5

Castle Tirrim 6 (214) [chi·rəm] *Caisteal tioram* (dry castle) iiB3 (see also Eilean Tirrim)

Ceann-Camuis-Raidh 162 [kyau·n ka·mish rōō·ɣ] (head of the red bay) iD7

Cinn-a'chreagan 127 [ki:n ə <u>chr</u>ā·kan] iiG10. This is the old name for the land on which Inverailort House stands.

Cliff 12 iiC1

Coroghon 74 [ko:rəghaw·n] iA8

Corran 15 [ko·rən] iG4

Corrie-Dhughaill 32 [ko·rə ghoo·əl] *Coire Dhúghaill* (the corrie of Dugald) iE6

Corrie-mhullen 128 [ko·rə voo·lən] *Coire a' mhuilinn* (the corrie of the mill) iC4

Craig-an-airgiod 58 [krā·k ən e·rəgət] *Creag an airgid* (the rock of the silver) iD3

Craig-an-Dùn 164 [krā·k ən doo·n] *Creag an dùin* (the rock of the fort) iiC4

Craig-an-t-Shagart 106 [krā·k ən ta·kərch] *Creag an t-sagairt* (the rock of the priest) iiG1

Crolen 173 [krō·lən] iE9

Dalelea 102 [da:lilay·] ii F2

Dalnambreack 42 [da:l nam bre·chk] *Dail nam breac* (the meadow of the salmon) ii D1/2

Dorlin House 6 iiB3

Drum-a-laoigh 119 [drūi·m ə loeuɣ] *Druim an laoigh* (the ridge of the calf) iiG2

Eigg 3 [ayg] iC6-7

Eignaig 130 [ay·gnik] iiB5

Eilean Fhionnan 32 (102) [eh·lan hē·ənan] *Eilean Fhiònain* (island of Finnan) iiF1 (see also Island Finnan)

Eilean-na-h-acarsaid 11 [eh·lan nə ha·hkərsech] *Eilean na h-acarsaid* (island of the anchorage) iD5

Eilean-nan-Gobhar 16 [eh·lan nən gō·war] *Eilean nan gobhar* (island of the goats) iiD8

Eilean-Raald 107 [eh·lan raa·əld]

Eilean Shona 6 (22) [eh·lan shō·na] ii A-C 4-5

Eilean Tirrim 5 [eh·lan chi·rəm] *Eilean Tioram* (the dry island) iiB3, so called because reached by causeway except at the highest tides.

Eriska 68 (142) [e·riskay]

Erroch 202 [e·rocht] iH6

Fassifern 144 [fa·sife:rn] iG6

Fort-William 3 iG5

Gaotal 156 [goeu·chəl] iD6; see also Guidale

Kilfinnan 98 [kilfi·nan] iI8

Kilmhorie 99 (131) [kil:mərē·] iD6; in the author's day the accent was still on the last syllable, retaining something of the original meaning of 'the Church of St Maolrubha' (compare 'Loch Maree'). Today however it is normally pronounced [kil mo·rɣ] in English speech.

Kinlochaline, Castle 61 [ki:n lochaa·lin] iE2

Kinloch-Aylort 13 [ki:n loch ī·lort] iiG10

Kinlochmoidart 6 [ki:n loch moi·dart] iiD/E3

Kinloch Morar 190 [ki:n loch mō·rar] iF7

Kinlochuachair 195 [ki:n loch ōō· əchər] iiE3

Kintail 24 [kintay·l] iF10

Kintra 58 [kintraa·] iiB1

Knock 193

Knoydart 2 [noi·dart] iD-F 7-9

Laig 133 [layg] iC6

Langal 15 (147) [la·ngal] iiD/E2

Leadnacloiche 142 [led na klo·chə] iiF5

Lochaber, Braes of 88 [loch a·ber] iI6-7

Loch Arkaig 32 [loch aa·rkayg] iG7-H7

Lochalsh 27 [locha·lsh]

Lochan 146 (141) [lo·chən] iiF4, the estate of Glenmoidart House.

Loch Aylort 1 [loch ī·lort] iiD8-G10

Loch Eilt 13 [loch ē·lt] iE6

Loch Etive 12 [loch e·tiv] iF1-H2

Loch Hourn 1 [loch hoo·rn] iE9-F9

Loch Lochy 28 [loch lo·chɣ] iH7-I8

Loch Moidart 1 iiC4-D3 (inner loch)

Loch Morar 1 [loch mō·rar] iD7-F7

Loch Moy 24

Loch-na-Fala 15 [lo:<u>ch</u> na fa·la] (loch of blood) iiC2

Loch-nan-Uamh 1 (143) [lo:<u>ch</u> nən oo·əv] iD6

Loch Nevis 1 iD8-F7/8

Loch Shiel 1 (2) [lo<u>ch</u> shē·l] iD4-F6

Loch Suinart 1 [lo<u>ch</u> su·nart] iD3-E4

Loch Teagus 14 [lo<u>ch</u> chē·akəs] iD3

Meoble 159 [mē·ōbəl] iE7

Mingarry 218 [mi·ngarɣ] iiD1

Mingarry, Castle [mi·ngarɣ] iC4

Morven iD-E 2-3

Mulroy 43 [mulroi·]

North Morar 2 [mō·rar] iD-F 7-8

Pole-a-bhainne 196 [pol: ə vaa·ny] *Poll a'bhainne* (the gully of the milk) iiH6

Polloch 13 [po:l lo-<u>ch</u>] iiH1

Polnish 32 [po:ləni·sh] iiF10

Port-a-bhata 109 (218) [po:rt ə vaa·ta] *Port a'bhàta* (the harbour of the boat) iiC4

Port-na-h-aifrinne 110 [po:rt na hī·rirɐ (locally)] *Port na h-aifrinn* (harbour of the Mass) iiD9

Risca 5 [ri·ska] iiB4

Rhu 172 [roo] iD6

Rhu Ardslignish 14 [roo:ə aa:rd sli·gnish] iC3

Rhu Ardtoe 11 [roo:ə aa:rd tō·] iiA3/4

Rhu Darach 12 [roo: da·ra<u>ch</u>] iiC1

Rhu Shamh-nan-Insir 81 [roo:ə hau·v nan i·nshir] of the several possible meanings for this place name none is entirely satisfactory; iB8

Roshven 6 [ro·shven] iiD8

Rudhasgor nam ban naomha 80 [roo:a skō·r nam ba·n noeu·va]

Rudha-sgùrr nam ban naomha (the headland of the holy women) iA8

Salen 13 [saa·len] iD4

Samalaman 147 [saa·maləman] iiB7

Samhnuich, Well 194 [sau·nēc̱h̲] iiD3

Sandy Island 79 iA8

Sandy Point 106 iiG1

Sanndaig 131 [sa·ndaig] iD6

Scardoish 15 [skaa·rdoi·sh] iiB3-C3

Sgeir nighinn-t-Sheumais 69 [ske·r nē:in hā·mish] *Sgeir nighinne Sheumais* (the rock of James's daughter) iiC4

Shiel, River 2 [shēl] iiB2-C1

Shielfoot 12 iiB2

Skipnish 111 [ski·pnish]

Smerissary 32 [smē·risərɣ] iiB7

South Morar 2 iD7-F7

Strontian 3 [strontē·ən] iE4

Suinart 13 [su·nart] iE4

Tirendrish 153 [tī:rəndri·sh] iH6

Tobermory 28 [tō:bər mō·rɣ] iC3

Tober-nan-ceann 72 [tō·pər nən kyau·n] *Tobar nan ceann* (well of the heads) iI8

Toghmore 47 [tō·mō·r]

Tom-a'chrodhaidh 24 [tō·mə c̱h̲ro·c̱h̲ɣ] *Tom a'chrochaidh* (the knoll of the hanging) iiB3

Tongoi 147 (Tongue 147) [tō·n goeu·i] iiB4. This place name is no longer in use, and neither of the spellings in the text fully indicates how it should be pronounced. The Gaelic original, *Tòn gaoithe*, gives us the pronunciation, and its meaning, 'windy anus', very aptly describes the slit of low land between Eilean Shona and Shona Beag.

Torloisk 194 [to:rloi·sk] iiE3

Torr-a-phrionsa 150 [tō·r ə frē·unsa] *Tòrr a'phrionnsa* (hill of the prince) iE/F5

Torr-na-breith 142 [tō:r na bray·] (hill of judgment) E/F2

Uist 3 [yū·ist]

Ulgary 146 [u·ləgərɣ] iiG6

Waternish 202 [va·ternish]

Personal Names: Alphabetical List

Alasdair-an-Oir 172 [a·laster ən aw·ir] *Alasdair an Òir* (Alexander of the Gold)

Alasdair Mac Mhaighstir Alasdair 117 (128) [a·laster ma<u>ch</u>k vī·shtir a·laster] (Alexander son of Mr Alexander; 'Mr' being the title given to a Minister of the Church, originally a reference to his Master's degree.)

Allan Dearg 87 [je·rak] (Red Allan)

Allan-Mac-Raonuill 102 [ma<u>ch</u>k roeu·nil] *Ailean mac Raghnaill* (Allan son of Ranald)

Allan Mac Ruari 24 [ma<u>ch</u>k roo·ərɣ] *Ailean mac Ruairidh* (Allan son of Roderick)

Allan-nan-Corc 30 [nan kaw·rk] (Allan of the Knives) — but should read 'Allan na Corc' *Ailean na Cuirce* (Allan of the Knive): cf. chapter II, note 4.

Allan-nan-Creach 99 [nan krā·<u>ch</u>] (Allan of the Plunderings)

Andrew MacDonald mac Aonghuis vich Ian 210 [ma<u>ch</u>kə noeu·ish vē<u>ch</u>k ē·ān] *mac Aonghais mhic Iain* (son of Angus, son of John).

Angus Beg 125 [bek] *beag* (Little Angus)

Angus Mac Eoin bhàin vich Eachen 205 [ma<u>ch</u>k Yō·in vaa·n vē<u>ch</u>k e·<u>ch</u>an] *mac Eòghainn bhàin mhic Eachainn* (son of fair-haired

Ewan, son of Hector)

Bean-a'ghlinne 214 [benə ghli·ny] (the wife of 'the Glen' — i.e., Glenaladale)

Brocair Sgiathanach 104 [bro·chker skē·anach] (the foxhunter from Skye)

Coll Bàn 171 [baan] (fair-haired Col)

Coll Ciotach 61 [ki·utach] (left-handed Col)

Coll mac Gillesbuic 61 [machk gile·spik] *mac Gilleasbuig* (son of Gillespie)

Diorbhail 37 [je·rəvel] (Dorothy)

Donald Dubh 27 [dōō] (dark Donald)

Donald Gorm 27 [go·rəm] (raven-haired Donald)

Donald Mor MacVarish 104 [mō·r machk va·rish] 'MacVarish' was a Moidart name, and until *c*.1800 confined to Moidart. From the time of the keeping of written records (by factors, etc) most families of this name changed to MacDonald.

Ian Caol MacDhunnachaidh vich Aonghais 120 [ē·ān coeu·l machk gho·nachɤ vē:chk ənoeu·ish) *Iain caol mac Dhonnchaidh mhic Aonghais* (Slim John, son of Duncan, son of Angus)

Ian Fràingeach 166 [fra·ngach] (French John)

Ian Og 102 [awg] *Òg* (the young(er) John)

Iseabal nighean Ian Mhòr 118 [ē·shəbal nē·an ē·ān vō·ir] *Iseabal nighean Iain mhòir* (Isabel daughter of big John)

MacCailin mòr 65 [machk ka·lin mōr] *Mac Cailein mór* (the great descendant of Colin — i.e., the Chief of Campbell)

Mac Dhonuill Ruaidh Bhig 41 [machk ghaw·(n)yil roo·ɤ vē:k] *mac Dhomhnaill ruaidh bhig* (son of little red-haired Donald)

MacShimie 42 [machk hē·mɤ] *mac Shìmidh* (son of Simon — i.e., Lovat).

Maighstear Alasdair 102 (118) [mī·shtir a·laster] *Maighstir Alasdair* (Mr Alexander, 'Mr' being the title given to a Minister of the

Church, originally a reference to his Master's degree.)

Maighstear Alasdair Mor Mac Aonghais vich Alasdair 178 [mī·shter a·laster mō·r ma<u>ch</u>k ənoeu·ish vē<u>ch</u>k a·laster] *Maighstir Alasdair mór mac Aonghais mhic Alasdair* (Big Mr Alexander, son of Angus, son of Alexander; 'Mr' being the title given to a Catholic priest — in the same way as to a Minister — originally in reference to his Master's degree.)

Neil Mòr-an-Eilean 101 [mōr ən yā·lan] *mór an eilein* (Big Neil of the Island)

Ranald Galda 37 [gau·lta] *gallda* (Ranald the Stranger)

Raonuil Bàn 30 [roeu·(n)əl baa·n] *Raghnall bàn* (fair-haired Ranald)

Raonull Mac Ailein Oig 81 [roeu·(n)əl ma<u>ch</u>k e·līn aw·ig] *Raghnall mac Ailein Òig* (Ranald, son of the young(er) Allan)

Raonull Mor a'Chrolen 4 [roeu·(n)əl mōr ə <u>chr</u>ō·len] *Raghnall mór Chròlain* (Big Ranald of Crolen farm)

Raonull-nan-Raonuillich 73 [roeu·(n)əl nan roeu·nəla<u>ch</u>] *Raghnall nan Raghnallach* (Ranald of Clanranald)

Raoul a'Phuirt 103 [roeu·(n)əl ə foo·irch] *Raghnall a'phuirt* (Ranald of the landing place)

Selection of Names from the Clanranald List of 1745 (pp 146ff)

Allan Du [e·līn doo·] *Ailean Dubh* (dark Allan)

Allan Mac Allister vic Murdo [e·līn ma<u>ch</u>k a·laster vē<u>ch</u>k vu·rə<u>ch</u>ɣ] *Ailean mac Alasdair mhic Mhurchaidh* (Allan, son of Alasdair, son of Murdo)

Allan MacCallane [e·līn ma<u>ch</u>k e·līn] *Ailean mac Ailein* (Allan, son of Allan)

Angus Mac Vorrich (see Ewan Mac Vorrich)

Calum Mac Gawry [ka·lum ma<u>ch</u>k gaw·rɤ] *Calum mac Goiridh* (Malcolm, son of Godfrey)

Downcan Mac Innish vich Ian [do·nəchəgh ma<u>ch</u>k ənoeu·ish vē<u>ch</u>k ē·ān] *Donnchadh mac Aonghais mhic Iain* (Duncan, son of Angus, son of John)

Ewan Mac Vorrich [e·owin ma<u>ch</u>k va·rish/voo·ri<u>ch</u>] — this is either *Eòghann mac Mharais* (Ewen MacVarish) or *Eòghann mac Mhuirich* (Ewen MacVurich)

Hugh MacVoddich [ma<u>ch</u>k ə vo·ti<u>ch</u>] *mac a'bhodaich* (apparently — Hugh son of the old man)

Ian MacYonill vic Ean vic Yonill Oig [ē·ān ma<u>ch</u>k ghō·(n)il vē<u>ch</u>k ē·ān vē<u>ch</u>k ghō·(n)il aw·ig] *Iain mac Dhomhnaill mhic Iain mhic Dhomhnaill òig* (John, son of Donald, son of John, son of the young(er) Donald)

Ian Og vic Ruari [ē·ān ōg vē<u>ch</u>k roo·ərɤ] *Iain òg mhic Ruairidh* (John the younger, (son of) the son of Roderick)

John MacIsaac the Violer (John MacIsaac the fiddler), 'Violer' being a transcription of the Gaelic *fidhleir* (fiddler).

John MacFinla vic Ean Roy [ma<u>ch</u>k hyoo·nleɤ vē<u>ch</u>k ē·ān roo·ɤ] *mac Fhionnlaigh mhic Iain ruaidh* (John, son of Finlay, son of red-haired John)

John MacInnes vic Ean vic Creul [ma<u>ch</u>k ənoeu·ish vē<u>ch</u>k ē·ān vē<u>ch</u>k roeu·(n)əl] *mac Aonghais mhic Iain mhic Raghnaill* (John, son of Angus, son of John, son of Ranald)

John Mac Leasbeck [ma<u>ch</u>k gile·spik] *mac Gilleasbuig* (John, son of Gillespie)

John Mac Neill Mor [ma<u>ch</u>k nē·l vō·ir] *mac Neil mhóir* (John, son of big Neil)

John Mac Yonill vic Creul [ē·ān ma<u>ch</u>k ghō·(n)il vē<u>ch</u>k roeu·(n)əl] *Iain mac Dhomhnaill mhic Raghnaill)* (John, son of Donald, son of Ranald)

Mac In vic Ean [ma<u>ch</u>k ē·ān vē<u>ch</u>k ē·ān] *mac Iain mhic Iain* (son of John, son of John)

Mac vic Yonill vic Creul [ma<u>ch</u>k vē<u>ch</u>k ghō·(n)il vē<u>ch</u>k roeu·(n)əl] *mac mhic Dhomhnaill mhic Raghnaill* (the son of the son of Donald, son of Ranald)

Patrick Mac Gillendrich [paa·drig ma<u>ch</u>k gila·ndrish] *Pàdraig mac Gilleanndrais)* (Patrick, son of Gillanders)

Ruari Mac Innish Mòir [roo·ərɣ ma<u>ch</u>k ənoeu·ish vō·ir] *Ruairidh mac Aonghais mhóir* (Roderick son of big Angus)

Appendix 2
Maps

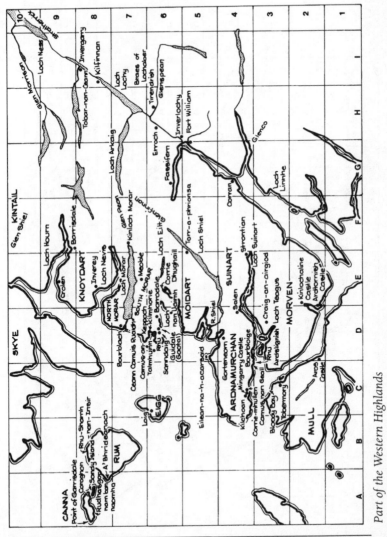

Part of the Western Highlands

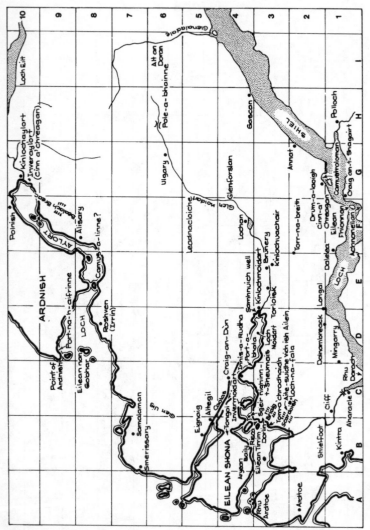

Moidart

Appendix 3
Genealogical Tables

Lords of the Isles

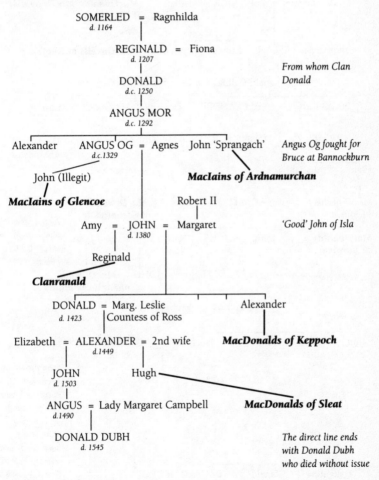

SOMERLED = Ragnhilda
d. 1164

REGINALD = Fiona
d. 1207

From whom Clan Donald

DONALD
d.c. 1250

ANGUS MOR
d.c. 1292

Alexander   ANGUS OG = Agnes   John 'Sprangach'
d.c.1329

Angus Og fought for Bruce at Bannockburn

John (Illegit)

MacIains of Ardnamurchan

MacIains of Glencoe

Robert II

Amy = JOHN = Margaret
d. 1380

'Good' John of Isla

Reginald

Clanranald

DONALD = Marg. Leslie   Alexander
d. 1423   Countess of Ross

MacDonalds of Keppoch

Elizabeth = ALEXANDER = 2nd wife
d.1449

JOHN   Hugh
d. 1503

ANGUS = Lady Margaret Campbell
d.1490

MacDonalds of Sleat

DONALD DUBH
d. 1545

The direct line ends with Donald Dubh who died without issue

Clanranald

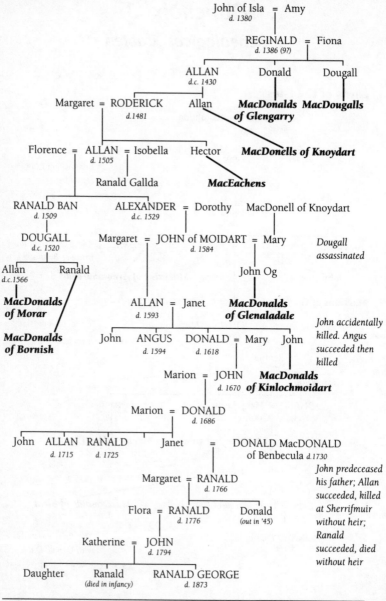

John of Isla = Amy
d. 1380

REGINALD = Fiona
d. 1386 (9?)

ALLAN — Donald — Dougall
d.c. 1430

Margaret = RODERICK — Allan — **MacDonalds of Glengarry** — **MacDougalls**
d.1481

Florence = ALLAN = Isobella — Hector — **MacDonells of Knoydart**
d. 1505

Ranald Gallda — **MacEachens**

RANALD BAN — ALEXANDER = Dorothy — MacDonell of Knoydart
d. 1509 — *d.c. 1529*

DOUGALL — Margaret = JOHN of MOIDART = Mary
d.c. 1520 — *d. 1584*

Dougall assassinated

Allan — Ranald
d.c.1566

MacDonalds of Morar

John Og

ALLAN = Janet — **MacDonalds of Glenaladale**
d. 1593

MacDonalds of Bornish

John accidentally killed. Angus succeeded then killed

John — ANGUS — DONALD = Mary — John
d. 1594 — *d. 1618*

Marion = JOHN — **MacDonalds of Kinlochmoidart**
d. 1670

Marion = DONALD
d. 1686

John — ALLAN — RANALD — Janet = DONALD MacDONALD of Benbecula *d.1730*
d. 1715 — *d. 1725*

John predeceased his father; Allan succeeded, killed at Sherrifmuir without heir; Ranald succeeded, died without heir

Margaret = RANALD
d. 1766

Flora = RANALD — Donald
d. 1776 — *(out in '45)*

Katherine = JOHN
d. 1794

Daughter — Ranald *(died in infancy)* — RANALD GEORGE
d. 1873

Kinlochmoidart

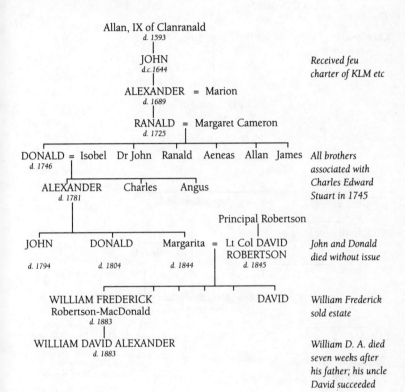

Allan, IX of Clanranald
d. 1593

JOHN
d.c.1644

*Received feu
charter of KLM etc*

ALEXANDER = Marion
d. 1689

RANALD = Margaret Cameron
d. 1725

DONALD = Isobel   Dr John   Ranald   Aeneas   Allan   James
d. 1746

ALEXANDER   Charles   Angus
d. 1781

*All brothers
associated with
Charles Edward
Stuart in 1745*

Principal Robertson

JOHN   DONALD   Margarita = Lt Col DAVID
ROBERTSON

d. 1794   *d. 1804*   *d. 1844*   *d. 1845*

*John and Donald
died without issue*

WILLIAM FREDERICK
Robertson-MacDonald
d. 1883

DAVID

*William Frederick
sold estate*

WILLIAM DAVID ALEXANDER
d. 1883

*William D. A. died
seven weeks after
his father; his uncle
David succeeded*

Glenaladale

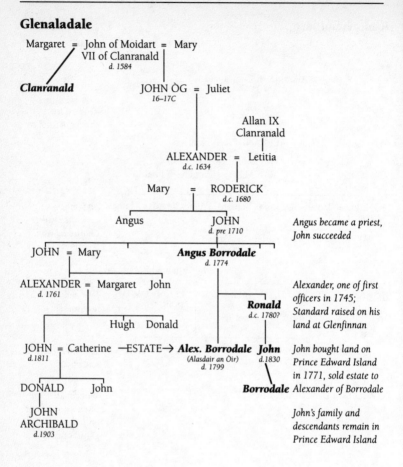

Margaret = John of Moidart = Mary
VII of Clanranald
d. 1584

Clanranald

JOHN ÒG = Juliet
16–17C

Allan IX
Clanranald

ALEXANDER = Letitia
d.c. 1634

Mary = RODERICK
d.c. 1680

Angus   JOHN
d. pre 1710

Angus became a priest, John succeeded

JOHN = Mary   **Angus Borrodale**
d. 1774

ALEXANDER = Margaret   John
d. 1761

Hugh   Donald

Ronald
d.c. 1780?

Alexander, one of first officers in 1745; Standard raised on his land at Glenfinnan

JOHN = Catherine —ESTATE→ **Alex. Borrodale**   **John**
d.1811   (Alasdair an Òir)   *d.1830*
                          d. 1799

DONALD   John

Borrodale

John bought land on Prince Edward Island in 1771, sold estate to Alexander of Borrodale

JOHN
ARCHIBALD
d.1903

John's family and descendants remain in Prince Edward Island

Showing also how the estate passed to the Borrodale family
(shown in bold italics – see the fuller Borrodale genealogical table on p.245).

Borrodale

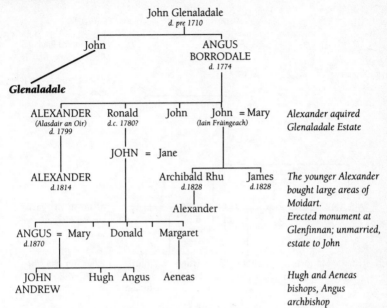

John Glenaladale
d. pre 1710

John

ANGUS
BORRODALE
d. 1774

Glenaladale

ALEXANDER
(Alasdair an Oir)
d. 1799

Ronald
d.c. 1780?

John

John = Mary
(Iain Fràingeach)

Alexander aquired
Glenaladale Estate

JOHN = Jane

ALEXANDER
d.1814

Archibald Rhu
d.1828

James
d.1828

The younger Alexander
bought large areas of
Moidart.

Alexander

Erected monument at
Glenfinnan; unmarried,
estate to John

ANGUS = Mary
d.1870

Donald

Margaret

JOHN
ANDREW

Hugh

Angus

Aeneas

Hugh and Aeneas
bishops, Angus
archbishop

Morar

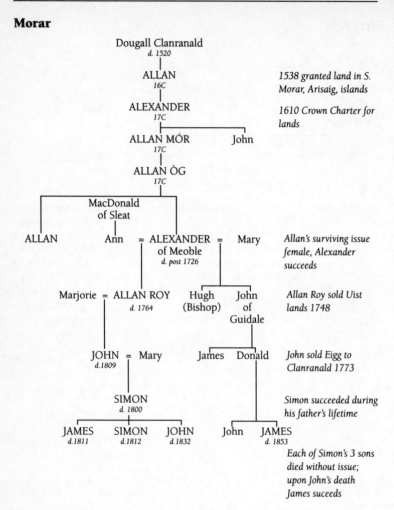

Dougall Clanranald
d. 1520

ALLAN
16C — 1538 granted land in S. Morar, Arisaig, islands

ALEXANDER
17C — 1610 Crown Charter for lands

ALLAN MÓR   John
17C

ALLAN ÒG
17C

MacDonald of Sleat

ALLAN   Ann = ALEXANDER = Mary — *Allan's surviving issue female, Alexander succeeds*
of Meoble
d. post 1726

Marjorie = ALLAN ROY   Hugh   John — *Allan Roy sold Uist lands 1748*
d. 1764   (Bishop) of
Guidale

JOHN = Mary   James Donald — *John sold Eigg to Clanranald 1773*
d.1809

SIMON — *Simon succeeded during his father's lifetime*
d. 1800

JAMES   SIMON   JOHN   John   JAMES
d.1811   *d.1812*   *d.1832*   *d. 1853*

Each of Simon's 3 sons died without issue; upon John's death James suceeds

Appendix 4
Suggestions for Further Reading

Should the reader wish to delve further into some of the events, personal histories or issues that Father Charles has written of, the suggestions below may be helpful. Readily accessible works only are cited, and manuscript and other archive sources are not included. The list is in no way exhaustive but the sources cited in it in most cases themselves include bibliographies. Where a large number of works exist for a topic — as for the '45, for example — I have chosen those that contain the most up-to-date information and bibliographies. For ease of reference the list is arranged alphabetically by topic.

Alasdair mac Mhaighstir Alasdair

MacDonald, A., and MacDonald, A. (eds), *The Poems of Alexander MacDonald* (Inverness, 1924) – texts, translations, introduction.

Black, R. *Mac Mhaighstir Alasdair – the Ardnamurchan years* (Coll, 1986).

MacDonald, N.H., 'Alasdair Mac Mhaighstir Alasdair – Alexander MacDonald The Jacobite Bard of Clanranald, *Clan Donald Magazine* No.9 (Edinburgh, 1981) pp 46-51.

Thomson, D. (ed), *Alasdair Mac Mhaighstir Alasdair Selected Poems* (Edinburgh 1996).

Canna

Campbell, J. L., *Canna, the Story of a Hebridean Island* (1984; 3rd ed, Edinburgh 1994); includes a chapter on Black Donald and the Cuckoo.

Castle Tioram

Aikman, C., *Castle Tioram in Moidart* (Oban, 1987) – a booklet.

Donaldson M. E. M., *Wanderings in the Western Highlands and Islands* (Paisley, n.d.) pp 32-39.

Clan Donald

MacDonald, Donald J. of Castleton, *Clan Donald* (Loanhead, 1978)
— includes chapters on leaders, genealogies; illustrated.

MacDonald, A. and MacDonald, A., *The Clan Donald*, 3 volumes
(Inverness 1895, 1900, 1904) — for long the standard work.

Ceannas nan Gàidheal The Headship of the Gael (Armadale Castle,
Skye, 1985) — booklet.

Clan Donald Magazine (Edinburgh) issues 1 (1959) — 13 (1995).

Clanranald

MacKenzie, A., *History of the MacDonalds of Clanranald* (Inverness,
1881).

MacDonald, Donald J., *op.cit.* chapter 19.

MacDonald, A. and MacDonald, A., *op. cit.*, vol 2, chaps 8–9.

Cameron, A., *The Book of Clanranald* — text, translation and
introduction to the original Red and Black Books of the family; in
MacBain, A. and Kennedy, J. (eds), *Reliquae Celticae* (Inverness,
1894), pp 138-309.

The forthcoming history of Clanranald by Norman H. MacDonald
(likely date of publishing 1996 or 1997) will add considerably to
existing works and correct a number of errors, particularly as to
the earlier history.

Claverhouse ('Bonnie Dundee')

Daviot, G., *Claverhouse* (London 1937).

Tayler, A. and H., *John Graham of Claverhouse* (London 1939).

Terry, C.S., *John Graham of Claverhouse, Viscount of Dundee, 1648-
1689* (London, 1905).

Dalriads *see* Scots

Eilean Fhionain

Cameron, A., ('North Argyll') *St. Finan's Isle, Eilean Fhianain, Its
Story* (Oban, 1957) — a booklet; includes also photograph and
biography of Father Charles.

Emigrations – Early 19th century

Bumstead, J.M., *The People's Clearance: Highland Emigration to British*

North America 1770-1815) (Edinburgh, 1982).

McLean, M., *The People of Glengarry – Highlanders in Transition 1745-1820* (Montreal, 1991) – deals in particular with Knoydart, covers both sides of the Atlantic.

Emigrations – after 1846

Devine, T.M., *The Great Highland Famine* (Edinburgh, 1988).

Hunter, J., *A Dance Called America: The Scottish Highlands, the United States and Canada* (Edinburgh, 1994) – treats of the eighteenth and nineteenth centuries; very full bibliography.

Forty-Five, The

Hook, M. and Ross, W., *The Forty-Five – the Last Jacobite Rebellion* (Edinburgh, 1995).

MacLean, F., *Bonnie Prince Charlie* (Edinburgh, 1988).

Scott-Moncrieff, L. (ed.) *The '45 – to Gather an Image Whole* (Edinburgh, 1988) – includes chapters on lesser known aspects of the rising.

Kelp Industry

Gray, M., 'The Kelp Industry in the Highlands and Islands' *Econ. Hist. Rev.*, 2nd series, iv, no.2, 1951.

Lead Mining

Cameron, A., ('North Argyll') 'A Page from the Past: the Lead Mines at Strontian', *Transactions Gaelic Society Inverness*, volume xxxviii, 1937-41.

Lordship of Isles *see* **bibliography for Clan Donald**

MacDonald, Alexander *see* **Alasdair mac Mhaighstir Alasdair**

MacDonald, Bishop Hugh *see* **bibliography for Priests**

Montrose

Buchan, J., *The Marquis of Montrose* (London, 1913) – by the celebrated author.

Cowan, E.J., *Montrose for Covenant and King* (London, 1977).

Hastings, M., *Montrose the King's Champion* (London, 1977).

Wedgwood, C.V., *Montrose* (London, 1952) – Collins' Brief Lives Series.

Wishart, Rev. G., *Memoirs of James Marquis of Montrose 1639-1650,* transl, with introduction, notes and original Latin text, by Murdoch, A.D., and Simpson, H.F. Morland (London 1893) – written by Montrose's chaplain.

Picts

Laing, L. and J., *The Picts and the Scots* (Stroud, 1993).

Ritchie, A., *Picts* (Edinburgh, 1989) – HMSO publication.

Ritchie, A., *The Kingdom of the Picts* (Edinburgh, 1977).

Wainwright, F.T., (ed.) *The Problem of the Picts* (Perth, 1980).

Priests, in W. Highlands, 17–19th century

Gordon, J.F.S., *Journal and Appendix to Scotichronicon and Monasticon* (Glasgow, 1867) – includes brief details of many of the priests, and a brief biography of Bishop Hugh MacDonald.

Anderson, W.J., and Forbes, F., 'Clergy Lists of the Highland District, 1732-1828', *Innes Review*, vol. xvii, 1966.

Johnson, C., 'Scottish Secular Clergy, 1830-1878: The Western District', *Innes Review,* vol. xl, no. 2, Autumn 1989.

Rough Bounds – Topography, Flora Fauna, etc

Darling, F., Fraser and Boyd, J. Morton, *Natural History in the Highlands and Islands* (1964; new ed. London, 1989).

Scalan

Johnson, C., *Developments in the Roman Catholic Church in Scotland 1789-1829* (Edinburgh, 1983) – chapter 8.

Watts, J.R., *The Story of Scalan for Young People* (Edinburgh, 1995) – covers the whole history briefly; several good articles have been written for particular aspects of Scalan, and these are listed in the bibliography.

McOwan, R., 'The College by the Burn', *The Scots Magazine*, June 1996.

Scots

Laing, L. and J., *The Picts and the Scots* (Stroud, 1993).

Menzies, G., (ed.) *Who Are the Scots?* (London, 1971) – BBC publication; chapter on the different peoples within Scotland, including the Scots.

Ritchie, A., and Breeze, D.J., *Invaders of Scotland* (Edinburgh, n.d.) – HMSO publication; covers different invaders, including the Scots.

Scots Colleges

Johnson, C., *Developments,* chapters 7, 13-15, 21, 22.

Seminaries, Highland

Blundell, O .,*The Catholic Highlands of Scotland*, 2 volumes (London, 1909 and 1917), volume 2.

Johnson, C., *Developments,* chapters 9 and 26.

Smuggling

MacDonald J., 'Smuggling in the Highlands', *Transactions Gaelic Soc. Inverness,* vol.xii, 1885-6 – contemporary with Father Charles.

Fraser, D., *The Smugglers* (Montrose 1971) – eighteenth century smuggling through the port of Montrose.

Society in Scotland for the Propagation of Christian Knowledge (SSPCK)

MacInnes, J. *The Evangelical Movement in the Highlands of Scotland 1688-1800* (Aberdeen, 1951).

Somerled

MacDonald, Donald J., *op.cit.* chapter 2.

MacDonald, A. and MacDonald A., *op.cit.* vol.I, chap.3.

Vikings

Crawford, B. E., *Scandinavian Scotland* (Leicester, 1987).

Ritchie, A. and Breeze, D.J., *Invaders.*

Wade, General

Salmond, J.B., *Wade in Scotland* (Edinburgh, 1934).

Whisky, Illicit Distilling

Devine, T. M., 'The Rise and Fall of Illicit Whisky-Making in Northern Scotland 1780-1840', *Scot. Hist. Rev.* no.54, 1975.

Glen, I.A., 'A Maker of Illicit Stills', *Scot. Studs.*, vol. 14, 1970.

General

Fairley, R.,(ed.) *Jemima – Paintings and Memoirs of a Victorian Lady* (Edinburgh, 1988) – a fascinating and vivid pictorial record of domestic and occasional events in North Moidart in the second half of the nineteenth century, from among the paintings of Jemima Blackburn of Roshven House.